THE TOILS OF UNDERSTANDING
AN ESSAY ON *THE PRESENT AGE*

by Husain Sarkar

MERCER UNIVERSITY PRESS

ISBN 0-86554-663-0   MUP/H492

The Toils of Understanding
An Essay on The Present Age
Copyright ©2000
Mercer University Press, Macon, Georgia USA

The paper used in this publication meets the minimum requirements
of American National Standard for Information Sciences—
Permanence of Paper for Printed Library Materials, ANSI Z39.48-1984. ∞

Library of Congress Cataloging-in-Publication Data

The toils of understanding : an essay on The present age / by Husain Sarkar.

LC Control Number:	99087102
Type of Material:	Book (Print, Microform, Electronic, etc.)
Brief Description:	Sarkar, Husain.
	The toils of understanding :
	an essay on The present age / by Husain Sarkar.
	Macon, Ga. : Mercer University Press, 2000.
	p. cm.
Projected Pub. Date:	0005

[CIP data not received from LOC at press time. See <http://catalog.loc.gov/>.]

CONTENTS

For my son

CASIM

who taught me,
among other things,
grammar,
his passion.

Toward the end of the night, he ordered his attendants to get provisions of water. Then he ordered us to depart. We did. When we had left Qaṣr Banī Muqātil and had gone on for a time, his head began to nod with drowsiness. He woke up, saying, " 'We belong to God and to Him we shall return.' Praise be to God, Lord of the universe!" He did that twice or three times; then his son 'Alī b. al-Husayn approached him and said to him, " 'We belong to God and to Him we shall return.' Praise be to God, Lord of the world. Father! May I be a sacrifice for you. Why are you praising God and repeating the verse of returning to Him?" He replied, "My son, I nodded off, and a horseman appeared to me, riding a horse, and he said: 'Men are traveling and the fates travel toward them.' Then I knew it was our death being announced to us." 'Alī said, "Father, may God not show you any evil. Are we not in the right?" He said, "Indeed, by Him to Whom all servants must return!" 'Alī said, "Then, father, we need have no concern, if we are going to die righteously." Al-Husayn replied, "May God give you the best reward a son can receive from his father."

—*The History of al-Tabari* 19:101

PREFACE

Short as this book is, it is longer than the one it is about: *The Present Age*. That book would teach a man that his life was either an endless monologue to an audience of One, or it was nothing.

There are three reasons why I wrote this book. First, I wanted to write my own script for that monologue. Then, I suppose, you might shrug and say, "This is a book in philosophy of religion. Why doesn't he say so?" Yes, I say so, but not if by that you mean that it discusses the proofs for the existence of God, the problem of evil, Pascal's wager, and similar things as are peddled in such books. Second, when I read Kierkegaard's most profound, bitter work, *Fear and Trembling*, I could not easily put it aside. The irresistible seduction of Kierkegaard's prose and my unfailing dismay at how Abraham and faith were portrayed insured that I kept reading it again, and yet again. But what exactly was wrong with it, I asked myself, and how could I convey it half as well? I knew I had to prepare arduously for that task. The work before you is part of that preparation for the eventual journey to Mount Moriah. Third, I wrote this book for my son, Casim Ali. He was to leave home soon and I thought he might carry with him something of my own making—a sort of a lunchbox for the road.

I am grateful to Louisiana State University for providing me with a research summer grant in 1996 which enabled me to do considerable amount of work on the manuscript. Also helpful was the sabbatical leave granted me for the spring semester 1998. To the University of Oxford I am thankful for permission to come as a visitor scholar during the Hilary Term 1998. Chapter 3 was published in *The Southern Journal of Philosophy* 37/2 (1999): 253-79, as "Kierkegaard: *Vox Populi, Vox Dei*." Chapter 5 was published in two parts in *Cogito* 12/3 (November 1998: 199-204, and 13/2 (August 1999): 133-38, as "Know Thyself: A Theory of Understanding." I am grateful to the editors, Nancy Simco and Carolyn Wilde, and the respective publishers, for their kind permission to publish the material here.

As this book evolved from its long-forgotten origin, I was not unmindful of the gifts I received: some in the form of papers and preprints; some in the form of written support; and some in the form of powerful criticisms. I read everything that was sent to me; gratefully acknowledged the support tendered; and honored the criticisms with a careful afterthought. Happily, I sometimes found I struck a chord in my benefactors. Yet, sometimes, I found others not just unmoved, but immovable: not even a sea of arguments would have washed away the lines of interpretation drawn firmly in the sand. But this is the rhythm of philosophy, and I have played it the best way I know how.

So I thank them all: Johannes Birringer, Robert J. Edgeworth, Alastair Hannay, Alasdair MacIntyre, Joseph V. Ricapito, and Anthony Rudd for generously applauding my timorous efforts in chapter 6, begotten through readings of Kierkegaard and Christopher Marlowe's *The Tragical History of the Life and Death of Doctor Faustus*. Alastair Hannay, both for his encouragement and criticisms of two earlier versions—I have benefited enormously from his writings. Alasdair MacIntyre, for his remarks on chapter 1 and strong encouragement on the cardinal second section of chapter 4; this has stood me in good stead. One lore among Kierkegaardians is that MacIntyre is un-Kierkegaardian and should be opposed; I have tried to show that the charges are unjust. Louis H. Mackey, for his very substantive criticisms on the whole manuscript which led me to reimagine and rethink central features of the story I was attempting to tell; he wanted me to make the book much longer, and, likely as not, I will regret not having adequately heeded his advice. Christopher Ricks, for his many, if scattered, comments. Robert C. Roberts, for detailed and trenchant observations on chapter 4. Anthony Rudd, for his comments on virtually every page of the manuscript; I have learned very much from his own book on Kierkegaard, but we have also disagreed as much. John Whittaker, for pleading on behalf of distinct ways of understanding, and the way—he thinks—is central to Kierkegaard. Ken Zagacki, for his concerted defense of passion in chapter 1. Finally, I thank my son for his unfailing help with my prose and with the page proofs.

As anyone will know, I, a new miner in this old, rich, and inexhaustible field, was incredibly fortunate in receiving help from some of the world's leading scholars in Kierkegaard. I hope I have not repaid unkindly, thus fulfilling the prophecy that no good deed ever goes unpunished. I hope even more that by offering a theory of understanding, I have raised some questions we should have long asked of Kierkegaard—even if it meant that they would have made that gentle Dane smile.

Friday, 5 February 1999   *Husain Sarkar*
Baton Rouge, Louisiana

A PREFATORY NOTE

Regarding the text under consideration here—*The Present Age*—please note the following.

The primary text is Søren Kierkegaard, *Two Ages: The Age of Revolution and the Present Age, A Literary Review* in the Hongs' translation (see the bibliography for publication information). *The Present Age* was originally the substantive concluding part III of a review of Thomasine Christine Gyllembourg-Ehrensvard's (nee Buntzen; 1773–1856) last novel, *Two Ages*, published on 30 October 1845. There is, in Kierkegaard's review, an introduction followed by part I which is a survey of the contents of the two parts representing the two ages. Part II offers an aesthetic interpretation of the novel, but appreciation of it is heavily dependent on the knowledge of the novel. Part III is vintage Kierkegaard: here Kierkegaard is drawing conclusions, laying down philosophical theses. Of this last part, *The Present Age* is the final section, preceded only by a brief section entitled *The Age of Revolution*.

Kierkegaard's review, almost as long as the novel, was published under the unassuming title, *A Literary Review*, on 30 March 1846. Kierkegaard had read Gyllembourg's earlier short novels—published anonymously and by her accomplished son, Johan Ludwig Heiberg (1791–1860)—and was much impressed. Gyllembourg wanted to depict in *Two Ages* two styles of thinking generated by two types of ages she had lived through: the age of revolution which was decisively marked by Rousseau and the French Revolution and the present age, the age of rationalism.

Kierkegaard's review was intended to commend her writings to the general public and to offer a withering criticism of the prevailing norms and culture of his society. This work is widely regarded as Kierkegaard's first, and largely the only, venture into social and political philosophy. *Of the Difference between a Genius and an Apostle*, also published in 1846, was part of a different book, *The Book on Adler*, published posthumously.

I note two things of interest. First, Kierkegaard wanted to turn rural pastor, and to abandon being an author. But he could not bring himself to do so. A compromise result was *Two Ages*—not exactly a review, not exactly a book. Second, he suffered intensely through the infamous *Corsair* affair. During January–February 1846 the *Corsair* launched a relentless campaign against Kierkegaard, lampooning him mercilessly. The public joined in. The public and the press became Kierkegaard's target in his review.

Of all the sections in the book, why focus on Kierkegaard's *The Present Age*? Two distinguished authorities on Kierkegaard, Howard V. Hong and Edna H. Hong, have said that the entire work is a revealing instance of how Kierkegaard read books. First, he read thoughtfully and appreciatively; second, he rejoiced over the complexities involved in a good book; and, finally, when he read he was "using a book as an occasion for his own thinking. [Kierkegaard wrote,] 'A thesis: great geniuses are essentially unable to read a book. While they are reading, their own development will always be greater than their understanding of the author.' The first two aspects of reading are exemplified in the introduction and in parts I and II; the third is represented by part III" (*Two Ages*, xii). Consequently, I undertook this task the better to understand Kierkegaard's genius and his views.

Following a hint from Louis H. Mackey and Anthony Rudd, I devised the following plan. The translation used here, the Hongs' translation, is now the standard in the field. But also in wide currency (partly because it is economical?) is the translation of Alexander Dru. The Dru translation has a further advantage in that it includes *Of the Difference between a Genius and an Apostle*. (The original Dru translation also included "Has a Man the Right to Let Himself Be Put to Death for the Truth?") It would be quite convenient for some, students in particular, to use the Dru translation in conjunction with this book. Consequently, I have referred to the pages of both translations. There are two numbers in parentheses: the first number refers to the pages of the Hong translation; the second refers to the pages of the Dru translation. The Dru translation, I should note, has several infelicities. Punctuation is sometimes altered, a few sentences, and even paragraphs are missing, and it does not contain the whole of Kierkegaard's review. The details of these references are supplied in the bibliography.

Chapter 1

THE SIGNATURES OF PASSION

In *The Present Age* Søren Aabye Kierkegaard treats his age unkindly. He thinks it is given to much talk and reflection, cleverness and calculation, but to little passion and deed. The present age is, he says, marked by its ability, virtuosity, and good sense; full of skill and inventiveness in creating illusions; signalled by much scope, but little intensity; an age of advertisement and publicity, without any profound or prodigious learning among the young; an age of the Public and the Press; filled with envy and *ressentiment*; ambiguous; apathetic and indolent; famed in statistical tables as having consumed large doses of information; run badly. The litany goes on. "I wonder," Kierkegaard lamented, "if there is a person anymore who ever makes just one big stupid blunder" (68, 33).[1] Is there no hope?

There is: it lies in the individual, a shade more in the outstanding individual. In such an age, as opposed to the passionate age, the outstanding individual has a dual task to perform: unlike prophets and judges of old, such an individual must continue to conceal himself but, like them, continue to work for others. His life may be exemplary, but he can never exert his authority—or else he ruins everything. Ultimately, each individual in the present age must save himself. His being saved cannot depend on the work of others. It cannot be a secondhand gift from God.

My interest in this book is circumscribed in two ways. First, I am primarily interested in philosophical argument, but this is not my way of saying that I have been careless with history or exegesis. Second, my aim

---

[1]The mood was in the air. In America, in May 1845, nine months before Kierkegaard published *The Present Age*, Ralph Waldo Emerson wrote in his journal: "Our virtue runs in a narrow rill: we have never a freshet. We ought to be subject to enthusiasms. One would like to see Boston and Massachusetts agitated like a wave with some generosity, mad for learning, for music, for philosophy, for association, for freedom, for art; but now it goes like a pedlar with its hand ever on its pocket, cautious, calculating" (*The Heart of Emerson's Journals*, 214).

is to analyze certain core arguments of *The Present Age*. Consequently, I look neither backward to consult what Kierkegaard has said before that work nor forward to what he will eventually say in his subsequent works, with three exceptions: in this chapter, I shall turn briefly to *Fear and Trembling*,[2] only to clarify the problems relating to *passion* and *understanding*. In the middle part of the book, I shall look at the cardinal problem posed in *Either/Or: A Fragment of Life*.[3] In the final chapter, I shall cite from *Of the Difference between a Genius and an Apostle*, one of the closest historical relatives of the work under discussion.[4]

In chapter 1, I aim to show that for all his disparagement of *reflection* and *understanding*, Kierkegaard needs them. This is the dominant theme

---

[2]Published on 13 October 1843, two and one-half years before *The Present Age* was published.

[3]The book was published on 20 February 1843 and, I think, no single paragraph better describes the main theme of *The Present Age*, which was to be published three and one-half years later, than the one on p. 48 of *Either/Or: A Fragment of Life*.

[4]A word about the propriety, or relevance, of using *Of the Difference between a Genius and an Apostle* here. There are several reasons to think there is an intimate link between these two books. First, the first draft of *The Book on Adler*, of which the former is a meager part, was completed in 1846, the same year *The Present Age* was published. Consequently, there is a historical connection. Second, Kierkegaard actually proposed changing the title of the book to *The Religious Confusion of the Present Age*, suggesting that the work is closely bonded with *The Present Age*. Third, Kierkegaard wrote not one but four prefaces for this book, one of them being the longest he had ever written. Walter Lowrie, whose translation I shall use in conjunction with the Dru translation, has this to say in his preface to *On Authority and Revelation: The Book on Adler, a Cycle of Ethicoreligious Essays*: "These prefaces make it abundantly clear that S.K. was not living in an ivory tower, as a poet or a theologian, unmindful of the social and political trends of his age. As 'a thinker,' as he preferred to call himself, he ruminated profoundly upon them, and with prophetic insight he traced their consequences into and well beyond our age, which has not yet outlived 'the convulsive period' " (xiii). Of *The Present Age*, Lowrie said: "His political and social views are expressed in *The Present Age*, but to that people have paid hardly any attention" (vii). Things have changed a little, one hopes, since Lowrie wrote his preface in 1954. But these comments from Lowrie make abundantly clear the connection between the two books.

of the book: that even when Kierkegaard is sympathetic to reflection, understanding, and Socrates, Kierkegaard's sympathy does not extend far enough, even for his own purposes. Chapter 2 analyses what leads to the destruction of man. In chapter 3, a case is made for the claim that Kierkegaard's social and political philosophy leaves several issues unattended, not least of them being the role of the individual in society and the foundations of that society. Chapter 4 shows why, on Kierkegaard's view, going inward is the only way out. In chapter 5, I offer a theory of understanding—an account of the stages that lead to self-knowledge; I do it in order to uncover the role understanding plays in a life in which faith also has a role to play. In chapter 6 the legendary Faust is made to confront a philosophical paradox, one which, I think, would have pleased Kierkegaard. Finally, in chapter 7, I want to show that there is a deep, intractable problem in the solution, the *hope*, Kierkegaard offers in *The Present Age*.

FIRST THINGS

For Kierkegaard, among the several culprits that corrupt "the present age" is *reflection*. It freezes one's ability to act, it adds to one's sorrows, and it is not easy to escape from its clutches. One can get hooked on it. "But one thing is sure, reflection, like knowledge, increases sorrow and beyond a doubt there is no task and effort more difficult for the individual as well as for the whole generation than to extricate oneself from the temptations of reflection" (77, 42). It is true that reflection increases possibilities, views, options—one's scope, extensity; but in the process it dampens passion or enthusiasm—one's intensity. "Generally speaking, compared to a passionate age, a reflective age devoid of passion *gains in extensity what it loses in intensity*" (97, 68). Finally, while reflection allows one the luxury of reviewing alternative lifestyles—Zen Buddhism, Shamanism, Taoism, Sikhism, Zoroastrianism—that in itself cannot corner the religious market, which is what saves an individual. "Reflection is and remains the most persistent, unyielding creditor in existence. Up to now it has cunningly bought up every possible outlook on life, but the eternal lifeview of the essentially religious it cannot buy" (89, 58). What it cannot buy is what passion sells.

As bad as reflection is, it is not in itself the corrupting force. "Reflection is not the evil; but the state of reflection, stagnation in reflection, is the abuse and the corruption that occasion retrogression by transforming the prerequisites into evasions" (96, 68).

First, reflection is bad only if it results in any form of escapism. When that happens, the net result would be retrogression towards an increasingly indolent moral life. Second, reflection offers a far greater degree of significance than passion. "Just as reflection is not the evil, so too a very reflective age certainly must also have its bright side simply because a considerable reflectiveness is the condition for a higher meaningfulness than that of immediate passion" (96, 67). The manner in which reflection awards greater significance is, presumably, by drawing the details of a significant picture of life: significance which "will account for itself in a higher existence-form" (76, 41). And when such significance finds itself well implanted, it will make possible the genuinely comic (82, 49). Third, "the prerequisite for acting more intensively is the thorough kneading of reflection" (111, 84). What is it to work through reflection; or, "the thorough kneading of reflection"? It can mean two things. Either it can mean to see through the deceit of reflection, thus enabling us to disdain it and save ourselves from becoming its victims or it might mean that our action is intensive only in proportion to how informed it is by reflection. Kierkegaard trades on this ambiguity. Fourth, reflection confers on an individual a greater capacity for action. When passion or enthusiasm enters to harness that additional capacity, it results in being nearer to what the individual should be "if enthusiasm intervenes and persuades the reflective powers to make a decision, and because a high degree of reflectiveness makes for a higher average quality of the prerequisites for action—if religiousness intervenes in the individual and takes over the prerequisites" (96, 67-68).

Kierkegaard speaks of the various stages of actions that are performed with enthusiasm. First is the stage of immediate enthusiasm; second is the stage of cleverness. Because the first stage does not calculate, the second stage assumes with certain cleverness that it is higher than the first—but that is only an appearance. Finally, there is the stage of the highest and most intensive enthusiasm. This final stage clearly perceives the shrewdest plan of action, but disdains it. This action will more often than not be misunderstood for awhile. For one thing, an enthusiastic action is never obvious, especially because it is opposed to the shrewd. Nor is it obvious, important though it is, whether the "average man"—Kierkegaard's phrase—will be able to escape the enchantment and seduction of cleverness, whether he will be able to dominate cleverness, cast it aside, and thus act. Or, will he only toy with possibilities and squander the deed? (111, 84).

How then must we understand the deed of Socrates? Socrates was charged with corrupting the youth, studying things in the sky and beneath the earth, and failing to believe in the gods of the city. Socrates protested his innocence, but the majority of 501 jurors thought otherwise. No doubt the result of envy and *ressentiment*? (82-83, 49-50). His old friend Crito urged him to escape from the prison, but Socrates, as we know, argued against doing so. Socrates ended up drinking the hemlock. The story is old; the story is repeatedly told; still, the story never fails to astonish.

Socrates' deed presumably had three stages. There was the stage of immediate enthusiasm, say, when he felt impelled to speak the unvarnished truth, "spoken at random,"[5] before the assembly; he got past the stage of cleverness, say, when he forestalled Crito's arguments to escape; and, finally, the last stage of the highest and most intensive enthusiasm when, with calm and self-assurance, he speaks with his friends in the final hour, then ends his life. In the eyes of Kierkegaard, Socrates

> was sufficiently prudent to perceive what he should do to be acquitted, but he disdained acting accordingly, just as he disdained the speech offered to him. For that very reason there is nothing obvious about his heroic death; even in death he went on being ironical by posing the problem to all the prudent whether he actually had been so very prudent, since he acted contrary to prudence. (111, 84-85)

Thus Socrates' deed is undersold. Socrates would have reasoned that Kierkegaard's three stages were not enough. Interposed between the second and the final stage, he would have said, is a stage of *understanding*. Let us call this the *third* stage. This stage is designed to explicitly warn of the distinction between cleverness and understanding. When this third stage is complete, then, and only then, can the highest and most intensive enthusiasm or passion, which Kierkegaard speaks of in the fourth stage, make a real difference and lead to a deed, the fifth stage. This fifth stage is, presumably, "a higher existence-form," in which is ultimately explained the significance designed in the fourth stage (76, 41).

---

[5]Plato, *The Trial and Death of Socrates*, 22. Hereafter, all page numbers in parentheses with a "P" prefix refer to the pages of this book.

In the absence of that intervening third stage, the character of the passion[6] gets transformed into something less than what it might have been.

STAGES OF AN ENTHUSIASTIC ACT

Schematically, then:

	Socrates	**Kierkegaard**
Stage 1	immediate enthusiasm (passion)	immediate enthusiasm (passion)
	(scale of energy)	
Stage 2	-----	cleverness
	(scale of cleverness)	
Stage 3	understanding	-----
	(scale of understanding)	
Stage 4	highest and most intensive enthusiasm (passion)	highest and most intensive enthusiasm (passion)
	(scale of passion)[7]	
Stage 5	deed	deed
	(scale of courage)	

Stage 1. Stage of Initial Gusto. As before, this is the stage where Socrates speaks before the assembly of Athenians, not in stylized phrases, he says, but "expressed in the first words that come to mind" (P 22).

---

[6]There is an argument from recent theories of emotions and passions that I shall not use. These theories analyze an emotion into three components: beliefs, attitudes, and feeling. A change in the first component would presumably bring about a change in the emotion. Thus, the highest passion of the final stage conjoined to the beliefs in the second stage would be different from the one conjoined to the beliefs in the third stage. See, Robert Nozick, *The Examined Life: Philosophical Meditations*, chap. 9. Such a view of passions immediately yields the intended conclusion.

[7]Might this stage also be described as yielding a *scale of faith*? Also chap. 5, 139-34, and chap. 7, n. 5.

These words stem, say, from immediate passion. Such passion presumably lies anywhere on the *scale of energy* (69, 34). In Socrates' case, it lay on the far side of high.

Stage 2. Stage of Holding Back. Socrates chides an anguished Crito:

> I am the kind of man who listens only to the argument that on reflection seems best to me. . . . I value and respect the same principles as before, and if we have no better arguments to bring up at this moment, be sure that I shall not agree with you, not even if the power of the majority were to frighten us with more bogeys, as if we were children, with threats of incarcerations and executions and confiscation of property. (P 46)

Crito's claims—we will be deprived of a friend; we shall be thought to value money more highly than our friends; we can take care of the informers; you, Socrates, will be neglecting your children; it is wrong to surrender one's life when one can save it; this whole thing is not only evil, but shameful (P 45-46)—are met with an unaverted gaze on their cleverness (P 24-27). Undoubtedly, it was with much the same attitude that Socrates bruised the sophists, poets, orators, politicians, and craftsmen (P 24-27) whose cleverness lay fairly higher on the *scale of cleverness* (69, 34) than Crito's, and was thus more difficult to combat. But note that a more serious reading will show that Socrates' arguments can dispel cleverness only by relying, at least implicitly, on a substantive argument provided in the next stage, the stage of understanding. What is clever is only so when a contrast of substance is available, not otherwise. Note also that there is no guile in Crito: his passion, surely, is in the right place, if not his argument.

Stage 3. Stage of Understanding. This is far and away the most important stage. Socrates' entire defense in the *Crito*, and hence his deed, get distorted in the absence of stage 3, the stage of understanding. Socrates had argued that he should not escape. That is what the speech of the Laws was designed to show. Namely, that Socrates had entered into a covenant with the city of Athens; that this covenant was freely entered into and not coerced; and judged by everything that Socrates did—he was born and nurtured there, he raised his children there, and he left the city less often "than the lame or the blind" (P 53)—the city had pleased him. This was all the more reason why he should keep his end of the covenant. It is wrong to inflict harm, said Socrates. Breaking a covenant, one from which one has profited, moreover, is inflicting harm. Therefore, Socrates concluded, far from escaping from the prison, he should do what the city had bid him do: die.

Unreservedly, Socrates had acted on the principle, "[O]ne must never in any way do wrong willingly. . . . Nor must one, when wronged, inflict wrong in return, as the majority believe, since one must never do wrong" (P 49). Socrates must be construed as acting on this principle, notwithstanding Kierkegaard's general condemnation of acting on principle. What is acting on principle?

> Principle, as the word indicates, is primary, that is, the substance, the idea in the unopened form of feeling and inspiration, and impels the individual by its inner drive. The person without passion lacks this; for him the principle becomes something external for which he is willing to do this or that or the opposite. The life of the person devoid of passion is not a self-manifesting and unfolding principle. (101, 73)

For Kierkegaard, it might be argued in defense, a principle, is something subjective, internal; initially, it is no more than a feeling, a feeling no more than an inner power, an inner power no more than what propels the deed. So closely linked are the principle, passion, and deed that if an individual lacked principle, he would lack passion; if that, then his deed would come untied from the principle. He could or would perform one deed just as gladly as its contrary. Consequently, he who is without passion reveals a haphazard development; his life tells no consistent story of his inwardness.

For Socrates, a principle is something objective, external; an undeveloped feeling and enthusiasm may echo that principle, but the principle is no less separate from the passion or inwardness of that individual. Indeed, if two individuals had the same feeling and enthusiasm, that would be an occasion to applaud a single principle to which both adhere rather than to announce two different principles to which these two individually subscribe. Such a principle must be proposed, developed, argued, and critically evaluated at stage 3. And so forth for other principles. When consistently adhered to—through passion—these principles will reveal a life that is lived consistently, nonhaphazardly. It is extremely difficult to see how one could do "this or that or the opposite," and yet be thought to act in accordance with a, or the same, principle! No wonder Kierkegaard concludes that in the absence of a passion, a principle "is some immense something to which even the most insignificant person adds his most insignificant act and becomes very self-important thereby" (101, 73).

Imagine: Aeschines of Athens was among the jurors who had tried Socrates. He had cast his vote in favor of Socrates through seeing what others in the jury, whom he secretly admired, were saying about Socrates and how they would vote to acquit him. Aeschines, eager to be in high company, casts his vote for Socrates for reasons he scarcely understands. Years later, he himself is accused of something trivial and put on trial. Aeschines, ardently desires to mimic Socrates—who had become posthumously quite famous—tells himself that he will not weep, nor bring his wife and children to court, and ends up giving a long-winded, highfalutin speech in court. This would be a case of an insignificant man attempting to add a significant principle (even to act justly) to an insignificant action, thus persuading himself of his self-importance.[8]

The case of Socrates is scarcely that. It is rather the case of something immense being added by the most significant Greek to the most

---

[8]This illustration was added at Alasdair MacIntyre's suggestion that I clarify the distinction between acting on a principle and merely attaching an insignificant act to a principle. The issue is quite complicated, but fortunately need not be fully treated here. Even so, let me say that in a more complete account, the following would have to be done. First, to combine and permute significant and insignificant act with significant and insignificant principle, and to illustrate each of the four cases. Second, to show how an act can be described, and evaluated, independently of the principle from which it was done; this would be necessary, else all actions would be significant in proportion to the significance of the principle from which the action flowed. This would raise the important question of what else, other than following a principle, makes an act valuable or significant? Thus, Aeschines could have acted genuinely from the Socratic principle never to do wrong, and yet the modest circumstances of his life and trial would not have conferred on him anything resembling the solemnity conferred on Socrates. Third, to offer a clearer description of how an act and a principle are connected which, among other things, would make clear why Socrates' act is connected to the principle in a way in which Aeschines's act is not, or at least not connected in the desired way. Fourth, to detail what it means to understand a principle. Fifth, to show how understanding, principle, and act are interconnected and to demonstrate the centrality of understanding. As the book unfolds, I attempt to do at least some of these things.

significant deed, and thus becoming a signpost by which the Athenians would be condemned by succeeding generations. Aristotle said, when having to face the trumped-up charges of impiety, that he would not let the Athenians "sin twice against philosophy."[9] Should not one act on principle? What would Socrates' deed be worth if he had not acted on principle? Is not the principle, on which he acted, provided by the third stage? And was not Socrates high—*very* high—on the *scale of understanding*? Kierkegaard clearly errs in inferring that acting on an objective, external principle is not the important thing from the entirely correct claim that an insignificant act cannot be transmuted into a significant one by attaching it to a principle. Agreed. One might as well try to transmute base metal into gold.

Also, stage 3 is utterly indispensable if an individual would be true to himself.

> [T]he individual in faithfulness to himself . . . [is] just like that constant number three Socrates speaks of so beautifully, which would rather suffer anything and everything than become a number four or even a very large round number, he would rather be something small, if still faithful to himself, than all sorts of things in contradiction to himself. (97, 68-69)

Socrates would have argued that even if it were the case that one ought to be true to oneself—should Thrasymachus or a present-day Serb be true to himself?—one would have to examine what it is that one must be true *to*—hedonism, Stoicism, Pythagoreanism, Sophism? That cannot be done without the understanding provided at stage 3. Once one has discovered what it is one should be true to, the next step is to act with passion in accordance with that discovery.

The third and the fourth stages can be readily linked in the Socratic view, the stage of understanding yielding the stage of the highest passion. In the *Phaedrus*, Socrates maintains, "What overpowering love knowledge would inspire if it could bring as clear an image of itself before our sight."[10] The third stage is the stage of knowledge bringing "as clear an image of itself before our sight." That knowledge would inspire overpowering love. That love would produce the requisite deed. So, there is

---

[9]Ps.-Ammonius, *Aristotelis Vita*. Quoted in Sir David Ross, *Aristotle*, 7.
[10]Plato, *Phaedrus and Letters VII and VIII*, 57.

passion, the passion of love, but it is ultimately based on, or emergent from, understanding, but no less powerful for that. Being high on the scale of understanding pushes one to being high on the scale of passion. One might say, when Socrates had gained in *scope*, he had gained in *intensity as well*. Kierkegaard appears to endorse something quite similar.

Kierkegaard says, "considerable reflectiveness is the condition for a higher meaningfulness than that of immediate passion—if enthusiasm intervenes and persuades the reflective powers to make a decision, and because a high degree of reflectiveness makes for a higher average quality of the prerequisites for action—if religiousness intervenes in the individual and takes over the prerequisites" (96, 67-68). The deeper one's understanding, the greater one's capacity for action. When one has passion, then, that passion is able to garner that higher capacity for action and produce a deed high on the scale of courage. One should aim to be as high as one can on both the scales of understanding and passion. Socrates was quite high on both scales. Hence, his awesome deed.

When I speak of understanding in this book, my concern is with humans and human understanding, and that, too, in a reasonably circumspect way. I am not pursuing a whole gamut of interesting questions, such as, What is it for us humans to understand a physical object, such as the universe for which we devise cosmologies? What is it to understand nonrational living creatures, like the baboon and the white shark, for which we devise evolutionary theories? What is it to understand a primitive community, such as the Kreen-Akrore of Brazil, for which we devise anthropological theories? Nor am I concerned with group or communal understanding. My primary concern is with an individual's understanding of himself or herself, but it is far from suggesting that the other forms and types of understanding have no bearing on the form or type with which I am occupied; they do have a bearing.[11] Nor am I concerned with certain kinds of understanding of *particular* things an individual might seek: Why do I suffer from constant depression? How shall I react to this cancer in my body? What shall I do without that loved one? What shall I do to secure my family's financial future? How shall I take care of my aging parents? What shall I do to aid the Tibetans? Once again, it is not my aim to suggest that the answers to these questions will not ulti-

---

[11]See chaps. 3 and 5.

mately influence the answers I am seeking, even less that those answers will not influence the way those particular questions are framed and answered.

An act of understanding is a complicated structure, itself embedded in a far more complex structure. A metaphysical theory of understanding should address questions such as, What is the structure of a particular act of understanding? What is the structure of the whole of understanding in which the particular act is embedded? Is it pyramidal, more-or-less rectangular, or circular in structure? When understanding changes, what principles allow for what changes? Which changes in understanding are deep? Which are superficial? What is the characteristic of understanding when it understands primary (the *cogito*, Euclidean axioms) or secondary (explanations for particular events, theorems) propositions? What structure and principles allow for a deep change as when an aesthete becomes ethical? Is Sir Karl Popper right when he argues in *Objective Knowledge* that there is isomorphism between the problem of characterizing the structure of understanding and the problem of characterizing the structure of what it understands? To succeed at the latter, he says, is to succeed at the former. I do not have answers to those questions, nor is the inquiry pursued here affected by that lack.

There is one question I do attempt to answer, but which cannot be stated easily. Let us say, a biologist, like Stephen Jay Gould, is interested in the question, What is the function of the antlers of the Irish elk? Well, he can easily specify the object of his investigation, namely, the antlers of the Irish elk. But I cannot do likewise for my project (other than trivially say, "Understanding"). Never was the Socratic point in *Meno* driven home to me more clearly than in writing this book. There Socrates confronts the reader with the dilemma. Either one searches for an object one does not know or for an object one does know. The first horn: One cannot search for an object one does not know because one would not know what to look for nor, should one stumble on to the object, would one know that one has succeeded in one's search. The other horn of the dilemma: there is no point in searching for an object one already knows. My task, here, is to make clear what this understanding, this object, is I wish to investigate. My hope is that as the book unfolds it will make clear both what that object is and what are its characteristics.

Consider the Socratic inquiry into virtues. There is a *specific inquiry* constituted by specific questions, such as, What is justice? What is piety?

What is courage? One might also say, there is a *general inquiry*, What is a virtue? General still, Why should one concern oneself about virtues at all? Socrates' answer is well known. Human beings seek happiness. There is only one road to that goal: living the virtuous life. One might say that the general inquiry provides the *framework* and the particular inquiry provides the *content*. Without the framework, it would be impossible to provide the content. Change the framework and the particular inquiry changes. For instance, adopt Buddha's view of life that happiness (as Buddha understands it, not as Socrates does) is only attainable if one learns to root out desire, or craving, which is the ultimate source of suffering,[12] the particular inquiry changes drastically. My aim is to try and provide a framework for understanding, not the content; but I recognize, as I said, that the content can impinge upon and change the framework as much as the framework can direct and change the content. Even if the boundary lines are blurred, there are large tracts of land that are clear, discernible, and unique to each inquiry.

I am embarked on understanding understanding where that understanding is engaged in a task of enormous and highest significance; the kind of understanding the oracle at Delphi admonished us to undertake when it said, "Know Thyself."

Stage 4. Stage of High Passion. This is the second most important stage. If reflection is not in itself evil, then, surely, passion should not in itself be regarded as good. To so conclude, it is enough to have read Suetonius's *The Lives of Twelve Ceasars.* Yet Kierkegaard several times no sooner approaches this issue than he recedes from it. For example: "the man who goes astray in passion may have just as good an excuse as the person who shrewdly realizes that he is letting himself be deceived by reflection . . . " (77, 41). "A passionate tumultuous age wants to *overthrow everything, set aside everything*" (77, 42); "a passionate age *accelerates, raises up and overthrows, elevates and debases*, . . . " (84, 51). "The forward thrust of the enthusiast may end with his downfall, . . . " (86, 54). "There is no such thing as a public in spirited, passionate, tumultuous times, even when a people want to actualize the idea of the barren desert, destroying and demoralizing everything" (90, 60). And, finally, "If

---

[12]See chap. 2, n. 22.

formerly authority and power were misused in the world and brought down upon themselves the nemesis of revolution, . . . " (108, 81).

So, an unkempt, untoward, ruthless, or runaway passion can destroy, raze to the ground, demolish, or tear down. We have every reason to fear it. This from Kierkegaard: "Morality is character. . . . As energy, immorality is also character. But it is equivocation to be neither one nor the other, . . . " (77-78, 43). In order that we keep away from forming an immoral character, should we not distinguish between a good passion and an evil one?

This point can be illustrated differently. The scales have much in common, but there is one significant difference between one of them and the rest. For example, to be on the high end of the scale of understanding is necessarily good; not so for the scale of immediate passion, cleverness, passion, and deed. Thus, while it is very important to be on the high side of the scale of understanding, it does not obviously apply, say, to the *scale of passion* or courage. One can be very passionate or courageous about the wrong things. It is essential, therefore, that before we pronounce on the worth of a strong passion or remarkable courage we determine whether it is good on the basis of understanding. This shows how indispensable is the scale of understanding. Hear the Apostate Angel in *Paradise Lost*:

> What though the field be lost?
> All is not lost; th' unconquerable Will,
> And study of revenge, immortal hate,
> And courage never to submit or yeild:
> And what is else not to be overcome?
> That Glory never shall his wrauth or might
> Extort from mee. To bow and sue for grace
> With suppliant knee, and deifie his power
> Who from the terrour of this Arm so late
> Doubted his Empire; that were low indeed,[13]

Satan's defiance requires passion, no doubt; he even speaks of it as "courage." But that is not what Kierkegaard has in mind. So it is imperative that we differentiate between a good passion high on the scale

---

[13]John Milton, *The Poetical Works of John Milton*, 8, ll. 105-14.

from an evil passion which may well be high on the scale too. This we can do only at stage 3.

Parallels between reflection and passion are aplenty, so that, when Kierkegaard thought it fit to condemn reflection for some reason, he should have condemned passion for a similar reason also, as in the following passage:

> With respect to goodness, the person who is enmeshed in his reflection certainly can be just as well intentioned as the passionate, resolute person, and conversely the man who goes astray in passion may have just as good an excuse as the person who shrewdly realizes that he is letting himself be deceived by reflection even though his fault never becomes obvious. (76-77, 41)

Here, of course, Kierkegaard is partly explicit: both, the man of reflection and the man of passion, can be well intentioned; both may have their excuses when the reflection and passion, respectively, run away with their man. But might not Kierkegaard have added that although the fault of a man whose passions run away with him has an excuse, he, *too*, is cleverly aware that he lets himself be deceived by his *passion*? Therefore, there can be deception in either case. One might say, let the man of reflection beware of his reflection as well as a man of passion beware of his passions, lest they destroy them. What alleviates *this* problem is only a clear understanding. Having understood that one has let oneself be deceived—is it, then, any longer deception?—one then must choose to act on that understanding. Whether one actually does so is a different matter.

Or, consider this passage: "Another danger in reflection is the impossibility of seeing whether it is a resolution reached by deliberation that saves a person from doing evil or whether it is fatigue brought on by deliberation that weakens one and prevents one from doing evil" (77, 41-42). Now, first, are not the results of passion even more dangerous and unforeseeable, especially when one can never tell whether the passion which saves a man from evil is reached after thorough consideration? Do not say, "No, they are not: because he is saved from evil," for precisely that is true of reflection. Nor must we omit to observe Kierkegaard implicitly recommending that a thorough consideration—understanding—might be useful. Socrates would have added, as I do in the schema, that such a consideration is a *sine qua non* for any decision.[14] Second, both reflection and passion can strain and drain a man. Might not the decision that saves a man from evil simply be the result of exhaustion from his passion?

Or, finally, this passage: The temptations of reflection "are so dialectical because one single clever fabrication is able to give the matter a sudden new turn, because reflection is able at any moment to reinterpret and allow one to escape somewhere, because even in the final moment of reflective decision it is possible to do it all over again" (77, 42). Nothing, perhaps, is truer of passion. At any moment, passion is capable of explaining everything quite differently and allowing one some way of escape. Clearly, more so with passion than reflection: reflection is slow, laborious, and tedious; passion is quick, virulent, and strong. One turn of passion can change and explain everything—or try to. It is fair to conclude that passion and reflection are too alike for one to be acquitted when the other is condemned.

The passions ought to be the slaves of understanding. Stage 4 is, and ought to be, held hostage to stage 3. If he had an option to live in an age in which the passions were hooked to a *false* view of life and an age in which a true view of life was *not* acted upon, which one would Kierkegaard have preferred? It is hard to say. If he had an option to live in an age in which the passions were hooked to a false view of life and an age in which a *true* view of life was acted upon, which one would Kierkegaard have preferred? That is *not* hard to say. He would have preferred the same age that Socrates would have preferred: as Socrates did when he said to the Athenians that he would prefer to live amongst those in Hades than with the Athenians here, although both act passionately. For reasons, alas, all too well known (P 41-42).

---

[14]"Now, you'll never find courage without passion, in a horse or a dog or any other creature, will you? I mean, you must have noticed how indomitable and invincible passion is. It always takes passion in a mind to make it capable of facing any situation without fear and without yielding, doesn't it?"

"Yes." . . .

"Now, don't you think there's another quality which a would be guardian needs as well? Don't you think that in addition to being naturally passionate he should also have a philosopher's love of knowledge?"

"Why?" he asked. "I don't see why." (Plato, *Republic*, 67 and 68.)

Just as Kierkegaard wants reflection to be followed by appropriate action to make that reflection true, good, or justified, so, too, must we require passion to be preceded (and followed also?) by appropriate reflection that makes the passion true, good, or justified. Then, *contra* Kierkegaard, neither intensity (passion) nor scope (understanding) need gain at the expense of the other. Scope will produce intensity, intensity will produce scope, and so on up the *spiral*,[15] like the two strands in a double helix: scope and intensity in harmony with each other, but neither complete nor adequate in itself—hence the possibility of rising. We might then conclude that an outstanding individual, like Socrates, or some other genius, will be on the high end of one scale only if he is on the high end of the other. Though, admittedly, an apostle, and only he, can or will be at the highest end of all these scales (save the scale of cleverness).

Let me, for the next few paragraphs, traverse in a similar direction but in a different exegetical wood. Consider *Fear and Trembling.* Too many things—irony, humor, understanding, Socratic ignorance, repentance, and faith—are related to passion as species to genus. Thus, we need to distinguish one species from another, say, faith from irony, even understanding from ignorance. "Just to make the celebrated Socratic distinction," says Kierkegaard, "between what one understands and what one does not understand requires passion; and even more, of course, [passion is necessary in order] to make the authentic Socratic movement, the movement of ignorance. What our generation lacks is not reflection but passion."[16] Again, with respect to irony and humor, Kierkegaard says, "I know that these two passions are essentially different from the passion of faith."[17]

---

[15]"Now, provided our community's constitution is given a good initial start," I said, "then it'll get into a spiral of growth. I mean, a good educational system, if maintained, engenders people of good character; and then people of good character, if they in their turn receive the benefits of an education of this kind become even better than their predecessors in every respect, but especially—as is the case with other creatures too—in that they produce better children" (Plato, *Republic*, 128). What is true of a community is doubly and easily true of an individual: an individual is to his later self or succeeding selves what a generation of a community is to its succeeding generations.

[16]*Fear and Trembling*, 42n.

[17]Kierkegaard, *Fear and Trembling*, 51. Recall, too, that Kierkegaard had

Socratic irony needs understanding no less than Socratic ignorance. Consequently, we need to determine not only how faith as a species of passion is different and distinct from other species of passion, but also determine what, if any, is faith's relation to the genus of understanding and how faith, if a species of understanding, is different and distinct from the other species of understanding. Indeed, Kierkegaard says, "Nevertheless I have faith . . . —that is, by virtue of the absurd. The absurd does not belong to the differences that lie within the proper domain of understanding. It is not identical with the improbable, the unexpected, the unforseen."[18]

It follows, significantly, that faith is not identical to any species in the genus of understanding, but is in a different category—the category or genus of the absurd. Is faith *sui generis*? To leave no room for doubt, how far faith, a passion, "the paradox of existence,"[19] goes beyond understanding, Kierkegaard asserts: "Nevertheless, to the understanding this having is no absurdity, for the understanding continues to be right in maintaining that in the finite world where it dominates this having was and continues to be an impossibility. The knight of faith realizes this just as clearly; consequently, he can be saved only by the absurd, and this he grasps by faith."[20]

The single most important set of questions in this context that can be formulated is this: Can a man of faith reach the category of the absurd without having traversed through the category of understanding? If so, the toils of understanding is quite unnecessary to reach faith, however useful it may be for other purposes. On the other hand, is going through the category of understanding, and finding it inadequate, necessary in order that the individual reaches, *as he* ought, the category of the absurd? The category of understanding may be utterly and indispensably needed as the tough line that *has* to be crossed—without it, can the absurd even be defined? If so, then even if understanding is eventually to be cast away, it is needed for the climb.

---

written his doctoral dissertation entitled "The Concept of Irony, with Continual Reference to Socrates."

[18]Kierkegaard, *Fear and Trembling*, 46.
[19]Kierkegaard, *Fear and Trembling*, 47.
[20]Kierkegaard, *Fear and Trembling*, 47.

Each individual lives in a cocoon of understanding, a cocoon developed over ages by the society in which he flourishes. It took years of labor—of learning and instruction—of thousands of men and women who preceded him. They observed, measured, experimented, tried and tested conjectures and, through deep and unremitting deliberation, they arrived at what they thought they, finally, understood. The poor, ill-informed, illiterate Indian believed the universe rested on a stone, the stone on an elephant, the elephant on a tortoise. What boundaries of understanding that initially enveloped him did he have to cross before he could believe that? How difficult would it be for Stephen Hawking to believe what the hapless Indian believed? Clearly, the line of improbability shifts in cohort with the shift in the line of what one deeply believes. If faith is belief in the absurd, and the absurd goes against the understanding, as Kierkegaard repeatedly says, then one must ask, Is not he who is the wisest who will have the most to struggle with the absurd than the fool amongst us? And, should he who is the wisest make the leap of faith, will that leap not be a grand one? And, might that not show that faith without understanding is not nearly as difficult as one with it, thus giving understanding a place in the Kierkegaardian work worthy of its name? Kierkegaard avers, "for that which unites all human life is passion, and faith is a passion."[21] He then cites in a footnote, with emphatic applause, Lessing, who wanted to demonstrate, from a purely aesthetic point of view, that grief can give birth to a witty remark. Lessing quotes the words of the grief-stricken English king, Edward II, on a particular occasion; and then, approvingly, the words of a peasant woman, quoted by Diderot. Lessing then says: "And consequently one must not seek the excuse for the witty expression of pain and sorrow in the fact that the person who said them was a distinguished, well-educated, intelligent, and also witty person; *for the passions make all men equal again*; but in this, that in the same situation probably every person, without exception, would have said the same thing."[22]

Too many questions cry out for an answer. Can passion unite all human life without understanding? Ought it? If it does, is there not a qualitative distinction between two lives united by passion, one in which

---

[21]Kierkegaard, *Fear and Trembling*, 67.
[22]Kierkegaard, *Fear and Trembling*, 67.

there is little or no understanding, and the other enriched by understanding, a truly Socratic life? In the example Kierkegaard cites, "the situation made it inevitable" what was to be said. Perhaps, courage was needed. The peasant woman had it no less than the king. One instance, no matter how significant, shows neither how a life can be united by passion alone, nor how that life will fare in another situation. How would a peasant woman have fared facing an assembly of Athenians on a trumped-up charge? Might she have fared just as well? Not solely in speaking the truth, but in speaking the truth with the kind of grandeur Socrates mustered? A peasant woman's grandeur? This is not to denigrate the peasant woman so much as to rejoice in the possibility of how uplifting and ennobling understanding can make us and, therefore, something to which all human beings ought to aspire. (Nor am I guilty of confusing understanding with being "a distinguished, well-educated, intelligent, and also witty person." I am willing to grant that understanding may yield such things without *being* any one of them; nor, yet, yield *any* of them and yet *be* what it is.)

Adapting an old, yet ingenious, idea of Robert Nozick,[23] one might say that an individual, say, Socrates, begins in life with an immediate passion for something or other (stage 1). He sees through some of the cleverness, in himself and in others (stage 2), and arrives at a provisional understanding of something moral (stage 3). His passions (stage 4) link with that understanding, and these produce a deed or two (stage 5). His deed, in conjunction with the harshness of the world, instruct him (71, 37). His reflection deepens, his energy and passion intensify. "But this extensity in turn may become the condition for a higher form if a corresponding intensity takes over what is extensively at its disposal" (97, 68). Reflecting on the end result of those deeds, he acquires—the start of a new cycle—a new immediate passion for something or other. Once again, he sees through some of the new cleverness, in himself and others, and acquires a deeper, better understanding of what is moral. He has inched up higher on the scale of understanding. When this happens, it is

---

[23]Robert Nozick, *Anarchy, State, and Utopia*, 212. Nozick is trying to understand how John Rawls's two principles of liberty can be understood to be acknowledged and agreed upon by all the parties in the original position.

attended by a higher passion; this passion is attended by a greater, more courageous deed. End of the second cycle, and the beginning of the third.

He rises again in the next cyclical round. And so on. And so Socrates grows older, and so he rises higher and higher especially on the scales of energy, understanding, passion, and courage, respectively. He refuses to try the generals *en masse*; he defies the Tyranny of the Thirty; he displays courage at Potidaea, Amphipolis, and Delium. He is pronounced the wisest of men. Such a five-stage cycle enables us to understand better, to use a phrase of F. H. Bradley, a man's station in life; that is, I aver, his station as a man.

There is then the issue of values or assets. There is no value in the absence of passion, one might say, and cite this passage:

> As an age without passion, it has assets of feeling in the erotic, no assets of enthusiasm and inwardness in politics and religion, no assets of domesticity, piety, and appreciation in daily life and social life. But existence mocks the wittiness that possesses no assets, even though the populace laughs shrilly. . . . But an age without passion has no assets: everything becomes, as it were, transaction in paper money. Certain phrases and observations circulate among the people, partly true and sensible, yet devoid of vitality. . . . (74, 39-40)

Stage 3 by itself displays only cold, representational ideas, phrases, and observations. Add stage 4, and these are transformed into values. Socrates might have responded that there are true representational ideas independent of anyone holding them. His talk about *form* as a separate, distinct, if immanent, reality[24] (P 7) is in line with this view. The whole attempt at stage 3, the stage of understanding, he would have said, is precisely to try and discover which representational ideas are true by which one should let one's life be governed. He might have conceded that, perhaps, a separate passion is required to put these ideas into practice.

Stage 5. Stage of Action. From the passion must proceed the deed. The more daring the deed, the higher it is on the *scale of courage*. Socrates' deed of drinking the hemlock ultimately proceeded from the fear of sinning against his soul. That fear cannot be understood without understanding the stage 3 he went through. On the other hand, Ralph Barton, artist and satirist, killed himself because he was bored. His 1931

---

[24]I need not take sides in this thorny issue in Platonic scholarship.

suicide note read, in part, that he was tired of devising ways "for getting through twenty-four hours of every day."[25] Assuming—quite falsely, I think—that the same amount of passion was required in each case to produce the requisite deed, what distinguishes Socrates' death from Barton's is that one was at a point on the scale of understanding from where the other could be seen to be only far, far behind.

Whatever is wrong with the present age, it is not that it has too much understanding and reflection; to go through the third stage is minimally required of it. What is wrong is that it has too little passion, if any.[26] Only when an individual in that age has acquired passion, over and above understanding and reflection, can the individual have any hope of being saved. And how, exactly, is an individual saved? That is the subject of chapter 4. But in the next chapter I concern myself with what destroys him.

---

[25]Barton goes on to say that he would be happy to leave his remains "to any medical school that fancies them, or soap can be made of them. In them I haven't the slightest interest except that I want them to cause as little bother as possible" (*American Literary Anecdotes*, ed. Robert Hendrickson, 19). Compare and contrast with this, Kierkegaard's remark on a bored suicide: "Not even a suicide these days does away with himself in desperation but deliberates on this step so long and so sensibly that he is strangled by calculation, making it a moot point whether or not he can be called a suicide" (68, 33).

[26]"They go to land-grant colleges, normal schools, and learn how to do the white man's work with refinement: home economics to prepare his food; teacher education to instruct black children in obedience; music to soothe the weary master and entertain his blunted soul. Here they learn the rest of the lesson begun in those soft houses with porch swings and pots of bleeding heart: how to behave. The careful development of thrift, patience, high morals, and good manners. In short, how to get rid of the funkiness. The dreadful funkiness of passion, the funkiness of nature, the funkiness of the wide range of human emotions.

"Whenever it erupts, this Funk, they wipe it away; where it crusts, they dissolve it; wherever it drips, flowers, or clings, they find it and fight it until it dies. They fight this battle all the way to the grave. The laugh that is a little too loud; the enunciation a little too round; the gesture a little too generous. They hold their behind in for fear of a sway too free; when they wear lipstick, they never cover the entire mouth for fear of lips too thick, and they worry, worry, worry about the edges of their hair." Toni Morrison, *The Bluest Eye*, 64.

Chapter 2

THE DESTRUCTION OF MAN

What, then, destroys a man? Kierkegaard claims in *The Present Age* that what destroys a man is reflection and cleverness, or the absence of passion. In brief, reflection and cleverness produce ambiguity; ambiguity produces tension; tension destroys significance of relationships; and that destroys the vital springs that make possible daring deeds. This in turn produces in the individual envy and *ressentiment* which results in the individual being chatty, formless, superficial, and given to flirtation and reasoning. Such an individual erects a barrier between himself and others; a collection of such individuals reinforces these barriers, which become increasingly difficult to overcome, and worsen the situation. The net result is the present society. In this society individuals constantly seek comfort in the wrong place: not within themselves, but in groups and associations. Such a society is marked by anonymity in the form of the Public and the Press. The Public is the Master Leveller who, in cohort with the Press, completes the task of destroying the individual, but, enigmatically, also provides him the ultimate way to save himself.

In this part of the essay, my aim is to construct an individual who stands utterly destroyed, to better understand later how he is saved. I shall argue that while much of what Kierkegaard teaches is true, there is a marked failure in his casting understanding in a minor role in the scheme of things. The stage of understanding is central not only in recognizing how an individual gets saved, but also how he is initially destroyed. So, a brief word about understanding.[1]

For Kierkegaard, reflection, understanding, and cleverness keep in each other's bad company; it is passion that stays away from them, and it is passion that saves an individual. I distinguish between reflection and understanding, on the one hand, and cleverness, on the other.[2] Kierke-

---

[1]The details are provided in chap. 1. I say enough here to make the present theme self-contained.

[2]Here is what the translators, the Hongs, say in their "Historical Introduc-

gaard is right about cleverness: it keeps the mind and soul of an individual tethered to the wrong post. But genuine understanding, as Socrates might have said, is what makes possible the saving of an individual. I let Kierkegaard have his fair half, too: understanding *by itself* will not accomplish much unless it has a solid collateral—passion. So I recommend a halfway house. One must interpose between the stage of cleverness and the stage of the highest and most intensive passion, the stage of understanding.

AMBIGUITY AND THE LAWS

Let us, then, begin with *ambiguity* and trace the causal flow.[3] With considerable emphasis, Kierkegaard:

> A passionate tumultuous age wants to *overthrow everything, set aside everything*. An age that is revolutionary but also reflecting and devoid

---

tion": "Robert Bretall points out that in Kierkegaard's review of *Two Ages* 'reflection' is the principal category . . . with the ambivalence typical of all Kierkegaard's categories.

"Versatile categories pose difficulties for translators. For the sake of distinction, in the translation of Kierkegaard's *Two Ages*, *Reflex* as reflected image and effect has been translated *reflexion*. The Danish *Reflexion* as deliberation has been translated as *reflection*, but this again is a complex term in Søren Kierkegaard's *Two Ages* and at times also has the meaning of calculating prudence or procrastinating indecision lacking in the passion of engagement" (ix).

I sort out that ambiguity by using *understanding* and *reflection* as meaning deliberation, and using *cleverness* as meaning calculating prudence or procrastinating indecision lacking in the passion of engagement. Stipulating how I shall use certain terms is easy; what is not so easy is to determine is whether I have been plausible and fair in my reading of Kierkegaard. Clearly, however, so much is riding on this term that no commentator on Kierkegaard's *The Present Age*, let alone the whole of *Two Ages*, can possibly remain neutral. Nowhere more than here must I leave the reader to judge how impartial I have been.

[3]This claims that there is a causal sequence here, namely, cleverness causing ambiguity, ambiguity causing tension, tension producing lack of significance, lack of significance causing certain kinds of dispositions, such as talkativeness. But such a claim is not central to my argument; I am quite prepared to accept the counterclaim that these are mutually tied and influencing, and not linked in a fashion reminiscent of one-way streets.

of passion changes the expression of power into *a dialectical tour de force: it lets everything remain but subtly drains the meaning out of it; rather than culminating in an uprising, it exhausts the inner actuality of relations in a tension of reflection that lets everything remain and yet has transformed the whole of existence into an equivocation that in its facticity is—while entirely privately [privatissime] a dialectical fraud interpolates a secret way of reading—that it is not.* (77, 42-43)

What makes for ambiguity, or equivocation, and what does it do? Ambiguity, when it enters into life, impairs "by a gnawing reflection . . . the qualitative disjunctions of the qualities" (78, 43). The qualitative distinctions are supplied by passions, which constitute "the coiled springs of life-relationships" (78, 43). Dry up those springs and the qualitative distinctions disappear. A passionate age will produce great deeds—a feat of works rather than a feat of dialectics, deeds rather than talk—which may well provide the destruction and overthrowing of existing things and relations. But its rebellion imbues with significance both what it destroys as well as what it subsequently will rebuild. By contrast, an age of reflection will produce no real deeds, let alone great ones.

Suppose a jewel lay at the far end of a frozen lake; here, the ice is hard, skatable, perfectly safe; there, the ice is thin, dangerous, and affording little or no hope of rescue should one crash in. In the passionate age, a man would have dared to go that far and retrieve the jewel.[4] The crowd would have watched him with bated breath; would have applauded his achievement, loudly and zealously; and, would have deeply bereaved his loss had he perished in the act. One in the crowd, say, would have been an ardent admirer, and the skater, the object of admiration. The proper relation between them would have been one in which "the admirer is inspired by the thought of being a man just like the distinguished person, is humbled by the awareness of not having been able to accomplish this

---

[4]Rivetted in my mind is the image on television of the man in a helicopter, hovering over the Potomac, in mid-winter, on a rescue mission. A plane had just crashed into the river, and there was fear that several would die of hypothermia. While the helicopters hovered and the rescuers contemplated what they should do, one man jumped some thirty feet into the river and saved an old woman—who assuredly would have died without that help. The hero was later recognized at a White House ceremony.

great thing himself, is ethically encouraged by the prototype to follow this exceptional man's example to the best of his ability" (72, 38).

Now in an age of reflection, things are otherwise. No one would have dared to go that far in the lake. But, instead, something else would have happened. A deft skater would have cleverly skirted the periphery of where the ice was unsafe. He would never have ventured beyond that point, let alone as far as where the jewel lay. Had he been so bold, the cowardly crowd would have exclaimed: "Ye gods, he is crazy, he is risking his life" (72, 38). Here the proper relation between the admirer and the object of admiration has imperceptibly, yet to the core, changed. The real task of securing the jewel has been transformed into an unreal trick of skirting the thin ice so as to only *appear* daring.

> Even at the giddy height of the fanfare and the volley of hurrahs, the celebrators at the banquet would have a shrewd and practical understanding that their hero's exploit was not all that good, that when all was said and done the party being held for him was fortuitous, since any one of the participants could have done almost the same thing with some practice in tricky turns. (72-73, 38)

Ambiguity has crept in. Daring and enthusiasm are replaced by skill and deceit.[5]

When ambiguity rules, inwardness is lost; then also is the significance of relationships lost. But when inwardness is lost, something else must take its place. Its place is occupied by tension. The admirer and the object of admiration—Kierkegaard calls them the "opposites"—for example, are no longer in a significant relation. Instead, the opposites "carefully watch each other, *and this tension is actually the termination of the relation*" (78, 44). Such was the end of the relationship between the skater and his

---

[5]"I was on the point of bringing up the subject of these people myself," Socrates says in *Euthydemus*, "not long ago. They are the one, Crito, whom Prodicus described as sitting on the fence between philosophy and state affairs, though they *think* they are the *ne plus ultra* of wisdom. . . . And why shouldn't they think they are clever? They reckon they don't overindulge in either philosophy or affairs of state, which is a highly reasonable stance, they maintain; they have an accessible foot in both camps, stand back from the risks and the disputes, and reap the benefits of their wisdom" (Plato, *Early Socratic Dialogues*, 373-74).

admirer. This is how significance is emptied from existing things and their relations. What transforms the relation between the object of admiration and the admirer, happens to other relationships, too, in the age of reflection: the relationship between a king and his subject; a father and his son; a schoolmaster and a pupil; a man and a woman (78-79, 44-45); and, for our own age, we might add: a physician and his patient; a garage mechanic and his customer; an attorney and his client; a dean and his faculty; owner of a funeral home and his patrons; a restaurant manager and busboys; a pastor and his parishioners. These relations are like the grandfather clock, says Kierkegaard, that goes on ticking and goes on chiming *one* semiregularly, regardless of the hour of the day. The faulty mechanism has taken over, but the clock no longer serves the purpose for which it was designed. So also with relationships: the outer form takes over; it no longer serves inwardness or as a vehicle for the expression of inwardness.

The above pairs are deemed *opposites*. The interests of the opposites are not necessarily in conflict; for example, the interests of a teacher and that of his pupil. Sometimes the interests of the opposites are in conflict, sometimes they are not. Sometimes the fulfillment of the interests of the one requires the fulfillment of the interests of the other. Sometimes each wants to be free of the interests of others. In Kierkegaardian terms: sometimes they can dispense with one another; sometimes not. Sometimes they are able to hold together; sometimes not.

Kierkegaard offers two laws. First, *the negative law*: opposites "cannot do without each other and they cannot stay together" (78, 44). Second, *the positive law*: opposites "can do without each other and they can stay together, or more positively, they cannot do without each other because of the mutual bond"[6] (78, 44). To these I add the remaining variants Kierkegaard omitted. Third, I shall call *the fundamental law*: opposites are unable to dispense with each other and are able to hold together. Fourth, I dub as, *the separation law*: opposites are able to dispense with each other and unable to hold together. Quite easily, we can rank these

---

[6]Kierkegaard then goes on to add: "or more positively, they cannot do without each other because of the mutual bond." But this is a slip; the two statements are not equivalent. The latter statement is stronger than the first and might be construed as being equivalent to the fundamental law.

laws. The negative law is the worst. It depicts a possibility of serious conflicts. If two individuals are unable to dispense with one another, nor, being together, can they hold together in harmony, then serious conflict is written into the relationship. They will be constantly warring individuals. Only a trifle better is the fourth law, the law of separation. If two individuals can dispense with each other and are unable to hold together, then there is no rationale for them to be together. They will be individuals in an unstable peace? Next in line, the second or positive law, is a law of latitude. If two individuals can dispense with one another, and, yet, if brought together can hold together, then such individuals may join together whenever they deem fit. They will be harmonious individuals. But it is the third law, the fundamental law, I take to be of utmost importance. If two individuals are unable to dispense with one another, and what is more, when brought together, they can hold themselves together, then their union would be not only an harmonious one, but a powerful, fulfilling, and lasting one as well. They will be passionate individuals. Which law yields the most passion or enthusiasm; which one the least? Which law is necessary for the individual to be saved; which law devastates the individual the most? Interestingly enough, when we discuss distinct communities below,[7] these alternatives prove useful.

THE NOISE OF *RESSENTIMENT*[8]

The inquiry has led us thus far. As in the case of the clever skater, we are to tacitly condemn the daring deed; our words may seem to take us toward the deed, but in no case must we actually do the deed for reflec-

---

[7]See chap. 3, 51-55.

[8]I shall use Alexander Dru's term, "ressentiment," which renders Kierkegaard's *misundeleseas*, to denote what the Hongs translate as *moral envy*. I hope that nothing said in this section ignores the warning in Robert L. Perkins's masterful article, "Envy as Personal Phenomenon and as Politics" (128-29), that one should not be guilty of the unwarranted inference that Kierkegaard was concerned about the same thing as Nietzsche. For a pithy distinction between Kierkegaard and Nietzsche, Merold Westphal offers this: When the break from Christianity is incomplete, with the herd retaining its morality while rejecting its metaphysics, then one has a Nietzschean resentment; however, when it is the metaphysics that is retained and the morality that is rejected, then one has a Kierkegaardian envy. See Westphal's "Kierkegaard's Sociology," 134.

tion has convinced us to be cautious and calculating: that the world will not sit up and applaud our deed; that we are likely to fail in that task; that we are better off hiring a fool to do it; and that, therefore, the balance sheet dictates it is silly to take such huge chances. We are invited to conclude:

> The distinction between good and evil is enervated by a loose, supercilious, theoretical acquaintance with evil, by an overbearing shrewdness which knows that the good is not appreciated or rewarded in this world—and thus it practically becomes stupidity. No one is carried away to great exploits by the good, no one is rushed into outrageous sins by evil, the one is just as good as the other, and yet for that very reason there is all the more to gossip about, for ambiguity and equivocation are titillating and stimulating. (78, 43)

No passage, more than this one, cries out for distinguishing between the stage of cleverness and the stage of understanding. Yes, it is our cleverness that: makes us superficial; daunts us to denounce acts of goodness as a form of stupidity, by smartly pointing to the harsh realities of the world and advocating grim caution, prudence, a scaled-down enthusiasm; gets the better of us and exults in what ambiguity offers in the way of stimulus; makes us gossip. But, No: it is not the failure of understanding. If we are to save ourselves, we will need—even if it is not ultimately sufficient, but only necessary—our understanding to outwit our cleverness; and it is our understanding that will instruct us on how shallow our cleverness has been. I can hear Socrates say: Unless we antecedently know which reflections the passions, the springs of life, must enlist (and which ones they must not), we might have lack of ambiguity but no assurance that the cause is a just one. Passions supply neither significance, clarity, contrast—nor unambiguity; knowledge and understanding do that.

Ambiguity has eventually produced tension which has this result.

> Ultimately the tension of reflection [says Kierkegaard] establishes itself as a principle, and just as *enthusiasm* is the unifying principle in a passionate age, so *envy* becomes the *negatively unifying* principle in a passionless and very reflective age. This must not promptly be interpreted ethically, as an accusation; no, reflection's idea, if it may be called that, is envy, and the envy is therefore two-sided, a selfishness in the individual and then again the selfishness of associates toward him. Reflection's envy in the individual frustrates an impassioned

decision on his part, and if he is on the verge of a decision, the reflective opposition of his associates stops him. (81, 47-48)

I amplify the unifying principle in this way. It is an axis, or a core plan, around which a life revolves. In a revolutionary or tumultuous age the axis around which words and deeds revolve is passion; in a reflective age the axis around which words and deeds revolve is envy. This envy destroys his ability to make passionate decisions. It imprisons his will and makes so many unrealistic demands on him as to make it easier for him not to *do* anything. Hence he will not devote himself to others. Envy is what surrounds him, and he by his own envy sustains that surrounding. "But the longer this goes on, the more reflection's envy will turn into ethical envy" (82, 49).

Here we distinguish the different forms of *ressentiment*. First, one might be resentful of the eminent, but joke about it. In the most passionate age, inferiors have always liked to joke about their superiors; but having joked about them, they return to a life form that acknowledges—yea, reveres—that distinction. Such an age gives *ressentiment* its proper character, and is thus saved from a dangerous disposition. Second, Aristides was told by a man that he could not bear the idea of Aristides' being called the only just man; that, says Kierkegaard, was more a commentary on him than on Aristides. Here there was envy, but unable to joke about it, he casts his vote to exile Aristides. But, at least, he clearly recognized the distinction between Aristides and himself.[9] Third, all but the worst character of *ressentiment*, is where there is failure to acknowledge the distinction, the inferior thinks he is equal to his superior, has no reason to joke about a distinction he does not believe exists, and thus unable to vent his *ressentiment*, he finds himself disposed to indolence or dangerous behavior. Finally, the worst alternative: It

---

[9]Perkins argues that the concept of envy portrayed by Dante, particularly in the *Purgatorio* as a personal phenomenon, was taken by Kierkegaard far beyond this into the broader realm of society and politics. He then goes on to show in nice detail how that notion, as used by Kierkegaard, is different from what it was in the hands of Nietzsche, Max Weber, and Max Scheler (even though the latter had more affinity with Kierkegaard than the other two). See "Envy as Personal Phenomenon and as Politics," esp. 128-31.

wants it to be taken as a joke, and when that apparently miscarries, wants it to be taken as an insult, and if that miscarries, claims that nothing was meant at all, that it is supposed to be a witticism, and if that miscarries, explains that it was not meant to be that either, that it was ethical satire, which in fact ought to be of some concern to people, and if that miscarries, says that is nothing anyone should pay attention to. (83, 50-51)

Among other things, this destruction of distinction results in want of character.

Characterless envy does not understand that excellence is excellence, does not understand that it is itself a negative acknowledgment of excellence but wants to degrade it, minimize it, until it actually is no longer excellence, and envy takes as its object not only the excellence which *is* but that which *is to come*. (83-84, 51)

It is difficult to comprehend *ressentiment*, even less how to remedy it, without the notion of understanding. There is false envy and there is true envy. Adapting Kierkegaard's illustrations, Miss Gusta envies Miss Marsden for being the first to have noticed that an actor had mispronounced a word as well as observe a member of the chorus smiling at him, and she was widely given credit for this, and it became a much-discussed topic in the salons. This is false envy. In order to rid herself not just of this particular envy, but envious disposition of this type, Miss Gusta needs to recognize that *this* is not something to waste her envy on. But this only comes through proper understanding of what is genuinely and intrinsically good. Otherwise, her relation to Marsden—pitying, dismissing, or hating her—and to her own envious disposition—denying it—will be a false one, leaving intact a disposition that is easily reactivated.

By contrast, there is true envy. He who condemned Aristides at least understood Aristides' eminence; he who condemned Socrates, may not have understood Socrates' eminence. The first is not a leveller of distinctions, although resentful—his is a case of true envy; the second is a leveller, yet not resentful. One should then infer that while mere cleverness is to be roundly condemned, reflection and understanding are necessary if one is to comprehend or get rid of envy and *ressentiment*. As the case of Aristides shows, understanding is not a sufficient condition—the will (in his case, to will not to envy) has also an important role to play—but it is just as surely a necessary condition, as the case of Socrates shows.

Robert L. Perkins:

> These three steps—tension, envy, and leveling—show a public charac-
> terlessness of demonic proportions. Kierkegaard has made a gigantic
> step beyond the descriptions of the disposition of envy offered by
> Dante. Kierkegaard has shown how envy has spread through his whole
> society and sapped it of its vitality, individuality, and religious inward-
> ness. The intellectual instrument was reflection and the means of
> dissemination was the press. Human life has been poisoned in the
> depths of the individual and the poison has spread to the full number of
> the public. Human degradation caused by this unholy trio is deep, wide,
> and pervasive. There is a single cure, but it is radical.[10]

And the radical cure is to take the leap into the arms of God. As Perkins frames it on the next page, "The leap called for is not according to prudence and it is against the understanding. Again, we face the incommensurable of the religious and the ugly ditch over which Lessing could not leap."

The central tenet of this book would suggest that a step be interposed between the degradation and the leap: the step of understanding. Take Dante's first example of envy. Sapia is banished from her native city of Siena.[11] She bears a grudge against her own countrymen for they can still call Siena their home.[12] So, she wishes evil upon them. On June 17, 1269, she, a widow, observes, perhaps even from the family castle of Castiglioncello, the battle of Colle. It was a battle between the Sienese Ghibellines and the Florentines Guelphs. Sapia devoutly prays for the Sienese's defeat; she had avowed to fling herself down from the window, if the Sienese won.[13] When the Sienese are defeated (and her own nephew

---

[10]Perkins, "Envy as Personal Phenomenon and as Politics," 126.

[11]The rationale for her banishment is anything but clear; it is rather important, though, for the philosophical tale. Dante has her saying, "Sapient I am not, although Sapia was my name; and at others' hurt I rejoiced far more than at my own good fortune" (Dante Alighieri, *The Divine Comedy: Purgatorio*, canto XIII, 109-11, p. 139). My account is wholly indebted to Charles S. Singleton's translation and learned commentary.

[12]Or is it because they unjustly banished her?

[13]Paget Toynbee, *Dante Dictionary*, 481.

is killed)—it was God's will anyway—she relishes every moment of it, and in her joyous rage she blasphemes, "Now I fear thee no more."[14]

How might Sapia save herself?[15] Not simply making a leap. She must first ask, was her envy true or false?[16] If it was false, she exercised herself—like Miss Gusta—over nothing. Her understanding would dispel her envy, and bring her to a natural remorse before God. If it was true envy, she needs to understand whether her curse on her countrymen was justly measured against the evil she suffered at their hands. If it was justly measured, will she, or ought she, to repent and say, "I mend my sinful life"?[17] If it was not justly measured, then it is Sapia's understanding that

---

[14]Not to leave this in mid-verse, the line continues: "as the blackbird did for a little fair weather" (Dante, *The Divine Comedy: Purgatorio*, canto XIII, 122-23, p. 139). Singleton cites Buti who comments on the last line thus: "The bird is very afraid of the cold and of bad weather. When the weather is bad, it goes into hiding; then, when fair weather returns, it comes forth and seems to make fun of every other bird. As in the fable about this bird, it is made to say, 'I do not fear you, Lord, for winter's over!' " (*The Divine Comedy: Purgatorio*, 282n.123).

[15]Not an altogether bad woman, Sapia: with her husband she had founded a hospice for wayfarers to which Clement IV had granted privileges (Paget Toynbee, *Dante Dictionary*, 481). But, by Sapia's own account, earning a place in purgatory was due neither to her good deeds nor repentance as to the honest Franciscan, Pier Pettinaio, Peter the combmaker (who refused to sell any comb with the slightest defect in it), who took pity on her and prayed for her.

[16]Dante, in fact, offers a taxonomy of three types of envy: "It follows, if I distinguish rightly, that evil we love is our neighbor's, and this love springs up in three ways in your clay. There is he that hopes to excel by the basement of his neighbor, and solely for his desires that he be cast down from his greatness. There is he that fears to lose power, favor, honor, and fame, because another is exalted, by which he is so saddened that he loves the contrary. And there is he who seems so outraged by injury that he becomes greedy of vengeance, and such a one must needs contrive another's hurt. This threefold love is wept for down here below" (*The Divine Comedy: Purgatorio*, canto XVII, 112-25, p. 187).

If Sapia is not guilty of the first two kinds of envy, then she is not concerned, not envious, over those who still retained the citizenship of Siena. If she is guilty of being "outraged by injury," that would explain her curse, but it would not explain how her feelings could be described as envious.

[17]Dante, *The Divine Comedy: Purgatorio*, canto III, 107, p. 137. Why should she say this? Even God punishes and his scales of justice are impeccable.

should bring her to her knees, and such falling down will then take her a step toward the leap that she must eventually make. And "so may grace soon clear the scum of her conscience."[18]

THE PROCESS OF LEVELING

What destroys an individual is the process of leveling. The process of leveling destroys difference, distinction, rank—to reduce everything to the same level as does an engineer a tract of land. This process can be initiated, or sustained, by a particular class, such as the clergy, the bourgeois, the peasants, the people. This constitutes the first movement of an abstract power within the concreteness of individuality.[19] None can arrest this process of leveling: neither a single, outstanding individual; nor a society or an association; nor nations with their distinctive individualities. The abstract leveling process is like a trade wind: it consumes everything in its path (87, 55-56). Yet, hope lies only in it, in this trade wind, for "by means of it every individual, each one separately, may in turn be religiously educated, in the highest sense may be helped to acquire the essentiality of the religious by means of the *examen rigorosum* [rigorous examination] of leveling" (87, 56).

---

[18]Dante, *The Divine Comedy: Purgatorio*, canto XIII, 89, p. 137. Purgatory should not only be the place of purging of sins, but a place where occurs the ultimate recognition—understanding—of how sinful one's life was because only then can remorse have significance. This is not exactly Dante, I know, for he says, "And my good master, 'This circle scourges the sin of envy, and therefore from love the cords of the whip are drawn' " (Dante, *The Divine Comedy: Purgatorio*, canto XIII, 37-39, p. 133). Singleton's commentary on this passage reads: "The scourge which goads the sinners toward the virtue that opposes envy, is made up of three thongs, three examples of love, of charity" (Dante, *The Divine Comedy: Purgatorio*, p. 274). To which I would add one more, the thong of *understanding*.

[19]This Kierkegaardian claim can be nicely explained in terms of Clifford Geertz's distinction between thick and thin descriptions of cultures. Here I can do no more than provide a hint, and leave the rest as an exercise for the reader. Geertz argues that one can provide fairly wide, general, and abstract descriptions of cultures. Such are the thin descriptions which are true of several cultures. However, as one zeroes in on a single culture, the descriptions become increasingly singular, particular, rich, and thick.

The drift in modern times, through its several changes, has been to bring about leveling. But many of its changes have not been abstract enough. There is a concrete reality attached to each such change as when one great man attacks another, resulting in making both weak; or, when an association becomes sufficiently powerful to bully an individual, to coerce his assent, to secure his unwilling enlistment to its cause. Here, there is a concrete reality to which blame, responsibility, even praise can be assigned. However, to effect relentless and powerful leveling, thinks Kierkegaard, one has to devise a phantom, a nothing; its spirit must be an abstraction. It must be such that it can be neither reviewed, nor represented; neither ashamed, inconstant, nor unfaithful; neither a nation, a generation, a community, a society, nor particular men. Such a phantom, he deems, is the Public. "The Public is the fairy tale of an age of prudence, leading individuals to fancy themselves greater than kings" (93, 63). In an age without passion, yet given to sedentary life and reflection, this phantom is helped by the Press, an abstraction in its own right.

The contrast with the age of passion or tumult is instructive. In such an age, there is no abstraction, the Public. Such an age may be divided into parties, and the Press takes sides with a concrete party, and consequently the Press dons a particular character. In antiquity, when societies were smaller in size, there could not have been a Public (nor, of course, was there a Press). The society gathered in the agora, say, and listened to a leader. Each individual found himself in a concrete situation, simultaneously in touch with several others present; that is what sustained him. ("But the existence of a public creates no situation and no community" [91, 61].) The leader was present when he was applauded or condemned; and when the crowd assented to his decision, each individual in the crowd assented to that decision and held himself accountable. No less accountable was he if elected to go with the minority opinion. In such a situation, "But the majority and the minority are, it is well to note, actual human beings" (91-92, 61). "But," in modern times, "to adopt the same opinion as the public is a deceptive consolation, for the public exists only *in abstracto*" (61). To align oneself to the public in this fashion does not—indeed, cannot—enable one to make a real commitment (93, 63).

When a society becomes large, or large enough, so that the individual is no longer held accountable in the way in which he was in antiquity, then the Press takes over and creates that abstraction, the Public. And as this Press becomes weaker, when it finds itself no longer in the grip of a barnstorming idea or event, the process of leveling becomes a harmful, sensual pleasure (94, 64). And so what is that Public? It is "made up of unsubstantial individuals who are never united or never can be united in the simultaneity of any situation or organization and yet are claimed to be a whole" (91, 60). Such a Public cannot sustain the individual; it is not a concrete reality to which an individual can relate himself. So that, "if someone adopts the opinion of the public today and tomorrow is hissed and booed, he is hissed and booed by the public" (92, 61). To adopt public opinion, seeking safety in numbers, perhaps, is to receive "a deceptive consolation" (92, 61). Consequently, "more and more individuals will aspire to be nobodies in order to become the public" (94, 64). Seeking shelter in the Public, this anonymity, provides an excuse to do nothing. What is more, it instills in one a wanton disregard for a teacher or a judge, an official or an artist, who is actually trying to *do* something.

This is how the Public destroys the individual. Note that the task of destruction is left really to the abstraction, the Public. Anything concrete, anything particular, can only accomplish the task approximately. "The public is the actual master of leveling, for when there is approximate leveling, something is doing the leveling, but the public is a monstrous nonentity" (91, 60). Such a Public destroys hands over fist everything that is concrete. "But once again this situation is the very expression of the fact that the single individual is assigned to himself" (91, 61). Oddly, in this devastation lies also the individual's hope. "But if the individual is not destroyed in the process, he will be educated by this very abstraction and this abstract discipline (in so far as he is not already educated in his own inwardness)" (92, 62). Or again: "the public is the cruel abstraction by which individuals will be religiously educated—or be destroyed" (93, 63-64).

Kierkegaard, we know, was mocked mercilessly in the press, especially in the *Corsair*. So Kierkegaard's example of the dog, "the sum of the literary world," is particularly poignant. The dog is set on an outstanding individual; the creature demeans him harrowingly, relentlessly. The Public sits on the porch in its rocking chair and watches the spectacle—without having to take blame for it. When the Public tires of this fun, it will then get the dog to stop. But, the Public will disclaim owning the dog; it will despise the dog, when that suits itself; it will be quite unrepentant; and, after awhile, it may even order that that nuisance of a dog be killed. This is how the Public levels: through a third party. "That is the basest kind of leveling"[20] (96, 67).

Suppose, however, someone were to commiserate with the man who is thus made to suffer and be humbled. No doubt this person thinks himself self-important, superior—after all he condemns what the others found amusing. (But he is, in fact, rootless, superficial, and sensate [96, 67].) And he opines that such mischievous episodes are a great calamity to that unfortunate individual, and that they should not have occurred. Kierkegaard would reply: "I cannot agree with that at all, for the person who desires assistance in reaching what is highest does benefit by experiencing such a thing and should desire it, even if others may be disturbed on his behalf" (95, 66). Far more significant is the continuation a few lines down:

> in their limitation they even derive self-importance from having sympathy for the victims of the attack, without grasping that in such a situation the victims are always the strongest, without grasping that here

---

[20]On the same page where the central theme of the novel is announced by Patrick Fenman, who has just been saved from death by Marcus Vallar, that, "We shall travel the world together as poor beggarly men, carrying our message to the planet, and everywhere we shall be spurned and everywhere we shall be glorified," there is this curious piece: " 'Dogs are enlightened beings,' said Gildas, 'they are saved. Perhaps a dog could save his master. Remember Judas's dog sitting under his chair in *The Last Supper* by Rubens in Brera' " (Iris Murdoch, *The Message to the Planet*, 131). Murdoch is hardly a stranger to Kierkegaard: see her *Metaphysics as a Guide to Morals*.

Or, consider this passage—written as if in deference to Kierkegaard—from Rainer Maria Rilke: "But wherever there is someone who gathers himself together, some solitary person, for example, who wants to rest roundly upon his whole circumstance, day and night, he immediately provokes the opposition, the contempt, the hatred of those degenerate objects which, in their own bad consciences, can no longer endure the knowledge that something can actually hold itself together and strive according to its own nature. Then they combine to harass and frighten and confuse him, and they know they can do that. Winking to one another, they begin the seduction, which then grows on into the infinite and sweeps all creatures, even God himself, against the solitary one, who will perhaps endure: the saint" (*The Notebooks of Malte Laurids Brigge*, 184).

it is dreadfully and yet ironically appropriate to say: Weep not for him, but weep for yourselves. (96, 66-67)

Let me make two key inquiries. First, what, precisely, is the role of misfortune, grief, or any harrowing experience, in achieving the highest or in becoming religious? Second, what, if any, is the role of understanding?

First, the saving role of misfortune: "the person who desires assistance in reaching what is highest does benefit by experiencing such a thing and should desire it" (95, 66). First, there is benefit in grief, calamity, or misfortune; second, therefore, one must desire it. Is this harsh treatment, levelled at the outstanding individual by the phantom Public, a necessary requirement for that individual to achieve the highest? So that, if there is no misfortune in his life, he will not be saved? Or, is it simply a sufficient condition? If there is misfortune in his life, he will—in the presence of other things—be saved. Though Kierkegaard never considers that question, or those questions, in quite that way, there is a strong implication that he thinks suffering is a necessary condition. Or, else, why should I desire it, if I could attain the highest without being miserable?

Kierkegaard's claim about misfortune is an unargued assumption even for its sufficiency as a saving factor. There is some *value* which we regard as the highest value, say, acknowledging God. There is some experience whose *structure* unravels that value; say, misery or misfortune that unravels the value of acknowledging God. Unless Kierkegaard can show how that kind of experience is connected to that value, he has no substantiated claim that only a particular kind of experience—grief, sadness, despair—will lead us to that value.[21]

---

[21] I do not doubt that suffering is a powerful factor in Christianity: "[A]nd he began to teach them that the Son of Man had to endure great suffering, and to be rejected by the elders, chief priests, and scribes; to be put to death . . . " (Mark 8:31 REB). Again: "How is it, then, that the scriptures say of the Son of Man that he is to endure great suffering and be treated with contempt?" (Mark 9:12 REB). My purpose here is to show that as a *philosophical* argument Kierkegaard needs an account of why this suffering is needed.

Nor is it clear, in this instance, of the end and means distinction. Suffering is not an end in itself, but as a means presumably to realizing the highest value in one's life. If so, one can make the same point in a different way: Kierkegaard

When Gautama Buddha was twenty-nine years old, he went out in his chariot with his charioteer. One day he encountered a very old man, decrepit; on another day, a very sick man, rolling in his excreta; on a third day, a dead man. On each occasion, the Prince asked his charioteer the meaning of what he had witnessed. His charioteer replied that it was the essence of man to grow old, to suffer sickness, and finally to die. One day, Buddha saw a Brahmin serenely going about his way; Buddha decided to follow that path. Buddha himself did not undergo the experiences of the men he had witnessed; although he was troubled enough by them to renounce his kingdom and the world and to seek a solution for human suffering.[22] (His charioteer witnessed the same thing, but, so far as we know, did not renounce the world.) If this was grief, it was a different form of grief from the grief that the first two men, whom he had witnessed, were experiencing. If Buddha has attained the highest, then Kierkegaard's claim, that if one wants to attain the highest one must desire harsh treatment, offers not just a few difficulties.

The question can be generalized: How do we justify that only certain experiences will lead us, or even point us, to certain values? This applies not only to Kierkegaard's view, but to other views as well. (a) Among the *philosophes* of the eighteenth century, different basic values were touted: ones that dealt with the *joie de vivre*, sexual delight, love of trivia, indulgence of senses, and a sense of commonplace fun.[23] What is the

---

has not shown that suffering is the only means to salvation.

[22]Buddha lets knowledge and understanding play indispensable roles in the lives of mendicants or monks. Thus, recall their roles in the four noble truths: first, diagnose suffering (*dukkha*); second, identify its cause which is "craving"; third, attempt the removal of the cause which will alleviate *dukkha*, and, fourth, pursue the Holy Eightfold Path or Middle Way (*Magga*) which leads to the cessation (*nirodha*) of *dukkha*. The Path consists of the following: (1) right view or understanding, (2) right directed thought, (3) right speech, (4) right action, (5) right livelihood, (6) right effort, (7) right mindfulness, and (8) right concentration. The same point put differently: ignorance is what leads to *dukkha*; and, understanding and right practice obliterates it. He who achieves salvation in this way is called *Arahat* and the state he arrives at is the state of *Nibhana*. For a succinct account, see Peter Harvey, *An Introduction to Buddhism: Teachings, History, and Practices*, chap. 3.

[23]It would be hard to find a nicer piece on the Enlightenment, within the

structure of those experiences? How do those experiences justify those values? (b) Bertrand Russell's "A Free Man's Worship,"[24] lists a variety of values of religion from a humanist perspective. What experiences give particular insight into those values? Which ones lead away from them? and Why? (c) Spinoza offers a view in which the highest value is the intellectual love of God.

> The more we understand particular things, the more do we understand God. . . .
>
> The intellectual love of the mind towards God is that very love whereby God loves himself, not in so far as he is infinite, but in so far as he can be explained through the essence of the human mind under the form of eternity; in other words, the intellectual love of the mind towards God is part of the infinite love wherewith God loves himself.[25]

What particular understandings clearly demonstrate that it led, or pointed, us to the love of God?[26] (d) Someone listens to Socrates questioning in the market place, and follows him about. He enjoys, for a while, other people's squeamishness and squirming, when they are examined, but soon

---

compass of that many pages, than Charles Taylor's, *Sources of the Self: The Making of the Modern Identity*, chap. 19, "Radical Enlightenment."

[24]Bertrand Russell, "A Free Man's Worship," in *The Basic Writings of Bertrand Russell 1903–1959*, 66-72.

[25]Benedict de Spinoza, *The Ethics*, part V, propositions XXIV and XXXVI, 260 and 264-65, respectively.

[26]Other than Socrates, Spinoza offers the best example of the philosophical thesis I am trying to illustrate. One simply cannot have the love of God, the highest value, without deep understanding of particular things. Take that away and the love of God degenerates into something else; or at least its full force and potential lessens to mere conventional piety. Spinoza does not offer any particular experiences that are sharp pointers of a genuine love of God in action in a way in which a *philosophe* might offer particular examples of experience in which one delights, and should delight, such as communal dance and festivity or the pleasures of an evening walk. As instructors in those values, think of the paintings: Auguste Renoir's *Le Moulin de la Galette*, Paul Cezanne's *Bacchanal* (*La Lutte d'amour*), and Henri Matisse's *Joy of Life*.

the inquiry is directed at himself. He learns what it is to be at the receiving end. One day he hears Socrates say,

> Good Sir, you are an Athenian, a citizen of the greatest city with the greatest reputation for both wisdom and power; are you not ashamed of your eagerness to possess as much wealth, reputation and honours as possible, while you do not care for nor give thought to wisdom or truth, or the best possible state of your soul. (P 32)

Then, he suddenly understands. Eventually, he comes to write the *Apology*. What experiences led this man to be saved? There was evidently no sorrow or grief that gripped him.

There, of course, does not have to be one single experience that points to the highest value; there might just as well be a cluster of experiences that collectively point in that direction. But these must tie themselves essentially to the fundamental value or values—which, then, saves the owner of those experiences. I have no such general theory of experience and value to offer.[27] But until such a theory is offered, Kierkegaard's claim will continue to remain a bland assumption. One can, of course, raise the standard question: Of the several values, competing for the best value, which one is the best, and how shall we determine that? Lastly, there is this interesting asymmetry: to espouse a religious value seems to entail, or call for, repentance; there seems to be nothing corresponding to it, should one turn secular. At best, regret at having wasted one's life in prayer and penance when one could have had fun and frolic.

Second of the two key inquiries: the issue of understanding. So as to sharply focus, let me repeat Kierkegaard's assertion:

> [I]n their limitation they even derive self-importance from having sympathy for the victims of the attack, without *grasping* that in such a situation the victims are always the strongest, without *grasping* that here

---

[27]For one detailed account of value, see Robert Nozick's *The Examined Life: Philosophical Meditations*. For Nozick, value is organic unity, and since there are degrees of organic unity, there are degrees of value. Nozick's view can capture several good examples in its net, but it ultimately fails since it tries to straddle between the unbridgeable Humean gulf between *is* and *ought*. Thus vipers, international conspiracy, corporate greed, hurricanes, NRA, and KKK, have no less a high degree of organicity than objects that do have value.

it is dreadfully and yet ironically appropriate to say: Weep not for him,
but weep for yourselves. (96, 66-67; my emphasis)

The stage of understanding—grasping—is utterly crucial here, *and not
only for him who commiserates*. This much is clear: he who commiserates
with the misery of the outstanding individual betrays ignorance or folly.
Had he understanding, had he reached that stage, far from finding anything to commiserate, he would have found everything which would have
led him to bemoan his fate, his existence. Thus, if he who commiserates
must escape from his prison, he clearly needs understanding, and not just
passion.

Imagine: Leah of Judeah brings food to John the Baptist in his prison.
She has not heard him preach in the desert, and seeing his present condition, she commiserates with him. "This is what you get when you mess
with king Herod." She fails, therefore; is lost. But if her failure is to
transform itself into success, there are three questions Kierkegaard would
urge her to ask of herself, and answer: First, why is that person, John the
Baptist, stronger than me? Second, isn't my alleged self-importance my
folly? Third, why must I weep over *my* fate rather than over *his*? These
questions are, surely, related. In fact, I surmise, the answer to the first
question provides the central key to the answers to the remaining two
questions. To *understand* that John the Baptist is stronger than her, she
has to understand what it is to be saved (what it is to have faith). Once
that is understood, she can then supply the answers to the remaining
questions. Need I claim that she can understand, or act on that understanding, without passion? No, I need not. I need only claim that passion
is sufficient neither to give her understanding nor the answers that she
needs to those three questions. Unless Leah reasons, answers these
questions, and comes to understand, she will either weep but not be
saved, or neither weep nor be saved.

But much more: The foregoing does not only apply to Leah or to him
who commiserates. John the Baptist, or the outstanding individual, who
is undergoing the harsh treatment, fails if he does not really understand
the demands that the leveling process is making on him, what it is doing
to him, and how and why he must surmount that process. If he succumbs,
and, say, pities himself, mourns his fate, seeks sympathizers, he fails; is
lost. His being so lost is a direct consequence of his failure to understand.
If he is saved, it is because he understands, and not in spite of it. Consequently, it is imperative that John the Baptist must ask himself, and

answer questions similar to the ones Leah is urged to ask. When he does, this will ensue: "Do not weep over me," John will say to himself,[28] "but weep over yourselves: for I am stronger than you. And your alleged self-importance is your folly; and that you shall learn when you have learnt to have faith, as I have."[29]

What, then, does the failure of understanding lead to both in the individual and in the society of which he is a part? This is what I consider next.

---

[28]As we shall see in chap. 7, he can say this only to himself; he is required not to tell it to others, and exert his authority. As we shall also see, though, this poses a difficult problem.

[29]This is not impious, or pompous. Only there is no false modesty, for, having said this, he will continue to preach in the Judaean wilderness, continue to wear as raiment a rough coat made of camel hair, eat locusts and wild honey, and preach the coming of one "whose sandals I am not worthy to remove" (Matthew 3:11 REB; see Matthew 3:1-12). At the very least, John the Baptist must *understand*. Or, I cannot make sense of his life and preaching.

Chapter 3

VOX POPULI, VOX DEI

When darkness ascends in an individual's life, his life withers. Part of this slow withering process we have studied; part still remains to be examined: it is the part where the individual is engaged in the process of leveling and the process of building or joining. The leveling of differences, inequalities, makes him feel equal to his betters. The effect seeps deep down in him and then surfaces in his everyday life. By now, if he is not subject to whims and fancies, he is subject to something worse: he joins the crowd. What is the basis of this joining together?

An individual may band with others for a variety of purposes: for defending his life and property; for protecting and securing his health and welfare; for fun, games, and frolic; for fashioning life plans according to his own dictates. The individual makes himself the center of that association. The association exists to serve him, his needs and desires; he makes himself the be-all and end-all of that association; he can dispense with it if it does not serve him. (Might the association dispense with him if he does not serve *it*? Will he unwittingly become its slave?) What voice runs that association? One finds that it is the voice of the people, not the voice of God. And, in this association, the individual will claim, he sees his salvation. The darkness deepens.

THE DARKER SIDE

The process of leveling can hardly be without devastating consequences. In part, it manifests itself in the everyday life of an individual given to reflection. And so from offering a general analysis of the present age, a broader picture, Kierkegaard offers, "concrete attributes of the reflexion of the present age in domestic and social life," the details in that picture. "Here," says he, "the dark side becomes apparent" (96, 67). In each case, Kierkegaard attempts to delineate the consequences on which we can get a firm, realistic grip. In each case, he shows that there is a blurring of vital distinctions. Thus asks—and answers—Kierkegaard:

What is *chatter*? It is the annulment of the passionate disjunction between being silent and speaking. (97, 69)

What is *formlessness*? It is the annulled passionate distinction between form and content. (100, 72)

What is *superficiality* and its characteristic propensity, "the exhibitionist tendency"? Superficiality is the annulled passionate distinction between hiddenness and revelation. (102, 75)

What is *philandering*? It is the annulled passionate distinction between essentially loving and being essentially debauched. (102, 75)

What does it mean *to be loquacious*? It is the annulled passionate disjunction between subjectivity and objectivity. (103, 76)

The darker side, then, of a man succumbing to reflection, in Kierkegaard's view, is that he will be talkative, formless, superficial, flirtatious, and given to reasoning that has no anchor in inwardness or subjectivity. These are devastating traits which one should, if possible, eliminate from one's nature or character. Indeed, they may even be signs of an absence of character. "Morality is character; character is something engraved (χαράσσω); but the sea has no character, nor does sand, nor abstract common sense either, for character is inwardness. As energy, immorality is also character. But it is equivocation when the qualitative disjunction of the qualities is impaired by a gnawing reflection" (77-78, 43).

Asked to develop parallels Kierkegaardian in style, I would offer the following.

- What is *conventional religion*? It is—using a more colloquial expression—the result of doing away with the vital distinction between worship and apostasy.
- What is a *commercial*? It is the result of doing away with the vital distinction between truth telling and utter deceit.
- What is a *job*? It is the result of doing away with the vital distinction between work as a form of religious expression[1] and drudgery.
- What is a *business associate*? It is the result of doing away with the vital distinction between a friend and a coconspirator.

---

[1]This is meant to capture Kierkegaard's point (79-80, 45) and the point of Charles Taylor's impeccable "God Loveth Adverbs," chap. 13 in *Sources of the Self: The Making of the Modern Identity*.

- What is mere *expertise* or *scholarship*? It is the result of doing away with the vital distinction between wisdom and ignorance.
- What is a *politician*? It is the result of doing away with the vital distinction between a visionary and a leader of self-seekers.
- What is a *talk show*? It is the result of doing away with the vital distinction between intimacy and gossip.
- What is *social welfare*? It is the result of doing away with the vital distinction between charity and heedlessness.
- What is a *poll*? It is the result of doing away with the vital distinction between knowledge of the particulars and knowledge of the universals.
- What is *gross national product*? It is the result of doing away with the vital distinction between the health of a nation and its phony smile.
- What is *seeking a well-paid profession*? It is the result of doing away with the vital distinction between you seeking the world and the world seeking you.[2]

One might continue the list. The ones I offer are justified on no other grounds than their intuitive soundness. They instruct on what it is we should stay away from—apostasy, utter deceit, ignorance, heedlessness, knowledge of the universals, and such—and what it is we should avidly pursue—worship, truth telling, wisdom, charity, knowledge of the particulars, and so on. These properties stated in isolation appear bland; they lose the color they have when inserted into rich contexts. One might propose old properties that do away with new distinctions, for example: What is *social welfare*? It is the result of doing away with the vital distinction between offering a hand and donating money. Or, far more interestingly, suggest new properties that do away with old distinctions, for example: What is *pity*? It is the result of doing away with the vital distinction between charity and heedlessness. One might have pursued a commonplace philosophical task: to ferret out those basic properties from which the others would follow. Kierkegaard understandably does not do so, nor will I.

My only concern for now is to ask, Can one be saved from this darker side without the help of understanding? In each instance, Kierke-

---

[2]See Kierkegaard on money (75, 40-41).

gaard urges that only passion can save us; I argue that our hope lies, at least in the *first* instance, in understanding. There at least must be a glimmer in us that something is wrong; minimally, we must be in a doxastic state.[3] For example, we have to understand what it is *to keep silent* if one is to rid oneself of the fault of talkativeness: no amount of passion will help if one does not know when one should talk and when one should not and what ill talkativeness perpetuates. Similarly, one has to understand what it is to be a *visionary* to avoid being a leader of self-seekers or to be a *politician* of the right kind because, without understanding what it is to be a visionary, no amount of passion can insure that one is on the path of righteousness. This is not to say that understanding what it is to be a visionary, or when one should keep silent, is a simple thing. It is not: an understanding of a host of other things would undoubtedly be required. The final act will also require will and passion. Clearly, understanding is necessary to dispel the surrounding and increasing darkness in one's everyday life. What else ensues with this darkness?

BANDING TOGETHER

When corruption has laced itself into the very fabric of the day-to-day existence of men, then men seek comfort in groups. This is one way in which they shirk, or avoid, individual responsibility. But one cannot be saved by joining a crowd. One can only be saved by standing against the crowd, and acknowledging one's eternal responsibility before God. A group, a community, or an association may be indispensable in building a cathedral or an outhouse, but one cannot obtain salvation by a joint enterprise. By the nature of the case, it is something one must do alone or not at all. Kierkegaard has this to say:

> Even if a small group of people had the courage to meet death, we today would not say that each individual had the courage to do that, for

---

[3]This initial state of *feeling* that moves us needs, I venture, a far more careful analysis than has been treated in the literature thus far. One might simply dismiss, or insist, that it is a passion. On the other hand, one might argue, that it is a vague belief-state—yet, a *belief*-state—with which a passion of varying degrees might be associated. Thus, it is passion that rides piggyback on an epistemic state. In the absence of that belief-state, the goad to know more, or better, will be lacking, and the effort may even be misdirected.

what the individual fears more than death is reflection's judgment upon him, reflection's objection to his wanting to venture something as an individual. . . . therefore ten would have to agree on something in which it is a contradiction to be more than one. . . . And what is the basis of this other than a disregard for the separation of the religious individual before God in the responsibility of eternity. When dismay commences at this point, one seeks comfort in company. (85-86, 53)

But why does banding together not help? What does it do? What effect does it have on the individual? *When* is joining together justifiable? Kierkegaard answers:

It is very doubtful, then, that the age will be saved by the idea of sociality, of association. On the contrary, this idea is the scepticism necessary for the proper development of individuality, inasmuch as every individual either is lost or, disciplined by the abstraction, finds himself religiously. In our age the principle of association (which at best can have validity with respect to material interests) is not affirmative but negative; it is an evasion, a dissipation, an illusion, whose dialectic is as follows: as it strengthens individuals, it vitiates them; it strengthens by numbers, by sticking together, but from the ethical point of view this is a weakening.[4] Not until the single individual has established an ethical stance despite the whole world, not until then can there be any question of genuinely uniting; otherwise it gets to be a union of people who separately are weak, a union as unbeautiful and depraved as a child marriage.[5] (106, 79)

---

[4] "I do not respond, I am not responsible, to the ultimate power if I lapse into the responses of the group, respond as one who among other things is also a Christian. . . . Kierkegaard's attack on mass Christianity was doubtless made with a somewhat inadequate interpretation of social institutions in mind. It was not quite fitting, but the truth that is in it was not overstated. 'When everyone is a Christian, no one is a Christian.' The faith that is not my own but a unit of a mass is not trust or loyalty. It may be a content of a common mind" (H. Richard Niebuhr, *The Responsible Self: An Essay in Christian Moral Philosophy*, 120-21). I owe this citation to J. Philip Woodland, a retired methodist pastor, who also corrected several of my infelicities.

[5] Ask: Why is the marriage of children as disgusting as it is harmful? Is it because they lack passion? Or is it rather because they lack maturity and understanding? Lacking understanding, they cannot enter into an informed, binding, responsible covenant.

This is a powerful credo for anyone interested in constructing a utopia.[6] Suppose the Nile annually inundates; it wreaks havoc along its banks and neighboring fields. While it deposits rich alluvial soil, the loss it inflicts outweighs the good it produces. Engineers and architects have a technical problem on their hands. They construct dams and canals. Consequently, the fields are no longer inundated, crops no longer ruined, and ecosystems no longer destabilized. The Nile now runs smoothly, as do its several artificially constructed tributaries. Applaud the engineers and architects.

This is the sort of analogy we have in mind when we try and solve human problems in society. Social planners play the roles of architects and engineers; the problems of untrained work force, environmental degradation, illiteracy, runaway population, lack of medical care, and inflation compare to the problems created by the inundating Nile; finally, humans take the place of fields. We want the social planners to devise a plan whereby humans without *themselves* changing, or changing a whole lot, will bring about a solution to these problems. (The fields themselves did not contribute anything in solving the problem of the inundation of the Nile, did they?) The humans will march in lockstep with the plans for social engineering, and thus alleviate the social problems. Thus, social problems are seen as technical problems.[7]

Kierkegaard's view goes far beyond this. Even if these, or some of these, problems are solved by group effort, these help the community out of the social and political morass, but not out of its real problems, namely, the ethical or religious ones. The latter problems can only be solved by the individuals transforming themselves—and by the nature of the case, thinks Kierkegaard, they must do so solitarily, unaided. One might say, the social and political problems are external problems, or as he calls them, "the material interests," which, if solved, strengthen the individuals separately and collectively. But that kind of strengthening "is an escape, a distraction, and an illusion." Being successful in solving external problems means being unsuccessful in solving internal problems,

---

[6]As I am, in constructing a utopia of scientists: see *A Theory of Method*, chap. 5, esp. sect. IV.

[7]It was Garett Hardin, "The Tragedy of the Commons," who challenged this assumption and warned about it a long time ago.

the ethical and religious problems—which we shall call, by analogy, "the spiritual interests." It is as if each field had to solve its own real problems once the Nile stopped ruining them. Not even a well-regulated Nile could do *that*. However, once the individuals have transformed themselves, by acquiring an ethical outlook in the face of odds, then, and only then, can there really be a "joining together."

Even this picture is not detailed enough. Let us distinguish several cases. I am painting in very broad strokes. Essentially, the four communities that are to be delineated are the result of permutation on *able to dispense with each other / unable to dispense with each other* and *able to hold together / unable to hold together*. In what follows, taking Kierkegaard's cue, I shall call an individual weak if he has not acquired an ethical outlook. (One way this can happen is by the danger and harsh judgment of existence on his thoughtlessness arousing the ethical in him [71, 37].) Otherwise, I shall call him *strong*[8] (106, 79). Imagine, first, a collection of individuals who are weak and who are scattered, not joined in an association. Let us call this the *community of the weak*. Here the negative law seems to be exemplified. The law says "opposites are unable to dispense with each other and unable to hold together." The opposites are the members of the community; they require one another insofar as community is to be possible at all, but not being strong they are driven

---

[8]My use of *ethical* is bit different from Kierkegaard's. For Kierkegaard, in the ultimate analysis, there is no such thing as the ethical that does not involve God indispensably and centrally. This is why he speaks of pagan virtues as "glittering vices," as the Church Fathers, Saint Augustine (*The City of God*, book XIX, chap. 25), and Lactantius had characterized them before him. My assumption is that a pagan can be virtuous even if he is an atheist, otherwise the charge of being unethical or immoral against the pagan would be true by definition; alternatively, I am attempting to keep virtue separate from grace.

The reader need only grant me this provisionally. Although it should be noted that it does sit well with Kierkegaard's description of the French Revolution as one in which individuals were moved by an ideal, and moved passionately, in contrast to the present age which lacks both ideals and passion. Must we conclude that an individual thus moved in that revolutionary age, who did not believe in God, but who shared the same passion, commitment, and huge risks as did a theist fellow revolutionary, was unethical?

apart from one another by their selfishness. Their selfishness is the reason they are unable to hold together.

Second, a collection of individuals who are weak and who find themselves numerically strengthened by joining into an association. Let us call this the *community of this-lifers*. This seems to be exemplified by the positive law. It states that "opposites are able to dispense with each other and are able to hold together." Here the members of the community have managed to become independent; but their material interests dictate that they should set aside their selfishness, or their envy, in order to further their material interests. Thus, they form an association. It would be the disgusting association of which Kierkegaard spoke.[9]

Third, a collection of individuals who are strong but not joined in an association. Let us call this the *community of the strong*—the result, perhaps, of the separation law. This law states that opposites are able to dispense with each other and unable to hold together. This law is exemplified when each member of the community has become ethical through the process Kierkegaard recognizes, but for a variety of reasons, perhaps, based on nothing more than contingent facts, they are unable to found an association. It is not their selfishness that has gotten in their way; it is, say, the inability to find a common goal.

---

[9]"Whenever they were together, fanfares cleared the way before them and they picked up Paris in one hand and put it calmly in their pocket. Victory was theirs for certain, so what did they care about down-at-heel boots and threadbare jackets when they could be conquerors at will? Their disdain went hand-in-hand with a boundless contempt for everything outside their art, for society, and, above all, for politics. What use had they for such sordid nonsense? Nothing but a lot of brainless old dodderers. Their youthful arrogance set them above all sense of justice and made them deliberately ignore all the claims of social life in their mad pursuit of their dreams of an artists' Utopia. There were times when it turned their heads completely, but it also gave them both strength and courage" (Emile Zola, *The Masterpiece*, 74).

Merold Westphal might describe this transformation thus: "This is not to say that the herd has no values; rather, a transvaluation of values has occurred in which moral values have been replaced by other values. The categories of the moral life are put out of play and no longer function as the condition of possible existence" ("Kierkegaard's Sociology," 142).

Fourth, and finally, a collection of individuals who are strong and who are joined into an association. Let us call this the *community of Utopia*.[10] Here, the fundamental law seems to be at work. This law states that opposites are unable to dispense with each other and are able to hold together. Here we have a community of citizens who have not only become ethical, but are bound together into a kind of society that Kierkegaard would laud. Such a society neither makes their behaviors uniform nor engenders, therefore, skepticism. There really is joining together here.[11] This is a Utopian community, not only of how one should be, but also of how a community should be modelled or structured.[12]

Merold Westphal in "Kierkegaard's Sociology," offers four kinds of societies: a subhuman society, an amoral society, a diabolical society, and

---

[10]"When individuals (each one individually) are essentially and passionately related to an idea and together are essentially related to the same idea, the relation is optimal and normative" (62). I owe this citation to Anthony Rudd. This is from an earlier part of *Two Ages*, from *The Age of Revolution*, and not from *The Present Age*, nor does Kierkegaard mention it later nor make any real use of it, such as in delineating a utopia.

[11]"Like all lovers," wrote John Bayley the novelist, in an article about his wife, Iris Murdoch, and their marriage, "I suppose, I wished to be a special case in quite the wrong sense—to be 'the one.' I felt that by telling me that she didn't want anyone to know of the novel's existence Iris was singling me out. But her instinct, in this regard, was, essentially, a kindly one. She wanted each of her friends to know her in the same pristine way. No groups, no sets. No comparing of notes between two about a third. This desire that each of her relationships should be special and separate, as innocent as in the Garden of Eden, was of great significance to Iris. Since what she felt about each of her friendships was totally genuine and without guile, there was no gradation among them, no comparisons made. Each one was whole in itself" ("Elegy for Iris," 47). Imagine a community of Iris Murdochs, and you imagine a community of Utopia.

[12]"If then one could contrive a state or an army should entirely consist of lovers and loved, it would be impossible for it to have a better organization than that which it would then enjoy through their avoidance of all dishonor and their mutual emulation; moreover, a handful of such men, fighting side by side, would defeat practically the whole world" (Plato, *The Symposium*, 43). Plato's vision was perhaps shaped by the Sacred Band of Thebes which was organized along these lines. A community of Utopia, duly adjusted by the present demands or constraints, might be such a Platonic community.

a society of glittering vices. They are intrinsically of great interest and I now briefly attend to the relationship between the Westphalian four communities with the four delineated here. To begin with, the Westphalian four societies are neither parallel to mine nor overtly rest on the four principles of association (in fact, Westphal recognizes only the two principles Kierkegaard himself has delineated).

The community of the weak could harbor all four of the Westphalian societies, but particularly the subhuman society and the amoral society, under its rubric. In chalking the community of the weak I have not particularly paid attention, as indeed Westphal has, to the aesthetic form of life Kierkegaard is deeply concerned with in *Either/Or: A Fragment of Life*. No human individual can get rid of his spiritual side, try as he might; but, he can ignore it, if he so chooses—and in so choosing he has sunk below the human level. Such an individual has not yet chosen the ethical.

The community of this-lifers has affinity with the diabolical society in that the herd, having pronounced that God is dead, turns amoral. Westphal says, "Kierkegaard sees the very amorality of the herd to be the ground of its eventually demonic self-deification."[13] But there is the following difference. I see it as possible for this-lifers to be ethical in a way in which Kierkegaard does not see it: for him the ethical must be eventually grounded in God. If it is not, then all attempts at constructing a just society that is not God-centered is eventually self-centered; hence, all such attempts lead eventually to demonic self-deification.[14]

The community of the strong and the Utopian community, given the last paragraph, might have a good deal in common with the society of glittering vices. Westphal takes the view of Kierkegaard, as did the Church Fathers, that in the absence of God virtues are merely glorified vices. Saint Augustine proves instructive. He says, "where there is no true justice there can be no 'association of men united by a common sense of right' [as Scipio had held]. . . . [J]ustice is that virtue which assigns to everyone his due. Then what kind of justice is it that takes a man away from the true God and subjects him to unclean demons?"[15]

---

[13]"Kierkegaard's Sociology," 145. For illustration, see n. 9 above.
[14]See n. 8 above.
[15]*The City of God*, 882.

Suppose, says Augustine later, one should say, " 'A people is the association of a multitude of rational beings united by a common agreement on the objects of their love.' . . . And, obviously, the better the objects of this agreement, the better the people; the worse the objects of love, the worse the people."[16] Consequently, one might argue against Augustine and Kierkegaard that, first, there might be an association of a multitude of rational beings that does not believe in God—say, a certain liberal community—and yet is run along the lines of justice commended by a Christian society *modulo* God. Second, this association is distinguished from the pagan association in that the former does not subject man to unclean demons or compel him to worship pagan gods. The liberal community does not have the worst objects of agreement as the pagan association does even if the liberal community does not have the best objects of agreement as the Christian community does. The object of their love is simply liberty, equality, and secular justice. Third, I do not see *this* community as being essentially selfish. But, Augustine's theory is underpinned by a powerful psychological claim: "For although the virtues are reckoned by some people to be genuine and honorable when they are related only to themselves and are sought for no other end, even then they are puffed up and proud, and so are to be counted vices rather than virtues."[17] (*The City of God*, 891). It is clear, I think, that in the Augustinian view no matter how humble a pagan—or a liberal—his virtues can only be alleged virtues. This, I claim, is at least not a necessary truth. Consequently, it is *possible* for a community of the strong or the Utopian community to have a marked family resemblance to the Westphalian society of glittering vices.

WHAT UTOPIA?

It is the community of utopia of which I see little recognition in Kierkegaard. There is no doubt that it is the result of Kierkegaard's curious view of what associations do and what it is for an individual to be saved. Kierkegaard's failure to weave the third stage, the stage of understanding, into his view becomes starkly noticeable here. Suppose a community of scientists formed into a community of *this-lifers*. Their aim is scientific

---

[16]*The City of God*, 890.
[17]*The City of God*, 891.

truth; but what motivates that search is greed, power, fame, and glory; and the association is structured to let them vent these desires in full so that in mad pursuit of these desires they will unwittingly fulfill the aims of science.[18]

But a Utopian society of scientists is one that is, surely, morally enlightened. Its pursuit of truth is constrained, above all, by moral notions and principles. Perhaps, in such a society the acquisition of truths might be a slower process; it may take decades where in the other community it might have taken only a few years; yet, such a society would prefer slower over quicker rates of return of truths; would prefer an ethical society over an unethical one, if for this reason only: that such a society would make it easier for an individual to be saved than not. *That*, in anyone's scheme, should be the only thing that matters. Unless, of course, the only thing that matters is how much of one's greed is satisfied and how many of one's desires for power, fame, and glory are fulfilled. Not an attractive picture, this. I state it not to commend it, but, with Kierkegaard, to warn against it.

Now here is the point of my analogy: even if a scientific society or group had the right aim (namely, the pursuit of truth), and other things (namely, greed, power, and glory) were of no importance, it would not follow that they could organize themselves into a rational society. They would still need a deep theory about what makes a scientific society—not

---

[18]This is no parody. Such a proposal has actually been made. See Philip Kitcher, "The Cognitive Division of Labor," esp. 21-22; see also Kitcher's *The Advancement of Science: Science without Legend, Objectivity without Illusions.* Kitcher is attempting the impossible task of reconciling sociology of knowledge with normative methodology. Our recent sociologists of science herald as their fresh, great, and stupendous discovery that the lives of scientists are nasty, brutish, and short. That the scientists labor under the burden of a distinctive social and political structure and individual values and that, as a result, their scientific work is no more than a reflection of that structure and those values. How, then, must a scientific Utopia be formed *respecting* these traits? Denouncing them only gives us an unrealistic airy-fairy picture of science. Or so it is argued. For that reason, Kitcher attempts to dovetail the norms of science with the sociology of science. I hold no truck with this bleak picture, nor with the philosophical enterprise it embodies. See my "The Task of Group Rationality: The Subjectivist's View," part I.

just the individual scientists in it—rational. (They will need a theory, too, for what makes an individual scientist rational.) This is true also for pursuers of ethical truth or seekers of spiritual interests. Even if each individual in the community, chastened by the harsh experience of the world yet not succumbing to it, has become ethical, it would not follow that they would immediately know how to form a just or good community. And they would require just as much understanding for knowing how to do that, how to form such a community, as for knowing what makes an individual ethical.

This is, clearly, not an unimportant task. If how an individual's passions and values are shaped, at least in part, depend upon the nature of the society around him—a commonplace theme in our society, for understanding, lightening responsibilities, or condoning deeds—then the chances of an individual's ethical or religious survival depend upon the structure and substance of that society.[19] To put the point in Kierkegaardian terms: if how the inner religious lives of individuals are shaped is dependent, at least in part, upon the history of their environment, then it is a crucially important task to fashion a society's environment so that individuals can religiously live and thrive.[20] If they do not become religiously or ethically free in such a society, then, perhaps, it may mitigate their ethical or religious degradation or deprivation. What should be the

---

[19]In the preface to the novel (published as a supplement in the Hongs' translation) *Two Ages*, which Kierkegaard is reviewing, Thomasine Gyllembourg, the author, writes: "This power of the spirit of the age over individuals' innermost feelings, over their completely private relationships and their judgment of themselves and others, the glaring contrast in which the very same human passions, virtues, and weaknesses appear in the various ages—this is what I have wished to depict as it has presented itself to me in my own experience and the experience of others" (155). In his review, Kierkegaard neither denies this significant effect nor confronts it.

[20]The single better and stronger statement than I have devised is this: "But in any case it is clear from a number of places in Kierkegaard's authorship that he regards both goals, the establishing of a harmonious society on the one hand and the fulfillment of true individuality on the other, as closely interwoven, even logically connected" (Alastair Hannay, *Kierkegaard*, 281).

structure and substance of that society?[21] The answer to that question rests inescapably on our understanding of both the individual and society.

Much more, in a good and just society it may be that individuals will reach ethical and religious heights hitherto undreamt of. Then, being saved and not being saved are crude, insufficient alternatives: we need speak of a scale of being saved, *a scale of salvation*. (Isn't there a moral hierarchy among men, and, for that matter, among saints and prophets?[22]) Such a scale should nicely dovetail with the other scales we spoke of earlier: the scale of understanding, the scale of passion, the scale of deed.[23] In a Utopian community, each individual would tend toward the high end of the scales of understanding, passion, and deed—or of being saved—that he would not be able to reach in the present age. The individuals in a Utopian community would not only be governed by what is true about the external world, the world of material interests, but also by what is true about the internal world, the world of spiritual interests, *and* how the two interests are linked. Think of monasteries, hospices, cloisters, and *ashrams* and, on a smaller scale, retreats and yoga centers. The individuals would work jointly in the belief that there is truth to be garnered about the spiritual or internal world, and that the acquisition of these truths may well depend upon the proper, rational, and just structure

---

[21]Kierkegaard is apparently not too interested in this problem. Thus Bruce H. Kirmmse: "To the limited degree to which SK takes a position on constitutional representative government *per se*, one cannot say that he was negatively disposed. However, it is not so much the principle of government espoused by one or another generation or group which here concerns SK but rather the way in which the principle is appropriated. Any honestly and passionately held idea which respects the individual as an integral unit and as the starting point for all further association would meet SK's criteria, and one can thus easily imagine quite a range of political systems—conservative, liberal, democratic, etc.—to which SK could assent" (*Kierkegaard: In Golden Age Denmark*, 270-71).

If one were not concerned about material interests, then one would be indifferent to which political system—say, conservative or democratic—was in place. One would not be interested in this political problem either, if one believes that material interests have *no* bearing on spiritual interests. But that, at least, is not self-evident.

[22]See chap. 5.

[23]See chap. 1, 6.

of the community in which they live as on anything else. Indeed, if it is true that what finally saves an individual is his passion, then that passion must be correctly linked, through understanding, to the truths about an individual and his society. And this passion would then produce the deeds that are worthy, just, good, and noble, and, should he make the leap, save him. No matter how we look at this, understanding, and not just passion, is of utter consequence.

Let me present this from the vantage point of "Call Me Ishmael—Call Everyone Ishmael." In this brilliant paper, Bruce H. Kirmmse traces in a nutshell the history of political thought from Adam Smith, through John Locke and Karl Marx, to Ferdinand Tonnies—while beginning and ending with Ishmael of the Old Testament: "He shall be a wild ass of a man, his hand against every man, and every man's hand against him; and he shall dwell over against all his kinsmen"[24]—to place in better philosophical perspective Kierkegaard's view of society and politics.

Imagine two societies: a liberal society and a society of Christians. The individuals in the liberal society have all read John Rawls's *A Theory of Justice*. They greatly admire the book, they have argued back and forth, and they all agree that for all their differences they should transform their society in the closest possible way into the one described in that book. Not only is there reason and agreement; there is also passion, a passion hitched to an idea, an ideal. The individuals in the society of Christians model their society on Christian tenets. They, too, have argued back and forth as to what these tenets are, and finally they are agreed not only about the kind of society they wish to engineer into existence, but to which they will give their undying allegiance.

Which society must Kierkegaard prefer? First, assume both societies flourish in a manner each would have itself flourish. Would, or should, Kierkegaard be indifferent between the two societies? Perhaps not. Kierkegaard might fear the hopelessly false assumption that the form and fabric of the society have no real bearing on the kind or type of men and women it will fashion. Thus, the liberal society allows an atheist, no less than a polytheist, to have a life plan and to live accordingly; and there can exist groups of such individuals. The result would be that a Christian individual would constantly be faced with trials and temptations inasmuch

---

[24]Genesis 16:12 RSV.

as he would constantly face non-Christian power, propaganda, and politics. These would make his life quite difficult, to say nothing of the lives
of his children and young adults. Kierkegaard cannot argue that these
trials and temptations will only serve to strengthen the individual, or that
the greater the trials the greater his victory will be should he overcome
them. He cannot so argue because he should then prefer the worst social
and political system which would put the greatest pressure on an individual (the kind prophets were subjected to?); or, he has nothing significant to say about social and political theory. Clearly, Kierkegaard must
choose, and give us reasons for his choice.

There are obvious variants. In which society does an individual have
a better chance of not losing himself, in a liberal society in which the
passion is still not lost or in a Christian society of the type Kierkegaard
bemoans?[25] Which society would Kierkegaard find less objectionable if
both societies were to lose their respective passions? Finally, and significantly, why is it obvious that he would prefer a Christian society in
which passion still rides over a liberal society in which passion has
faded? Why could not a striving individual be equally instructed ethically
in both cases (if not more in the latter case)?

Second, a liberal society is grounded in the voice and reason of the
people, not that of God—witness Rawls's key argument in the original
position. There is a veil of ignorance imposed on the individuals deciding
what form of society they wish to have. What they do not know in this
condition is their sex, economic background, class position, social status,
natural assets and abilities, intelligence and strength, psychological pro-
pensities, conceptions of the good, rational plan of life,[26] *and*, by implication, religion, and anything else that is "arbitrary from a moral point of
view."[27] These individuals reason using a maximin strategy that would
best serve their self-interest, but in a manner that does not violate the
self-interests of others.[28] Not only that, Rawls expects that individuals will

---

[25]Kirmmse, "Call Me Ishmael—Call Everyone Ishmael," 168-69.

[26]John Rawls, *A Theory of Justice*, chap. 3, art. 24, esp. p. 137.

[27]"Intuitively, the most obvious injustice of the system of natural liberty is
that it permits distributive shares to be improperly influenced by these factors so
arbitrary from a moral point of view" (Rawls, *A Theory of Justice*, 72).

[28]The maximin strategy advises that "we are to adopt the alternative the
worst outcome of which is superior to the worst outcomes of the others" (Rawls,

comply with these principles, and be known to comply with them, to ensure the stability of the society through public knowledge that each individual is pulling his or her weight in sustaining the society they have collectively created.[29]

Well, here's Kierkegaard:

all doubt has ultimately its stronghold in the illusion of temporal existence that we are a lot of us, pretty much the whole of humanity, which in the end can jolly well overawe God and be itself the Christ. And pantheism is an acoustic illusion that confounds *vox populi* with *vox dei*.[30]

And here's Westphal:

Living in a godless society the individual "seeks comfort in company." This company is "a something more" than the individuals who make it up. But it is not a human We that transcends the human I's who make it up. It is no voluntary association as Locke would have it, nor a moral commonwealth as Rousseau and Kant would have it, nor the incarnate spirit of a nation as Fichte and Hegel would have it. It is "an abstract power," that, though not human, holds human beings in bondage. It is a "demon." Through satanic pride a demonic power has been conjured up, and modern mass society is itself this demonic power.[31]

A Theory of Justice, 153). Is this just the kind of prudence Kierkegaard warned against?

[29]"It is an important feature of a conception of justice that it should generate its own support" (Rawls, *A Theory of Justice*, 138). Not only must one subscribe to the system, but one must do so in a manner that supports, sustains, and strengthens the system.

[30]*The Point of View for my Work as an Author*, 145. "Every individual," Kierkegaard says in *Training in Christianity*, "ought to live in fear and trembling, and so too there is no established order which can do without fear and trembling. Fear and trembling signifies that one is in a process of becoming, and every individual man, and the race as well, is or should be conscious of being in process of becoming. And fear and trembling signifies that a God exists—a fact which no man and no established order dare for an instant forget" (89).

[31]"Kierkegaard's Sociology," 147. See also Westphal's *Kierkegaard's Critique of Reason and Society*, chap. 3, esp. 30-32. I cite this passage because it neatly and substantially captures Kierkegaard's intent. Yet, I am puzzled why Westphal qualifies it as he does. Unless an individual is related to God as he

should be, his being a member in a God-oriented society will not help him; likewise, if his society is godless, his being related to God as he should be will not be enough to create a society human beings should live in.

In any event, the ultimate foundation of society in Locke, Rousseau, and Kant, is the reason of man, not the voice of God. Thus, Locke's society is fundamentally secular. "The toleration," says Locke, "of those that differ from others in Matters of Religion, is so agreeable to the Gospel of Jesus Christ, and to the genuine Reason of Mankind, that it seems monstrous for Men to be so blind as not to perceive the Necessity and Advantage of it, in so clear a Light" (*A Letter concerning Toleration*, 234).

Notwithstanding, Locke advocates a sharp separation between the Church and the Commonwealth, "each of them [must] contain itself within its own Bounds, the one attending to the worldly Welfare of the Commonwealth, the other to the Salvation of Souls" (*A Letter concerning Toleration*, 254). The State will secure to each individual his just "possession of the Things belonging to this Life" while the Church is to be engaged "in regulating . . . Men's Lives according to the Rules of Virtue and Piety" (*A Letter Concerning Toleration*, 235). Importantly, where there is conflict between Church and State, Locke clearly seems to favor the State. "Whatsoever is lawful in the Commonwealth," says Locke, "cannot be prohibited by the Magistrate in the Church. . . . those Things that are prejudicial to the Commonweal of a People in their ordinary Use, and are therefore forbidden by Laws, those Things ought not to be permitted to Churches in their sacred rites" (*A Letter concerning Toleration*, 245).

Rousseau's society is secular in its intent, too. Consult books I and II of *On the Social Contract*, for example, and one hears not a religious word in the discussion pertaining to the first convention, social compact, private and general will, sovereignty of man, on laws, on government, and such. Rousseau's great legislator (book II, chap. VII) could have been as pagan as you wish. Nor should one be misled by Rousseau's talk about "a moral and collective body" (24) and "the sanctity of the contract" (25)—for "moral" and "sanctity" here are not religious concepts. For criticism of what passed for Christianity in Rousseau's day see the early pages of chap. VIII, "Of Civil Religion," of that book. Rousseau even thinks ill of the lay Christian view. "Thus there remains the religion of man or Christianity (not that of today, but that of the Gospel, which is completely different). Through this holy, sublime, true religion, men, in being the children of the same God, all acknowledge one another as brothers, and the society that unites them is not dissolved even at death" (102). What would Rousseau advocate in dealing with an individual who does not wish to be a Christian, not even in Rousseau's sense? It is abundantly clear that Rousseau

Clearly, Kierkegaard cannot, or ought not, approve a society that has been ultimately founded on *vox populi*, no matter how philosophically smart that voice.

Distinguish two kinds of societies, a traditional society (*Gemeinschaft*) and the modern society (*Gessellschaft*) or the present age.[32] The traditional society is founded on a corporate idea, built upon natural ties

---

would rise to the individual's defense.

Kant's view is hardly one which Kierkegaard would endorse, given *Fear and Trembling* (see esp. the Hongs' notes on 348-49) and since Rawls is Kant's great intellectual descendant, I venture Kierkegaard would not be too pleased with Rawls either. See George B. Connell, "Judge William's Theonomous Ethics," for some solid arguments in favor of the view that Kantian ethics is sealed off from Kierkegaardian ethics. Parenthetically, Connell's idea can be usefully generalized. He notes Judge William's view that what makes the bond of marriage firm is God, in the absence of Whom marriages can just as easily be dissolved as created. Might one, then, show that it is only the presence of God which firms up the relationship between individuals by virtue of which they are true citizens and constitute a true community?

As for Fichte and Hegel, even if the Commonwealth were the incarnate spirit of a nation, that would not satisfy Kierkegaard; he would demand that the individual first become an individual before he becomes a partner in the unfolding of his nation's history. "It is Christian heroism—a rarity, to be sure— to venture wholly to become oneself, an individual human being, this specific individual human being, alone before God, alone in this prodigious strenuousness, and this prodigious responsibility; but it is not Christian heroism to be taken in by the idea of man in the abstract or to play the wonder game with world history" (*The Sickness unto Death*, 5). Would participating in any nation, any unfolding, be ethically satisfactory?

It is my claim that Kierkegaard never did give social and political philosophy much thought for the simple reason that he was primarily concerned about the individual in whatever society that individual lived. It is clearly not my argument that social and political philosophy can be dispensed with so much as to show—gesture in the right direction—that Kierkegaard's options in that field are considerably narrow. The task of finding a political theory that squares nicely with Kierkegaard's fundamental view of man is a deeply intriguing and worthwhile task.

[32]The argument of this paragraph is indebted to the German sociologist Ferdinand Tonnies. See Kirmmse, "Call Me Ishmael—Call Everyone Ishmael," 164.

and natural will, while the latter society is market-oriented and individual-
istic, inasmuch as it centers upon the rational will which highlights our
self-interest. There is no separate question of justice or fairness other than
what is determined by impersonal market forces. The modern society
dissolves all natural ties that an individual bears to another so he can
more effectively transact business, sell property, change attitudes, and
adapt to the discoveries in science. Clearly, the traditional society would
be more constraining, and that would have impact on economic and social
development, as Adam Smith foresaw and forewarned. "The State, too,"
says Ferdinand Tonnies, "feels the restrictive influence of these ties, and
hastens the tendency toward their dissolution, and considers enlightened,
greedy, and practical people as its most useful subjects."[33]

Such individuals, with such nasty characteristics, are presumably
essential if the tasks of the state are to be performed, and those are essential social and economic tasks. But religiousness is not to be confused
with the task of politics. Kirmmse trenchantly remarks:

> The proper sphere of politics, of "the public," is clear. It is the task of
> the state to see to it that various things that people need are available
> to them reliably and at reasonable cost. This is the case with roads and
> highways, street illumination, public water supply, and public safety. So,
> society argues, why not also purchase "eternal blessedness" in bulk and
> distribute it at lowest cost?[34]

But while one can purchase the former, one cannot, surely, purchase the
latter. So Kierkegaard can justly cry out, "there is nothing which makes
me so uneasy as anything which tastes of even the merest trace of this
disastrous confounding of politics and Christianity."[35]

---

[33]Quoted in Kirmmse, "Call Me Ishmael—Call Everyone Ishmael," 166.

[34]"Call Me Ishmael—Call Everyone Ishmael," 170-71.

[35]Kirmmse, "Call Me Ishmael—Call Everyone Ishmael," 170-71. For my purposes the footnote attached to the quote from Kierkegaard is of some importance:
"However," says Kirmmse, "to say that politics and Christianity shouldn't be
confounded with each other is not to say they have nothing to do with each
other. . . . The implication is that the state is only able to be truly a state (i.e.,
a useful, but limited, relative institution) when its members are aware that they
exist before the absolute (God) and so refuse to absolutize/deify the state"
(180n.52). What kind of society or Utopia would such individuals who "are

Thus, Kierkegaard pits the "Neighbor" against the crass "Individual." The passage from Kirmmse is long, yet a paraphrase will not do:

> But Kierkegaard's insistence upon "the individual" as the appropriate unit for the modern age does not mean that he promotes solipsistic self-absorption for it is only as an "individual" before God that we first experience our "Neighbor." In the self-interested individualism of Ishmael in the market-based *Gessellschaft*, the other person is an object to be manipulated for one's private gain. . . . [T]he other person is not seen or loved in his/her own right, but only egoistically, as "the second I." It is only when one has become "an individual before God" that one is capable of seeing the other person as one's Neighbor, as "the first person you see," as "the first Thou" rather than the "second I."[36]

None of this can be questioned; it is vintage Kierkegaard. But I am interested in the *implications* of these claims. The traditional society dissipated, and the modern society emerged. There were gains no less than losses. Say, Smithian goals were achieved, Kierkegaardian ones were lost. One might describe a slow evolutionary process whereby the values of the individuals in the traditional society came to be replaced by the values of the present age, and one might identify and offer a causal account for the transformation of the values that eventually led to the downfall of the traditional society. What transformations would be wrought on the present age as individuals brought to bear on it Kierkegaardian values? My impulse is simply to say, "Good ones—unconditionally." But I pause. Would such a society evolve into a society that is a kindred of the older one? If so, will it face social and economic problems of a similar sort, making some future Adam Smith usher in new economic ideas as his Scottish namesake had done in the past?

Kierkegaard himself had strenuously fought to undermine the illusory notions of what is Christianity in his society *and*—please note—"to attack the governmental and social apparatus that perpetuates these illusions."[37] Would it be fair, or unfair, to say that no matter what the political system—democratic, socialist, liberal, or conservative—the illusions

---

aware that they exist before the absolute" prefer? Or, would they be indifferent among political systems?

[36]Kirmmse, "Call Me Ishmael—Call Everyone Ishmael," 177.

[37]Kirmmse, "Call Me Ishmael—Call Everyone Ishmael," 174.

would be more or less the same (and hence not worth the fight against the governmental and social apparatus) *or* different enough to warrant a Christian to fight for the overthrow of a particular political system and to replace it with a better, or at least a less sordid, one? Given this context, consider the issue of taxes. Kierkegaard says, "paying taxes to Caesar [is] the most indifferent thing of all, i.e., something one must do without wasting one word or one moment in talking about it, in order to have all the more time in which to render unto God what is God's."[38] The greatest danger in paying too much attention to the state is to deify the state. "The deification of the Established Order makes everything worldly."[39] Now the running of the state does not involve just things like water pipeline, sewerage system, electric lines, waste disposal system, and such, but also how the tax dollars are used for other purposes, such as welfare, prevention of racial and sexual discrimination, abortion, criminal punishment and death, war and war-related research, education, environmental protection, medicine and homes for the sick and the elderly, genetic engineering, mental illness, and dying. Should an individual leave these to the governmental and social apparatus, too, "in order to have all the more time in which to render unto God what is God's"? Or, might he fear the illusions his inaction will perpetuate? If an individual is related to God, he is saved; but, then, he must *return* to society and confront the issues of justice.[40] Might he protest that his tax dollars are used to sustain an

---

[38]Kirmmse, "Call Me Ishmael—Call Everyone Ishmael," 171.

[39]Kirmmse, "Call Me Ishmael—Call Everyone Ishmael," 171.

[40]It is clear, I think, that such an individual who isolates himself from such responsibilities bears the full brunt of Kierkegaard's attack on mysticism in *Either/Or: A Fragment of Life* (see esp. 535-44 and 582), once his arguments are duly and easily modified. Elsewhere Kierkegaard says, "For although the ethical individual might refer to himself as his own editor, he is at the same time fully aware of his editorial responsibility to himself, insofar as what he chooses has a decisive influence on him personally, *to the scheme of things in which he lives*, and to God" (551; my emphasis).

Again: "He must open his self in respect of his whole concretion, but to that concretion also belong those factors specifically to do with taking an active part in the world. So his movement will be from himself, *through the world*, to himself" (561; my emphasis). Much of Kierkegaard's discussion is in the context of the three virtues: personal, civic, and religious or contemplative (see 535-37).

intrinsically bad political system? Might he do nothing? What does such an individual do?[41]

What should a Kierkegaardian Utopia look like? Tonnies says that, "in the *Gemeinschaft* they [the individuals composing the society] remain essentially united in spite of all separating factors, whereas in the *Gessellschaft* they are essentially separated in spite of all uniting factors."[42] Can a natural will be reconciled with a rational will? Is it even

---

It follows that who fails to be active in the world—thus exercising both his personal and civic virtues—fails, in the ultimate analysis, to make the essential movement back to himself, fails to win religious virtue. One might defend Kierkegaard by saying that an individual can be active in the world without being active in politics, but such special pleading, if it is not to be *ad hoc* needs good independent support, given its initial implausibility.

Kierkegaard may have got the point of Jesus just right. E. P. Sanders in *The Historical Figure of Jesus* says, "In every single case it is God who does whatever has to be done, except that individuals who live right will enter the kingdom. There is no evidence at all for the view that individuals can get together with others and *create* the kingdom by reforming social, religious, and political institutions" (179). See also esp. 178-80 and 183. I know just enough of John P. Meier's magisterial *A Marginal Jew: Rethinking the Historical Jesus*, part two, *Message*, chapters 14-16, to know how inordinately complex these issues are. Meier's chap. 14 treats the notion of the kingdom of God as it occurs in the Old Testament, Psuedepigrapha, and in the Qumran texts; the next two chapters, as that notion occurs in the New Testament.

[41]Saint Augustine says, " 'Blessed is the people, whose God is the Lord.' It follows that a people alienated from that God must be wretched. Yet even such a people loves a peace of its own, which is not to be rejected. . . . Meanwhile, however, it is important for us also that this people should possess this peace in this life, since so long as the two cities are intermingled we also make use of the peace of Babylon. . . . That is why the Apostle instructs the Church to pray for kings of that city and those in high positions, adding these words: 'that we may lead a quiet and peaceful life with all devotion and love' " (*The City of God*, 892).

There's the rub. Given the problems that kings, prime ministers, presidents, senators, congressmen, parliamentarians, and such let loose on society through a corrupt, or godless, political structure, should the people of God pray for these rulers and lead a quiet and peaceful life with all devotion and love? Is this what Kierkegaard would recommend too?

[42]Quoted in Kirmmse, "Call Me Ishmael—Call Everyone Ishmael," 164.

possible for a society to be formed from the pluses of both types of societies, *Gemeinschaft* and *Gessellschaft*, and the minuses of neither?

Kierkegaard misses this view because of his slant. He looks at the ethical or religious problem as if he were focusing on a Peter in a society of Judases, so that Kierkegaard has only focused on, or slanted toward, a society exemplified by the negative law, a society exemplified in the present age. No doubt an outstanding individual would have to call upon the full reserve of his moral fiber to fight against the leveling process of *that* community. But, for a moment, dwell upon the possibility of a Judas in a society of Peters. *This* Judas must no less make the leap himself and cannot be aided by all the Peters around him; he, too, cannot get the gift of God secondhand. Yet, his chances are immeasurably improved, given that he faces less ambiguity, tension, envy, and *ressentiment* around him. Why, then, should we not form a society in which an individual has no more difficult a time than that Judas would, than be satisfied with a society in which that Peter is given such a hard time?[43]

Finally, consider Alastair Hannay:

> Since it is certainly Kierkegaard's general view that a harmonious society depends first of all on its moral center, and that individuals are that center's only proper location, this also engenders a certain unclarity about Kierkegaard's actual attitude to the corporate state and its organs. Does he, or would he, believe that the corporate state must eventually go? Or even that it must go immediately?[44]

Hannay usefully reminds us, first, that Kierkegaard answers those questions in the affirmative in "A Cycle of Ethicoreligious Treatises"; second, that Kierkegaard is writing in 1848 (two years after the publication of *The Present Age*), when Europe was in political turmoil and there was war over the Schleswig-Holstein dispute; and, third, that Kierkegaard is convinced that when the turmoil is over, politicians—no less than popes and Jesuits, "emperors, kings, generals, and diplomats"—will have to be

---

[43]Thus, I notice and heed Kirmmse's warning: "We must not seek our salvation in some new and perfected set of political constellations or social relations" ("Call Me Ishmael—Call Everyone Ishmael," 167). My argument is not to seek salvation in a new political order so much as to seek a political order in which salvation is possible for most—not just for a select band of religious geniuses.

[44]*Kierkegaard*, 296.

replaced by the Fourth Estate by which he does not mean established religion so much as men and women unconditionally obedient to God.

Let us suppose that a handful of individuals in the society have acquired a moral outlook and are on the brink of conducting "a moral revolution."[45] These are the individuals who are clearly not in it for personal gain or reward, and they may even see their task as a punishment.

> How, asks Kierkegaard, can the political dream of equality (*Lighed*) be realized in time, the very "medium of differentiation"? What politicians fail to see, in their "impatience" with the eternal, is that absolute equality not only cannot be achieved but cannot even be conceived in worldly terms. True equality (*Menneske-Lighed*, human sameness) and humanity (*Menneskelighed*) can only be achieved in "the religious." However "impractical" it may seem to a politician, "the religious is eternity's transfiguration [i.e. true representation] of [his] fondest dream."[46]

Grant this, for the sake of argument. Even so, such a view does not answer the following queries. What is the relationship between true or absolute equality and what I shall call temporal or relative equality, in which a politician or even a political philosopher may be interested? Might absolute equality profoundly affect relative equality, but relative equality have no effect on absolute equality? Or, would Kierkegaard argue that they have nothing to do with one another? What kind of political structure—democratic, conservative, or whatever—will the moral individuals of the Fourth Estate (*Ukjendelige*, "the unrecognizable") set up or assist in setting up?[47] What would be the aim of such a

---

[45]Hannay, *Kierkegaard*, 297.

[46]Hannay, *Kierkegaard*, 277.

[47]Westphal says, "We should not be surprised, then, if Kierkegaard's politics is more like Marx's than Plato's in its form—if it emerges indirectly, through a critique of what he believes is the overriding sociopolitical defect of the theory and practice of his times rather than as a positive description of the institutions of the society he deems most rational," and then, a few pages later, that several writers have "reiterated and refined Kierkegaard's claim that the fundamental political question is not the shape of society's institutions but the quality of its spirit. Character is more basic than constitution" (*Kierkegaard's Critique of Reason and Society*, 33 and 40). This should reinforce my claim that Kierkegaard has not offered any social and political theory, even one *he* deems most rational, as an alternative to the ones prevailing then, and that it would be an interesting

state?[48] For instance, will it be for a just distribution of goods and services[49] or will the state be designed to make it more possible for individuals to become unconditionally obedient to God?

There are two distinct, but related problems. *Problem A*: What form and structure of the society must there now be that will slowly enable us to reach a Utopian society (one in which individuals become unconditionally obedient to God)? *Problem B*: What form and structure of the society must there be in a Utopian state?[50] Finally, given that achieving absolute

---

task to construct one that fits in with his philosophical views about the individual. Yet, more: I see quality of spirit anchored in character (just as Kierkegaard sees morality anchored in character [77, 43]) and character as substantially shaped by the institutions in which an individual lives; consequently, we need institutions that will shape the human character as it ought to be or, at the very least, institutions that will not damage them virtually beyond repair.

[48]This is an important question because after the moral revolution there still will be a need for the state. As Hannay says, "When the time comes for the Fourth Estate to establish itself, and that is *not* when the services of the corporate state are no longer required, as in the Marxist theory of the withering of the state, [then it will be] finally clear that the functions in question cannot be *served by* the corporate state" (*Kierkegaard*, 297). What functions are these? What noncorporate state will serve these functions?

[49]But "from a Christian point of view," Hannay says, explicating Kierkegaard, "people should be satisfied with the position they are given by birth, class, circumstances, education, and living conditions. Again, his view seems to be that there is nothing *inherently* right or wrong about such differences of status; what matters is whether they take effect in a Christian or an un-Christian way. To deny that such differences are acceptable is to suppose that there is some blueprint, 'the pure human being,' which provides a model for everyone. But 'Christianity is too serious to rave on about the pure human being. . . . [I]t simply wants a person not to damage his soul by abusing [the] difference' " (*Kierkegaard*, 295). Let us say, for now, that differences should not be washed away; people should learn to be satisfied with their positions in society. Nevertheless, what are the non-Christian ways by which the differences take effect? For *these* are not justified. Will the Fourth Estate create a noncorporate state in which at least these differences are eliminated? What rights, equalities, and justices are violated when one acts in an un-Christian way? What form and structure of a noncorporate state will best preserve these for the individuals in that state?

[50]For some related concerns, see Hannay, *Kierkegaard*, 281-82.

equality is a hopeless or impossible task, will the moral individuals of the Fourth Estate be utterly unconcerned about creating and sustaining any particular form of the state?

One readily recognizes a *paradox* facing Kierkegaard: either Kierkegaard must recommend that the moral individuals of the Fourth Estate work to create and sustain a particular form or structure of the noncorporate state or that they not so work. If he recommends that they should so work, then Kierkegaard must admit that the form and structure of a noncorporate state has an important bearing on the religious transformation of the individual (or else why recommend it?—pay and do what Caesar asks and be done with it). If Kierkegaard recommends that they should not so work, then Kierkegaard must admit that the form and structure of a noncorporate state has no bearing on the religious transformation of the individual, in which case it is extremely difficult to see why Kierkegaard should concern himself with politics at all.

To avert misunderstanding, the argument is not that once the right political form of the state is in place the individuals will have to make no effort of their own—anymore than it was suggested that once the Nile is dammed, individual fields will flourish without any effort being put in tilling, sowing, and harvesting. Just as the arts may flourish, but not necessarily so, once society provides them with the right environment and incentive, so might an individual morally flourish, or flourish better, in the right social circumstances. "It is tempting, and consistent with what Kierkegaard says in a number of places," says Hannay, "to interpret him as believing *both* that the end-state's being in the minds of some individuals is at least a necessary condition of its being eventually realized in fact, *and* that entering (properly) into the religious life is at least a necessary condition of anyone's having the idea of that end-state in mind in such a way as to dispose him to act in ways likely to bring it into being."[51] Point taken, but should the Fourth Estate attempt to create a society in which there is a higher probability of individuals having the idea of that end-state in mind than in an alternative society? Or, is the likelihood of individuals acquiring that idea the same in any randomly selected forms and structures of society? This question is directly related to Problem A above.

---

[51] *Kierkegaard*, 282-83.

There is a question Kierkegaard should have faced: What bearing religious transformation can have on the corporate state? Hannay's implication is that once an individual has attained the religious, through steps Kierkegaard recommends, then he should think and do things which might affect the corporate state. *How*? What *sorts* of things might he consider? Might he consider the effect a particular decision will have on the form and structure of the state which in turn will have effect on the character, disposition, values of the individuals? Or, might he simply ignore this as a possibility? No decision of his and other like-minded citizens, he might say, will have any long-term effects on the citizenry. Thus stated, it clearly sounds absurd. But I think that is not quite Hannay's fear. Hannay's real, but implied, concern runs as follows: Religious transformation can be achieved through the correct doctoring or fashioning of the corporate state; a perfect corporate state, a utopia, will produce perfect religiosity in individuals without, or hardly any, effort on their part. If that is the fear, there is no occasion for it.

Let me distinguish two types of proposals: a *negative* proposal and a *positive* proposal. A positive proposal claims to transform the lives of the individuals through a proper structuring of the state or society the individuals will live in. A negative proposal is primarily concerned with forestalling, blocking, or escaping a society that produces the ill consequences of a distorted psychological development, gross political inequalities, and the despicable economic conditions of individuals in it. Should a society be successfully structured along the lines of the negative proposal, the individuals in that society will still have to make choices and decisions to gain the eternal, but they will not be as severely handicapped in doing so as they would be, say, in a hideously immoral society. My aim, therefore, is not to take the burden away from the individual and place it squarely in the hands of the corporate state so much as it is to lessen that burden.

To be sure, I am not claiming that the society in which the negative proposal has been instituted will be envy-free, will not be watered down, and will not be corrupted; and, surely, the history of the attempts at instituting theocracy—think only of the attempts in our own century—should shock us into taking a bit more realistic stance. But here is my worry: Either there is no difference between a near-utopia (with whatever corruption is present in it), on the one hand, and the most miserably immoral society one can think of, on the other, or there is a difference. The first disjunct is simply false. The second disjunct, I venture, is true. But let us see precisely in what sense I need it to be true. Not in all the senses, but only in this: fewer people will be less handicapped in attempting to transform their religious lives in the alleged near-utopia than in any other alternative structure. If that is all that is offered me—and I need no more—my arguments go through.

As individuals become ethical the probability of a community becoming ethical is greatly increased. As a community becomes ethical the probability of an individual in that society becoming ethical is greatly increased, or such a community at least will facilitate the ethical transition of an individual. At both stages, understanding plays a clear role. Understanding is required if an individual is to correctly assess his moral failure. And when he has understood why he has failed, he will have a better chance of freeing himself from what levels him. This I take to be, quintessentially, the Socratic doctrine.

What destroys an individual is a variety of things: cleverness, that outperforms his substance; ambiguity, that replaces the clarity afforded by his passion; leveling, that recants distinctions; talk, that does double duty for itself and deed. What is so insidious is that the corruption often takes place unnoticed. The individual declines morally but does not know he has declined: worse yet, he might think he is on the moral *rise*. Kierkegaard has taught us what the root causes and signs of moral decay are in our speech and deed. Is there then no exit?

> When individuals are not turned inward in quiet contentment, in inner satisfaction, in religious sensitiveness, but in a relation of reflection are oriented to externalities and to each other, when no important event ties the loose threads together in the unanimity of a crucial change—(97-98, 69)

then is the time to run away from that lifestyle. That is a time when men should scream for a catastrophe: for nothing else will show them the exit.

Chapter 4

EXIT TO INWARDNESS

Imprisoned as he is in reflection, how does he escape? In a phrase, through *inwardness of religion.*

> The individual must first of all break out of the prison in which his own reflection holds him, and if he succeeds, he still does not stand in the open but in the vast penitentiary built by the reflection of his associates, and to this he is again related through the reflection-relation in himself, and this can be broken only by religious inwardness, however much he sees through the falseness of the relation. (81, 48)

There are, consequently, two obstacles in his path: (1) the reflection in himself; (2) the reflection of the society around him. Further, reflection has created both selfishness in himself and in others:

> reflection's idea, if it may be called that, is envy, and the envy is therefore two-sided, a selfishness in the individual and then again the selfishness of associates toward him. Reflection's envy in the individual frustrates an impassioned decision on his part, and if he is on the verge of decision, the reflective opposition of his associates stops him. (81, 47-48)

The task before us is to answer the following questions. How shall the individual escape from both these prisons? What is the nature of that escape, and what is the nature of *him* who escapes? In this escape or exit, what is the role of passion? What, if any, is the role of understanding? And when he escapes, *to* what does he escape? Is there a fundamental principle governing the authentic existence of one who has escaped? Among the questions also to be addressed in this chapter are: What is the relation the individual has to the reflection within himself? What is the relation he has to the reflection around him (as a result of his own relation to his own reflection)? Why and how are the two reflections connected? Can he break the bonds of his own reflection without escaping into the inwardness of religion? Can he possibly escape from the first prison without also breaking from the second? Why can he break from the second prison only after he has broken through the first? And then, too, only through religion? What is more difficult: breaking through the first prison or the second? Do we require some notion of degrees of escape?

THE TWO PRISONS

Imagine: Sarah Wylcott has been for several years an Atlanta socialite. Unmarried, black, and brilliant (educated at a prestigious Ivy League school), she has managed to rise in society and politics, tempered neither by principles, societal needs, nor fairness. Net result: she has enormous wealth and wields powerful influence. This is the life she dreamt of, this is the life she has achieved—all of this while she is just thirty-nine. This is, shall we say, phase 1 of her life: *The Ways of Evil.*

One day she visits north Louisiana, her place of origin, and the utter depression of the place gets to her; but she survives. Her cleverness is much too clever for the real. She damns, spits, and curses the ignorant and destitute folks who live adopting a lifestyle of hell, and not having the nerves, or the brains, to get out of it as she had once managed to do. In this I can clearly see selfishness, produced by reflection; yet, I cannot see, as Kierkegaard can, envy. Say this is phase 2 of her life: *The Ways of Cleverness.* These two phases are, of course, connected. Kierkegaard may very plausibly argue that evil is possible only to the extent that cleverness is possible in much the same way Socrates had argued that moral viciousness is only possible when the individual is unwise or ignorant of his true good. (This should not be seen as discounting the role of the will: utterly important for Kierkegaard, not so for Socrates.)

But, as a result of Sarah's visit, something sits in her soul, gnawing at her, having come there uninvited, unannounced. It wrecks her. It has been her "negative Prime Mover," in Gordon D. Marino's rather apt phrase. She loses the innocence of evil; she slowly perceives the falseness of her situation; she feels a misfit in her environment. That feeling grows into an ineradicable sense of isolation. She gathers enough courage to defy the trappings of her station in life, to the dismay of her ambitious family and friends. Sarah Wylcott returns, with her wealth, to the depressed, illiterate, and devastated county in northern Louisiana. This is her moral courage as she singles herself out from the world. This courage and singling herself out is intertwined with a sense of a commitment to these in the here-and-now, without a thought for the Other or the Hereafter. She is much too imbued with a clear sense of her own finitude. She rolls up her sleeves to work. To fiercely counteract or forestall the forces, human and otherwise (that corrupt and render the young helpless by keeping them in bondage to poverty and ignorance), she fights for help: for girls and women, black and white.[1] She starts a school, several medical clinics, and a few simple trade schools for the older women. She creates something of a force. For her, "it will be genuinely educative to live in an age of leveling" (88, 56). This is phase 3 of her life: *The Ways of Good.*

One more thing about Sarah: she believes God does not exist. When much later in life she comes to believe in God, we shall say she has embarked on phase 4 of her life: *The Ways of Faith.* This is her exit.

Whatever else may be true of Sarah, the following condemnation is not:

> Everyone is well informed; we all know everything, every course to take and the alternative courses, but no one is willing to take it. If one person eventually were to surmount his own reflection and act, a thousand reflections from outside would immediately create opposition to him because only a proposal to consider the matter further is received with rising enthusiasm, and a proposal for action is met with indolence. Some in their snobbish self-satisfaction would consider the enthusiasm of those who act ridiculous; others would be envious because he was the one who began it when they *knew* just as well as he what should be done—but still did not do it. (104-105, 77-78)

It is surely true that Sarah Wylcott has abandoned the life of ambiguity, tension, envy, and *ressentiment*, and chosen the life of passion. She not only works continually, but labors also to conceal herself (109, 82). If this is not inwardness, Kierkegaard never spoke of it. The purpose of this

---

[1]This example was inspired by a news story: "A Rare School Blooms in Chad's Unlikely Soil," *New York Times*, 12 June 1996. It was the story of Achta Abakar fighting her society that prevented the education of very young Muslim girls, prevented in part by tradition and in part by utter poverty (the girls were needed to baby-sit siblings and bring water and firewood from miles away). The only woman teacher among 116 teachers working in 160 schools, Achta Abakar was told by the village chief, "You can't make a school out of nothing." So, she opened a one-room school house, with one crude blackboard, for a handful of children who sat on straw mats. Her work moved Unicef and World Bank to offer help to Chad for educating young girls.

illustration is to make bold the claim that it is possible to realize inwardness, passion, without at the same time it being an inwardness whose
stamp is essentially religious. If I call this the *inwardness of humanism*,
what distinguishes it from the inwardness of religion of which Kierkegaard speaks? Is there not a leap of faith involved here as well? That
secular faith says: "Act morally for here and now, and improve the plight
of man; and man so raised will need no God for comfort or support; man
so raised will only need fellow man. Such a man will rise to his height
as only a man can rise."[2]

Or, can Sarah Wylcott's life be wholly explained in terms of her
understanding, without recourse to faith? Would reflection be necessarily
involved in this form of inwardness where it would be wholly absent in
religious inwardness? If so, why? Kierkegaard offers no such argument,
and presupposes that all real escapes from reflection are religious escapes.
Even if Kierkegaard is ultimately right that the most complete escape is
religious, we may still need to offer grades of escapes as much as one
might offer different forms of escape. One might escape to art, another
to science, still another to social uplifting, a fourth to God.

> The individual does not belong to God, to himself, to the beloved, to his
> art, to his scholarship; no, just as a serf belongs to an estate, so the
> individual realizes that in every respect he belongs to an abstraction in
> which reflection subordinates him. (85, 53)

Being committed to art or science may still confine us to a far greater
degree of reflection than being committed to social uplifting; and, in art
or science one's escape from reflection may vary proportionally to how
much one has escaped from selfishness. Perhaps, Sarah Wylcott's life exhibits a steady increase in the degree of escape from reflection, even if
she has not quite exited from it until she reaches phase 4. Or, should we

---

[2]"I allow the justness of the poet's exclamation on the endless projects of
human race, *Man, and forever!* The world itself probably is not immortal. . . .
It is a sufficient incitement to human endeavours, that such a government [a
perfect commonwealth] would flourish for many ages; without pretending to
bestow, on any work of man, that immortality, which the Almighty seems to
have refused to his own productions." David Hume, "Idea of a Perfect
Commonwealth," *Essays: Moral, Political, and Literary*, 528-29.

conclude that until she reaches the final phase her entrapment in reflection is not a whit less in phase 3 as it was in phase 2 or phase 1?

For the purpose of obvious comparisons, consider the following table.[3]

Religious Point of View	Secular Point of View
religious isolation	a feeling of emptiness
religious courage	gathering of moral wit
singled out by religion	handpicked by moral law
eternal responsibility	here-and-now responsibility
infinite freedom of religion	conscious of his finitude
singling out of the individual	singling oneself out
before God	from the World

How might a secularist describe the life of Sarah Wylcott thus far? The first phase of her life requires very little comment: it was a dreary, immoral life. But then her visit to northern Louisiana, her original home, changed things remarkably. Her attempts at being clever were only partially successful, and then too only for a time. This cleverness of hers, of course, is to be understood in secular terms; a cleverness partly governed by her ignorance of what is morally good and evil, partly a matter of self-deception (a Kierkegaardian notion, in fact, drained of what is religious in it).[4] Pretty soon, she began to feel isolated from her environment, produced by a feeling of emptiness, where before she was so much at home in it. This feeling deepened over time until she started—to steal a phrase of Socrates—to take her life in her own hands, and began to perceive the moral falseness of her way of life. Here began her gathering of moral wit. Within this frame of time was the moment moral law entered and possessed her, the moment in which she surrenders in fullness of faith to

---

[3]Most of the concepts under the rubric of a religious point of view can be found in the Kierkegaardian text (86-88, 52-56); the concepts under the secular point of view were devised by analogy.

[4]Asked to pick a single paragraph from anywhere in or out of Kierkegaard which best describes how one deceives oneself, obscures knowing, and thereby saves oneself from proper willing and acting, I can do no better than cite the long, solitary paragraph in *The Sickness unto Death*, 94. Note, however, that the self-deception Kierkegaard speaks of, and warns against, applies to some like Sarah Wylcott no less than it does to a religious person.

humanism. The impact of the moment when one chooses oneself (in one's eternal validity), which Kierkegaard describes in *Either/Or: A Fragment of Life*, can just as much describe Sarah Wylcott when she made the momentous decision to cast away her former life: "the experience of having loved gives to a man's nature a harmony that is never entirely lost; now I want to say that choosing gives to a man's nature a solemnity, a quiet dignity, that is never entirely lost."[5]

Sarah Wylcott dons solemnity, a quiet dignity. (How and where must we locate reflection in Sarah Wylcott in this moment? Or is it that this is just part of her surrendering to God which in time she will come to realize? How, exactly, would this moment differ from one when she turns to God?) The moral law in conjunction with her wealth and influence, dictated a sense of responsibility to her folks, here and now, and not in any highfalutin sense of *sub specie aeternitatis*. It was daring because she had to resist the enormous pressures from the World to continue her usual lifestyle (no doubt in part for its own benefit); it was daring because she must have had to struggle with the forces within herself that she herself had shaped and created for nearly a whole life. With no other prospect than just the good she might accomplish in this world, she acts in the full consciousness of her finitude, fallibility and all. This was also Sarah Wylcott's way of singling herself out from the rest of the World.[6]

No doubt, this is only an ethical form of life. What is of interest are some such questions as these: Are these descriptions adequate so far as the ethical form of life goes? Does it capture at least part of the truth? Or, is it that these descriptions themselves are mistaken since they miss the truth of the religious form of life? For instance, it is not that if one

---

[5]*Either/Or*, 490.

[6]In *Fear and Trembling*, Kierkegaard says: "But life has tasks enough also for the person who does not come to faith, and if he loves these honestly, his life will not be wasted, even if it is never comparable to the lives of those who perceived and grasped the highest" (122). On this reckoning, Sarah Wylcott's life is not wasted, even if her own life now does not rise as high as it will when she attains the final stage, *The Ways of Faith*, when she will perceive and grasp the highest. But the question is: Is she ethical? And, if not, why has her life not been wasted? Might an aesthete not love his talents honestly, and cultivate them? If so, what distinguishes, if anything, his life from that of Sarah Wylcott, if neither life is wasted?

kept within ethical bounds, one could describe truthfully Sarah Wylcott's life, after her return from her place of origin, as one where she senses emptiness. It is, in fact, to *misdescribe* what she is feeling. What passes for a feeling of emptiness is already a religious state or disposition, even though the agent herself would not acknowledge it to be so. Or, the description of her as singling herself out from the rest of her World is already a singling out, if only partially, before God. Are these descriptions entirely mistaken, or do they contain any partial, but ethical, truth such that in the full correct description of Sarah Wylcott, at a particular stage in her life, not only will the central vocabulary be religious, it must also be ethical?

To illustrate further how far in parallel lines the religious and secular lives can go, consider the following passage from Kierkegaard:

> This danger is foreign to immediate inspiration and enthusiasm, which therefore needs the *impetus* of highest enthusiasm to break through. And this highest enthusiasm is not rhetorical balderdash about a higher and a still-higher and highest-of-all goal; it is recognizable by its category: it acts against the understanding. But immediate goodnaturedness does not know the danger of reflection, either, that goodnaturedness could be confused with weakness; for this very reason a religious *impetus* has to follow reflection in order to get goodnaturedness afloat.[7] (111-12, 85)

Sarah Wylcott's decision to abandon her old life for a new one might almost be described in the vocabulary of the present passage. She has an intense immediate enthusiasm, and she is as heedless of danger now as she once was when she arm-wrestled with the rich and the powerful. (What was that danger then? What is it now?) She certainly has not engaged in rhetorical twaddle: she has consciously put behind her her political form of life; clearly, she has acted against understanding. In her goodness and weakness are not confused; but—and this is the main point—her impetus to set that goodness afloat, with her wealth, influence, and work, is not a *religious* impetus, but a secular one. Why must something of the evils of reflection remain still with her?

Kierkegaard offers a curious relationship between the prison of reflection within oneself and the prison of reflection without (in which others

---

[7]This passage should have been part of our discussion in chap. 1; it was saved for this chapter to illustrate the present issue.

are encased and which also imprisons the individual). Kierkegaard asks that first an individual free himself from his own prison of reflection—but that will not enable him to free himself from the second prison. That will be possible only through religion. Let us examine this in four parts. First, why is primacy given to escaping from the first prison? Why should an individual not try to escape first from the prison of reflection that the world imposes on him? It is often only by seeing the falseness of the world that one can be brought to a religious awakening—awakening I say, because it is not the same as escaping the first prison in which one has imprisoned oneself. For a long trial awaits the individual to escape from that tougher prison once he has escaped from the walls of the outside prison.

Second, Kierkegaard says that no one will ultimately be able to escape the prison of reflection imposed by the world without escaping it through religion. This is hard to fathom. No individual can escape from reflection save through religion? What sense can be attached to an escape from the prison of reflection of oneself which is not religious? If it is religious, what *more* is required to escape from the reflection of the second prison? After all, they are both religious escapes. The first escape is evidently not sufficient for the second, so what aspect of religiosity is required for the second but not for the first?

Third, perhaps there is a more realistic account. There might be a closely interconnected dual escape from the two prisons. Thus: insofar as I understand the falseness of the world and escape from it, I also stand a better chance of understanding the falseness within me and escape from it. Likewise, the better I come to understand the obstacle of reflection within me, and escape from it, the more likely will I be able to understand the prison of reflection the world imposes on me and escape from it. On this view, neither the escape from the first prison, nor escape from the second, is given primacy. Which prison one escapes from first is purely a matter of chance, accident, or gift of Nature. But, once the escaping has begun, each step of escape from one prison will quicken the step of escape from the second. With luck, this may have a spiraling effect; and, the process of escape may later become so swift and intense that the individual himself may be unable to sift or distinguish the two escapes.

Fourth, and finally, Kierkegaard has so phrased his view—"to this [the reflection of his associates] he is again related through the reflection relation in himself"—that it suggests that his relation to his own reflection is the *cause* of his relation to the reflection around him. Consequently, removing the cause would arguably remove the effect. Thus, the only crucial escape is from the prison of own one's reflection; with the occurrence of that escape the escape from the other prison would be a natural offshoot, and would not require any special, additional effort.

Has Sarah Wylcott become an outstanding woman? No, she herself prevents any such notion about her from circulating.

> [S]he only becomes an essentially human being in the full sense of equality. This is the idea of religiousness. But the education is rigorous and the returns are apparently very small—apparently, for if the individual is unwilling to learn to be satisfied with himself in the essentiality of the religious life before God, to be satisfied with ruling over [herself] . . . then [s]he will not escape from reflection. (88-89, 57)

Thus it appears that Kierkegaard has worked the notion of equality into the idea of religion, a notion that the case of Sarah Wylcott is supposed to query.[8]

---

[8]Now Robert C. Roberts complains that my portrait of Sarah Wylcott is woefully incomplete. It is. I plead guilty. Consequently, he thinks, it is difficult to decipher if her movements were not after all essentially religious, and not, as I have been arguing, ethical, but without God playing any role in her life. "Can there be," one might ask, "a secular Mother Teresa?" (As I write this, it is Saturday, September 6, 1997, the day after Mother Teresa's death, and so I find it hard to treat it as just a rhetorical question.)

In the terminology of *Either/Or: A Fragment of Life* (489), I could have described in greater detail Sarah Wylcott's outward works—the particularities of the things she did in connection with the workshops, schools, and her particular dealings with particular women and children—and her inward works—her reasons, motivations, desires, aims, hopes, struggles, needs, choices, and such; in short, her realm of freedom. Had I performed this task somewhat adequately, might it have been enough? Perhaps not. "This is all very well," I can hear Roberts say, "but I still do not know enough about her desires, goals, and choices, and what went into them or into the making of them, to determine if she was ethical, since the religious element is missing. Or, perhaps, it is not missing so much as implied or presupposed by these things and it is just that she is innocent of them, these religious implications or presuppositions having not yet found their way into her self-consciousness."

There are two notions of equality. First, the notion of equality before Man—call this the secular notion of equality. Second, the notion of equality before God—call this the religious notion of equality, one for which Kierkegaard is arguing. Granting this distinction, there are several routes along which the argument might proceed. First, one can argue that the secular notion is insufficient and that it would inevitably involve the individual touting it, or being trapped, in reflection. Or, second, one might argue that the notion is useful, but goes only part of the way: it is completed by the surplus in the religious notion of equality. Or, third, the two notions are essentially vastly different, whatever their surface and superficial similarities. The third view is what Kierkegaard seems to have in mind when he says, "Thus eternal life is also a kind of leveling, and yet it is not so, for the denominator is this: to be an essentially human person in the religious sense" (96, 67).

I might respond to Roberts: "But what do you mean *missing*? This is a piece of fiction, and I portrayed what should be there. The fiction illustrates a philosophical view, not the other way around. There are no such implications or presuppositions that you think you see in there."

"But if your philosophical view is mistaken?"

"And if it isn't? . . . "

And so on to an inconclusive end?

Princess Diana (I write this on the day of her funeral), on the best available evidence, had no religious pretensions worth reporting. She had one foot firmly planted in the life of the aesthete—she lived in the world of parties, fashions, sports, and music—and she relished it by all accounts. (When she was invited to the White House, Nancy Reagan reports, John Travolta was also invited at Lady Diana's request and then she expressed a desire to dance with Travolta. At another time, she asked Elton John, the latter reports, to invite Richard Gere to his party in her honor where she sat with the actor all night long, starry-eyed, sitting cross-legged on the floor. Other details may be found by consulting the twenty-one issues of *People* magazine in which she was featured on the cover.) No Mother Teresa she. But, and this is the point for now, her other foot was firmly planted in the realm of the ethical. She helped, assisted, cared for, with all her royal might, children suffering from aids, cancer victims, people injured and maimed by land mines, the homeless, and the helpless. Is it not logically possible that this doting mother of two, who also happened to be an English princess, could have done all that she did and yet not believed in God?

I take this to affect deeply what Kierkegaard means by passion. Sarah Wylcott has none of the characteristics of a man or woman destroyed: there is no ambiguity, no tension, no envy, no *ressentiment* in her. And, yet, she has no proper idea of equality before God since she does not believe in God. She, therefore, has no passion in the requisite sense.

What follows is a brief statement of what is a fairly complicated argument. In *Either/Or: A Fragment of Life*, Kierkegaard has woven so tight a conceptual net that given his premises it follows that no one who does not believe in God can be ethical. Thus:

Step 1. An individual is confronted with a choice between living the life of an aesthete and the ethical life.

Step 2. What, exactly, is that choice? "My either/or does not denote in the first instance the choice between good and evil, it denotes the choice whereby one chooses good and evil or excludes them" (*Either/Or: A Fragment of Life*, 486).

Step 3. How can that individual be aided in making the right choice? "Only when one can get a person to stand at the crossroads in such a way that he has no expedient but to choose, does he choose what is right" (*Either/Or: A Fragment of Life*, 486).

Step 4. What choice is right? "[Y]ou will again see why I kept on saying in the above that the either/or I proposed between living aesthetically and ethically is not a perfect dilemma, because there is really only one option. Through choosing it I do not really choose between good and evil, I choose the good, but by virtue of choosing the good I choose the option between good and evil" (*Either/Or: A Fragment of Life*, 520).

Step 5. Is there something prior (or concomitant—it does not matter here) the individual needs to do before he chooses the only option he really has? "So now he owns himself as posited by himself, that is, as chosen by himself, as free;

(*Step 6*) but when he owns himself in this way, an absolute difference appears, that between good and evil. So long as he has not chosen himself this difference remains latent" (*Either/Or: A Fragment of Life*, 523).

Step 7. What, then, is it to choose himself? "It is to bind oneself for an eternity to an eternal power" (*Either/Or: A Fragment of Life*, 486).

It follows, ineluctably I think, that no one, neither Sarah Wylcott nor anyone else, who has not bound himself to God for an eternity has available to him the categories of good and evil (in their absolute difference). Therefore, no one but a theist can be ethical.

Ill-Defined Selves, Arbitrary Reasons[9]

What is Sarah Wylcott's self? One can take the view that there is a pure self that thinks, reasons, reflects, and makes decisions, such as the decision whether to continue her previous life or to take a leap into a kind of life she hitherto did not know. Let us call this *the theory of pure self.* Alternatively, one can take the view that the self is nothing more than the sum of its parts, and its parts are defined by its roles, and its roles take form and substance from the society in which they play their parts. Let us call this *the theory of social self.*[10] Thus, Sarah Wylcott can be a bank

---

[9]This is my only diversion from the pages of *The Present Age*. My reason is this. A book—*any* book—on Kierkegaard must treat, even if only sketchily, as this section does, an issue of paramount importance, particularly for Kierkegaard: to wit, What is the role of reason in an ethical life? Several of Kierkegaard's recent commentators, inordinately sympathetic to his cause, aver that the choice Kierkegaard advocates is rational but not dispassionate. Minority opinion, on the other hand, has it that passion may, at best, be a necessary condition, but could not begin to be a sufficient condition for fear of rampant relativism and irrationalism. The majority argument is distinctive, learned; the minority opinion, patient, probing. It is my task, in this section, to show that the widely prevalent view on this topic misses what is most intriguing and unique in Kierkegaard, that, in any event, the common view leads to consequences Kierkegaard would, or should, have had reason to dread.

Here I jostle with eight significant recent works on this issue in Kierkegaard: George B. Connell's "Judge William's Theonomous Ethics"; C. Stephen Evans's *Passionate Reason: Making Sense of Kierkegaard's Philosophical Fragments*; Alastair Hannay's introduction to his translation of Kierkegaard's *Either/Or: A Fragment of Life* as well as his *Kierkegaard*; Alasdair MacIntyre's *After Virtue: A Study in Moral Theory*; Gordon D. Marino's "The Place of Reason in Kierkegaard's Ethics; Robert C. Roberts's "Kierkegaard, Wittgenstein, and a Method of 'Virtue Ethics' "; and, finally, Anthony Rudd's *Kierkegaard and the Limits of the Ethical*.

Given the direction of my enterprise, it is not my purpose to enter into a detailed argument for or against these texts; in any event, I do not have the space for that. I cite them here to acknowledge that they have powerfully shaped my arguments and counterarguments; and, that they have enabled me to finely chisel the philosophical point I wish to make.

[10]MacIntyre attributes (as does Rudd) the former theory to Jean-Paul Sartre

teller, a vice president of an insurance company, a provost, or a disk jockey; but had she lived in the times of Socrates, Ashoka the Great, or St. Thomas Aquinas, she could arguably have been none of those things.

Take Otto Neurath's famous raft analogy in the field of epistemology. If there is something wrong with the raft on high seas, one cannot stand out of the raft to repair it; one does with it what one can by staying on it. So also, Neurath thought, one cannot alter one's system of beliefs from some outside vantage point; whatever repairing or casting out of beliefs needs to be done must be done from within the system. Similarly, for the case at hand, Sarah Wylcott has a self and that self is the sum total of her roles. If she wishes to cast away a role or two from her life, or adopt fresh ones, she has no other self she can view, speak to, or address from and no other self from the vantage point of which she can engage in reasoning about those decisions. Her decision making must stem from the vantage point of these other roles that is now her self.

The theory of pure self is best approached through a critical look at the theory of social self. Let us suppose a self is identical to the sum total of its roles. Consider the case in which there are subroles distinct from the main role. For example, Sarah Wylcott in education (main role) might be a teacher, a principal, a counselor, or an administrator (subroles) in a school or university. If she wishes to determine in which subrole(s) she should cast herself, she can do so by invoking the main role that also supplies the criteria or measures of success. But consider a different case. Sarah Wylcott juggles different main roles, say, being a mother, a physician, and the chief administrator of a national charity association. Each major role has its own criteria of success and there is no *a priori* reason to think that these criteria will not conflict sometimes, if not often and in most important circumstances. Suppose she is constantly confronted by moral dilemmas, and decides to give up playing one of the major roles: say she gives up being the chief administrator of the national charity association.[11] What is the self that makes the decision, and by what criterion or criteria? This is a significant question.

---

and the latter to Erving Goffman.

[11]We do well to remind ourselves of Bernard Williams's remark: "While the standards can be in this way logically welded to the title, the title is not logically welded to the man" (*Morality: An Introduction to Ethics*, 66).

Let us consider the second half of the question first. The criteria by which she judges her performance as a mother and the criteria by which she judges her performance as the chief administrator of the national charity association have little in common—they are incommensurable, as they say. So, by what criteria does she opt out of one major role, while highlighting the other major role in her life? Or what if she wants to inculcate an interest in jazz or pottery, thus pursuing a new and different role? One might say in the first case, although not entirely persuasively, that she had donned the role of mother when judging her role as administrator and deemed the first role more important. In the latter case, evidently no such argument can be made. So, it would appear that the decision is entirely arbitrary when it comes to making decisions among major, main roles.

(Parenthetically, observe that happiness is not the basic criterion which brings unity into a life of apparent disunity. For what makes an individual happy is not a constant thing: he might be the happiest when a rake, and then just as suddenly and unaccountably decide that what would make him most happy is to be a recluse.[12])

Consider the first half of the question now. *Who—what* self—is making these fundamental decisions? "But what, then, is this self of mine?" asks Kierkegaard, and answers thus:

> [H]ave you ever heard a person seriously wish that he could become someone else? So far is that from being so, that it is precisely typical of what are called unfortunates that it is they who cling most tightly to themselves, that despite all their sufferings they would not for all the world want to be someone else. . . . As for the man with many wishes, he still thinks of always remaining himself though everything has changed. So there is something in him that is absolute in relation to everything, something whereby he is the one he is, even if the change he obtains through his wish were the greatest possible.[13]

---

[12]"A person who aesthetically considers a whole range of life-tasks . . . is more likely to arrive at a multiplicity than an either/or, because here the factor of self-determination in the choice is not given an ethical emphasis, and because, if one does not choose absolutely, one chooses for that moment only and can, for that reason, choose something else the next instant" (Kierkegaard, *Either/Or: A Fragment of Life*, 485).

[13]Kierkegaard, *Either/Or: A Fragment of Life*, 516-17. This is not to claim

Once again, Kierkegaard:

> He now discovers that the self he chooses contains an infinite multiplicity inasmuch as it has a history, a history in which he acknowledges identity with himself. This is history of a different sort, for in this history he stands in relation to other individuals of the race and to the race as a whole, and in this history there is something painful, yet he is only the one he is, with this history. Therefore it needs courage to choose oneself, for just when he seems to be becoming more isolated, he is entering more deeply than ever into the roots through which he is linked with the whole.[14]

This is the empirical or social self. Kierkegaard's point is that no individual can act in isolation from, or outside the context of, society and history, not that there is no individual outside of that context; not that, once you deprive that individual of history, he ceases to be, let alone ceases to be that unique individual.

Suppose at some time i a self is the sum total of roles, R_1, R_2, R_3, ..., R_z. When, at some time j this self no longer desires to be, say, R_m and is reasoning to abandon playing this role, how is this self, poised to make a decision, to be understood? Is it R_1, R_2, R_3, ..., R_z *minus* R_m? But, by the same token, it could question whether it wishes to pursue a

---

that Kierkegaard was touting a theory of pure self, although I think he came nearer to it than not. For while Kierkegaard had wanted nothing to do with the pure Cartesian ego, without the muddiness of being concrete—it was only as that concrete self one made decisions—he wanted to maintain a theory of ego that, at least in one clear sense, transcended the boundaries of history and society, as in the quotation in the next paragraph in the text.

Or consider: "But who, then, am I? Let no one ask about that. If it did not occur to anyone to ask before, then I am saved, for I am now over the worst of it. Moreover, I am not worth asking about, for I am the least of all, and people make me very bashful by asking this question. I am pure being and thus almost less than nothing. I am the pure being that is everywhere present but yet not noticeable, for I am continually being annulled.

"I am like the line with the arithmetical problem above and the answer below—who cares about the line?" (Kierkegaard, *Stages on Life's Way*, 86).

At least one point of the passage is lost if read only as a sign of his insignificance.

[14]Kierkegaard, *Either/Or: A Fragment of Life*, 518.

whole sleuth of roles, R_k, R_p, R_s, . . . , R_w. What, then, is that I, that self, that is doing the thinking, reasoning, and reflecting? What would arguing with oneself, in such a case, be like? Would it be a rapid-fire succession of selves, each self arguing with another? Is there a democracy of selves? But in virtue of what, then, is it the *same self*?[15] Is it after all a pure self?[16] Might one say that a self without roles is blind, a role without self is empty (nonexistent)?

What difference would a theory of self make to the question of what *reasons*, if any, Sarah Wylcott had to move from the life or ways of evil to the life of ways of good? Is there an impartial, independent, and objective ethical reality, and do reasons give us access to that reality? Or is there really no such reality at all and, consequently, neither any reasons that are ultimately not just arbitrary, subjective preferences of an individual? The nature of self seems to make no difference to that central question. Here is an argument for that claim. Either ethical reality is objective or it is not. First, assume an objective ethical reality. Then, if it is accessible at all, it would be accessible to the pure self just as much as

---

[15]Perhaps this argument might recall a similar one from the "Second Meditation" of Descartes's *Meditations on First Philosophy*. Descartes had there argued that a piece of wax is neither its color, fragrance, nor the sound it emits, and so on, and therefore it is none of these essentially. Not many philosophers find that particular argument attractive (because, they argue, a man's hair color, for instance, might be a variable, it does not follow that a man need have no color of hair). At any rate, that argument has only the most superficial similarity with the present argument. To say that a self is a pure self is not to say that it is nothing, even if it is to say it is not to be defined in terms of its roles. For the hundreds of thousands of gloves there are in the world that fit a hand more or less well, there is one, say, that fits it uniquely, perfectly. Those many gloves are those many roles the hand can fit into, but the hand is something different and distinct in its own right from those many gloves. Similarly, a self can exist in a multiplicity of societies, and can take on a multiplicity of roles; but it would not follow that the self is identical to any one role or to a set of roles. Add to it an Aristotelean suggestion: a hand has a unique function, and that function is best performed by that one glove that fits it ideally. Likewise, the self is soul and it dons various social roles. The soul has in all eternity a fundamental nature and function—its infinitude, as Kierkegaard says in *The Sickness unto Death*, which it cannot abrogate or deny; and, in the ultimate analysis, a soul evaluates its various and multifarious roles in the light of what is good for the soul. Back to *telos*?

[16]See, MacIntyre, *After Virtue: A Study in Moral Theory*, esp. 31-32.

to the social self. In short, both the pure and the social self would, through reason, be able to discover the objective ethical reality. Second, assume there is no such objective reality. Then, the pure self would be making a decision no less arbitrary than the social self. Third, if one were to argue that moral reality would be accessible only to the pure self and not to the social self, and hence reasoning about ethical matters only possible for the pure self, then that objection can be easily met. Whether a human being is a pure or social self is not something *he* determines; that is an ontological given. It would follow that if the given were that we are merely social selves, there would be nothing we could do to save ourselves from failure to reason in ethics. On the other hand, if we were pure selves, then none could deprive us from reasoning in the ethical sphere. A similar argument can be made if one were to claim that moral reality is accessible only to the social self and not to the pure self.

Let us assume, therefore, that our natures do not intrinsically deprive us of the ability to reason in ethical matters and that, if there is an objective ethical reality which we would wish our reasons to discover, we must have a criterion for judging the worth of our argument or rational discourse. Could there be a reason or reasons for Sarah Wylcott to move from any form of life to an ethical form of life? Or, is such a decision wholly arbitrary? Let us distinguish two cases. First, once I have adopted an ethical form of life, I may still have to struggle with problems from *within* it. Such problems, even when they lead to insoluble moral dilemmas, do not immediately warrant the judgment that the ethical form of life is a-rational. Consequently, we are not discussing the role of reason from within an ethical life. Second, I am going to leave aside the task of evaluating two nonmoral forms of life and whether reason can play a decisive role in determining which alternative between them is the right choice. Perhaps this is only a variant on the problem that concerns us; perhaps not.

It is difficult to improve upon R. M. Hare:

> Thus a complete justification of a decision would consist of a complete account of its effects together with a complete account of the principles which it observed, and the effect of observing those principles. . . . If the enquirer still goes on to ask him 'But why should I live like that?' then there is no further answer to give him, because we have already,

ex hypothesi, said everything that could be included in the further answer.[17]

The trouble with this sort of justification account is that it is palpably a double-edged sword. Sarah Wylcott asks the question, 'Why should I live an ethical life?' In Hare-like fashion, we delineate (a) the ethical principles, (b) the effect of observing those ethical principles, and (c) a complete account of the effects of the decision to lead an ethical life. This is our justification for why she should live an ethical life. The earlier Sarah Wylcott, then, rises to the occasion and offers us, in not one whit less Hare-like fashion, a justification for an aesthetic life or the life she led in phase 1 or phase 2: (a') the aesthetic principles, (b') the effect of observing those aesthetic principles, and (c') a complete account of the effects of the decision to lead an aesthetic life. This would have been her justification for why she should live an aesthetical life.

Let me elaborate. Hare's account leaves the justification of fundamental principles, that drive the entire system. untouched (nor, I hastily add, was it Hare's purpose to show that such principles are justified). Basic principles cannot be justified: you either accept them or not. But one does not accept or reject them for reasons, for reasons cannot be offered. Here they lie outside the perimeter of their proper scope and domain. One cannot persuade even in terms of effects: delineating the effects of espousing the principles is one thing, but one does not know whether those effects are something one should accept or reject until one has accepted the basic point of view. Sarah Wylcott at the stage of cleverness did not find certain things persuasive, the very things which eventually led her to abandon her former form of life. Once she had accepted the ethical point of view, *then* she could see the reasons for doing what she ended up doing; so long as she was tethered to her earlier life she could see no rationale in, nor be persuaded of, the form of life she pursued later. Consequently, Kierkegaard would admonish that the fundamental problem is one of arbitrating between (a) and (a'). Everything falls into place, and seems to offer virtually no interesting philosophical difficulty once that fundamental decision has been made. That decision is a matter of will and not a matter of reason; hence the accusation of his critics that Kierkegaard is, in the ultimate analysis, irrational.

---

[17]*The Language of Morals*, 69.

How might Kierkegaard be defended? Here's one way.

> A scientific theory may be tested quite objectively, but the test of an ethical theory lies precisely within human subjectivity. Ultimately, the only ground I may have for believing in the truth of an ethical theory is that I have found fulfillment as a result of living in a way that it recommends; or that I have experienced a lack of fulfillment as a result of living in a way that is significantly different.[18]

Likewise, for religious beliefs. Consequently, the accent falls on the subjective, on passion; the objective is insufficient though necessary. "Kierkegaard is not saying here that God's existence is somehow relative to, or dependent on, the faith of His believers, but that God as a subject, can only be known through another subject's relation to Him. Attempts to know God objectively miss the living God by turning Him into an object or a purely conceptual being."[19]

In this view, truth and falsity are not just simply ascribed to propositions, but, much more importantly, to a way of life. Consequently, one does not simply pay attention to the overt beliefs of an individual moral agent but to his life as lived to determine his true beliefs. One might have true beliefs but live the life of a sinner—one's anguish over one's deeds, one's repentance would serve as marks of one's real beliefs. One might also have false beliefs and live the life of a saint. The psychology of unconscious beliefs—whatever the method of determining these (Freudian, Jungian, or Adlerian)—is important because it will unveil the true nature of the man. *"When the question about truth is asked subjectively, the individual's relation is reflected upon subjectively. If only the how of this relationship is in truth, the individual is in truth, even if he in this way were to relate himself to untruth."*[20] This is where passion enters and occupies the king's chair. What relates the individual authentically is passion, not a belief in a set of propositions, however true. Thus, no amount of knowledge can initiate an individual into an appropriate relationship with the truth. Only passion can do so.

---

[18]Rudd, *Kierkegaard and the Limits of the Ethical*, 60.
[19]Rudd, *Kierkegaard and the Limits of the Ethical*, 61; also see 62-63.
[20]Kierkegaard, *Concluding Unscientific Postscript*, 1:199.

THE SIGNATURES OF PASSION

It is thus worth examining again the signatures of passion. First, let us grant that one cannot understand a form of life, especially an alien one, by merely being a Quinean observer armed with a theory,[21] and without being a participant. One understands the meanings of beliefs held in that community, and the values it espouses by living the life lived by its people. What sort of passion is evoked in its ethical form of life? When I listen to Mozart or Schubert I experience musical delight; that delight varies in duration, quality, and intensity, depending on a variety of my subjective states, such as moods and dispositions. However, when I listen to Indian classical music and delight in a *raga* or enjoy the *tabla*, *veena*, or *sitar*, my musical passion then belongs to a different scale and order. That delight also varies in duration, quality, and intensity, depending on a variety of my subjective states. This is not offered simply as an auto-biographical report.

Suppose there is some merit in this. Let me then add that one cannot genuinely appreciate Indian classical music without knowing, and living, not only an Indian form of life, but also to some extent being on the same scale and order of passion as an Indian is when he delights in that kind of music. There is one kind of passion for understanding or appreciating Western classical music, a different passion for understanding or appreciating Indian classical music.[22] Do appreciations of different ethical systems belong to parallel universes of passion too? Herodotus describes a tribe which, when it thundered and rained, came out of its dwellings armed, and shot arrows at the sky. Asked what exactly they were doing, they replied that they were shooting at lesser gods for threatening them with natural disaster, and making it clear to these second-class deities that they, the people of the tribe, were not going to be intimidated by them

---

[21]See Rudd's perceptive discussion of Quine and Davidson, *Kierkegaard and the Limits of the Ethical*, 40-45.

[22]"A work of art may be truthful—it may express or focus reality for us; this is the case, indeed, with music, which so often gives us the sense of expressing deep truths which are quite impossible to translate into propositions" (Rudd, *Kierkegaard and the Limits of the Ethical*, 65). Could they be translated—I am not being facetious—into different music? A baleful passage in one tradition of music just says one thing as a similar passage in another tradition?

and, consequently, would not propitiate them but propitiate only the gods they believed supreme.[23] There is one religion of the Herodotean tribe, and there is the Christianity of Kierkegaard. Imagine the passion that a member of the tribe feels and compare it to the passion of an honest and devout Christian. Are these two passions on the same scale, except that they are at different points on that scale? Or, as in the case of music, they are on vastly different planes? If so, what is the connection, if any, between these types of passion, and what connects or links them?

There is the issue of understanding and the issue of truth. If passion is important, as it avowedly is for Kierkegaard, its importance can be readily understood from the point of view of understanding. Unless you feel the passion as an Indian does (within a range that reasonable people can agree on), you simply have not understood Indian music, whatever else your mental repertoire enables you to do with that experience. In a similar fashion, unless one feels the passion—the anger, the defiance, the love one bears to one's own deities—one could not be said to have understood what the tribe Herodotus wrote about was doing. (And would one be said to have understood them only if one felt the passion to a point where one *too* would be willing to come out armed and shoot arrows at the threatening sky?) But truth is a different matter. Whether the fundamental beliefs of the tribe are true, or the Christian dogmas are true (or, for that matter, the dogmas of any other religion), is not, and cannot be, a matter of subjectivity.

So, when Kierkegaard says that subjective truth is an *"objective uncertainty, held fast through appropriation with the most passionate inwardness,"*[24] any believer of any religion might just as honestly claim that there is an objective uncertainty in what he believes, but that he nevertheless renders it a subjective truth given that he believes what he believes with intense passion, the most passionate inwardness. Kierkegaard was intrigued by the Carpocratian sect that held that salvation was found by living through all the possibilities of good and evil. Certainly Kierkegaard did not advocate that one should actually lead an evil life, but drama, arts, poetry, and literature can make vivid the unfathomable evil in certain forms of life. (I pass over the following point: if one is choosing between

---

[23]Herodotus, *The Histories.*
[24]Kierkegaard, *Concluding Unscientific Postscript,* 203.

different forms of ethical life, this is hardly the right recommendation; it blatantly begs the question. What is possibly evil from the point of view of the spectator may be a deep good from the perspective of the participant, and *vice versa*.) But, let us say, someone does decide to experiment with several different religions; he lives them all. One might even say that he has a genuine understanding of each of the religions he has lived; he has an appropriate passion for each religious practice. Indeed, each community boasts of a Kierkegaard who is able to delineate in powerful prose the value and worth of the religious enterprise that the experimenting individual has embarked upon, and the evils inherent in the alternative approaches. Yet, when the moment of ultimate decision arrives, the experimenter asks himself, "What do I do?" Unless he has a criterion or criteria by which he can judge these different religions or different ethical systems, his fundamental choice is simply an irrational—or an a-rational—choice.

Nor can the notion of nearness make any sense. Minimally, Kierkegaard wants to say that one who concentrates on an idol with an infinite passion, though he is an idolater, yet he is nearer to the truth than one who believes in the true God and has no passion. A skeptic might aver that Kierkegaard unfairly presupposes the truth of his view. Consider Sarah Wylcott. Look at her from a humanist point of view, and she appears nearer to the truth when she is at phase 3 than someone who is a theist; look at Sarah Wylcott from a theist point of view, and she appears nearer to the truth when she is at phase 3 and nearer still when she is at phase 4.

C. Stephen Evans offers a theory of the perspectival nature of human reason, a slight improvement, he avers, over Alvin Plantinga's, "Reformed Epistemology."[25] Evans claims that

> Human reason is not a neutral arbiter of religious truth, but always expresses the character of the reasoner. . . . [Consequently,] if I find Christian faith objectionable on rational grounds, that may imply something about Christian faith, but it may also imply something about me.[26]

---

[25]So termed in "Justification and Theism," *Faith and Philosophy* 4/4 (1987): 403-26.
[26]Evans, *Passionate Reason*, 178.

Now, in Plantinga's view, knowledge is the product, or by-product, of the functioning, or exercising, of human cognitive faculties, when these faculties are functioning normally, that is, when they are functioning in a normal(?) environment as they were designed to function. Adapting Plantinga's view, Evans says,

> The Christian who takes Climacus's view of faith will surely say that with respect to essential truth, our cognitive faculties are impaired by sin. . . . Truth, at least essential truth, is the product of the restoration and healing of our cognitive faculties . . . [which] is one that is made possible by the transformation of the knower through an encounter with Christ.[27]

It is extremely difficult to see how this escapes the charge of irrationality or arbitrariness. Here is why. First, a Hindu polytheist might readily agree with nearly all of Plantinga and Evans: namely, we have cognitive faculties and these faculties were designed to function in particular ways and in particular environments. When these faculties are so used, they are then best for the soul of the user; when not, the soul is impaired. Now comes the key Aristotlean question. What is the good for the soul for which these faculties were designed in the first place? The Christian has one view of the good; the Hindu, another. The Christian has a view of sin, but so does the Hindu polytheist; the former regards living in Christ as cardinal to a Christian way of life, the Hindu bows before Vishnu or Brahman (or . . .). From a Christian perspective, were a Hindu to criticize Christian faith, that may imply something about Christian faith, but it may also be a commentary on the Hindu; from the Hindu point of view, a Christian who criticizes the Hindu view of life may imply something about Hinduism, but the critic may also speak volumes about himself. *Why* should one prefer the view one is urged to prefer?

Finally, consider this. Let us suppose we were to confine our attention not to the character of the reasoner, but only to that which is reasoned about: Christianity and Hinduism, say. If there are good arguments indicating preference of Christianity over Hinduism, based on the initial propositions of the two religions and their implications, we have no reason to be concerned then about the character of the reasoner. On

---

[27]*Passionate Reason*, 181.

the other hand, if there is a tie, it is not clear how resorting to the character of the reasoner would settle *anything.*

There is no better Wittgensteinian reading of Kierkegaard than Robert
C. Roberts's "Kierkegaard, Wittgenstein, and a Method of 'Virtue
Ethics.' " Roberts attempts to show how the grammar of faith, in particular the Christian grammar of faith, works. In *Works of Love*, Roberts says,
Kierkegaard locates the concept of love—which is nonpreferential and
distinct from erotic love, love that "blossoms," or love of a friend, love
in which a Christian cannot be deceived—within a family of concepts:
consolation, envy and arrogance, self-renunciation, upbuilding, mistrust,
judging others, courage, hope, honor and shame, justice, domineering,
reduplication, discovery of sins, and forgiveness. This grammar indicates
how various concepts are linked, displays aspects of their use, and does
not purport to be a short-formula dictionary definition; it is, in the
language of Sir Peter Strawson, not merely descriptive, but quite often
revisionary. Kierkegaard's task is not simply to inform how the word is
used, but to put a Christian on notice, serve a reminder, when its use has
degenerated into something else.[28] Well, this is Christian grammar: but
how about Kantian grammar, Aristotelian grammar, Hindu grammar, or
Zoroastrian grammar?

If Wittgenstein's *Remarks on the Foundations of Mathematics*
exhibits, in Michael Dummett's honest phrase, "a full-blooded conven-
tionalism,"[29] then such a description might arguably be apt for Wittgenstein's later work, *Philosophical Investigations.* From this latter work, I
have in mind a passage such as this:

> One human being can be a complete enigma to another. We learn this
> when we come into a strange country with entirely strange traditions;
> and, what is more, even given a mastery of the country's language. We
> do not understand the people. (And not because of not knowing what
> they are saying to themselves.) We cannot find our feet with them.

A Hindu, I infer, might not find his feet with a Christian, and vice versa.

I conclude that if Wittgenstein is a relativist then so is Kierkegaard.
One might speak of the grammar of faith, as Roberts does, but if that

---

[28]See what it means, for example, in Kierkegaard's view to be feeding the
poor and making it out to be a feast; or, what it is to sorrow.

[29]"Wittgenstein's Philosophy of Mathematics," 425.

grammar is tied to a particular form of religious life, then there is a grammar of faith for each religion. The problem of rational choice among different grammars of faith then becomes even more glaring.[30] Undoubtedly, Roberts might respond by saying that viewing a Kierkegaardian text through a Wittgensteinian lens does not import all the features of Wittgenstein's philosophy, just those features which highlight the virtues of Kierkegaard's texts. So be it. For now, I am only concerned to point out the possible threat of irrationality with which one might charge Kierkegaard on such a reading, and what might have to be done to avert such a charge.

Consider now some of Roberts's specific arguments.

As Wittgenstein's and Kierkegaard's labors suggest, rationality is gentler and more variegated than such apologists suppose. Rationality does come in a variety of rival and incompatible forms. But the overlap between those forms is no accident. It is often traceable to our common humanity. And it is enough to enable the grammarian some deeply human way of life and thought to speak fetchingly to people outside his or her tradition.[31]

And his point is beautifully illustrated from Epictetus. Should one meet a man groaning and weeping for grief, says Epictetus to a disciple—take the advice, says Roberts, "as reflecting the grammar of Stoic compassion'—then "as far as conversation goes . . . do not disdain to accommodate yourself to him and, if need be, to groan with him. Take heed, however, not to groan inwardly, too."[32] A Stoic, confronted by a genuine instance of Christian compassion, in which there was not only an outward

---

[30]Roberts himself states the problem sharply: "If we lean hard on the metaphor of grammar, we may seem to deprive ourselves of an important application of the concept of truth. Spanish, Hebrew, and Mandarin have different grammars, but the differences are only to be noted, not adjudicated. Similarly, Nietzsche's ethics, Stoicism, and Christianity have different concepts, with different depth grammars, in terms of which human beings are understood and formed in their self-understanding. But these ways of understanding and living seem, on the face of it, to be in competition with one another in a way that Spanish, Hebrew, and Mandarin are not" ("Kierkegaard, Wittgenstein, and a Method of 'Virtue Ethics,' " 159).

[31]"Kierkegaard, Wittgenstein, and a Method of 'Virtue Ethics,' " 164.

[32]"Kierkegaard, Wittgenstein, and a Method of 'Virtue Ethics,' " 163.

show of comfort giving, but a sharing of an internal sorrow as well, might conclude that the self-protection of the Stoic approach is not in cohort with human nature. "Despite the pain involved in Christian compassion, he may come to feel that the human solidarity embodied in the emotion fulfills human nature better than the detachment characteristic of Stoicism."[33] The Christian compassion echoes in him, and that echo is not entirely foreign news; he may come to feel the value and need for fellowship, and finally admit to himself, what he had dimly felt all along, that "the Stoic way of life was oppressively lonely."[34]

To reiterate Roberts's central proposition: "Rationality does come in a variety of rival and incompatible forms. But the overlap between those forms is no accident. It is often traceable to our common humanity." Consequently, the grammar-of-faith argument can be examined from three perspectives. First, we might challenge the notion of "our common humanity." Second, one might argue that "our common humanity" is understood in distinct ways given the grammar of faith one adopts. Third, should two or more grammars get us to respond just the way we should respond, given our common humanity, other arguments would have to be adduced in order to settle the issue as to which grammar of faith is right.

For the sake of argument, let me concede the first point with only the observation that "our common humanity" may, in fact, not be a natural kind term.

Second, consider how a Stoic might respond to the Epictetus example. From within the grammar of each faith, there is a right way of speaking and a wrong way. There are also innumerable possibilities of illusion, temptations to follow the false path. A Stoic might argue that when a fellow Stoic sees Christian compassion taking away or minimizing his loneliness, assuring fellowship, then this is precisely the danger he faces to his authentic Stoic existence. It is a fact of nature, of our common humanity, from the Stoic point of view, that each individual is an island of loneliness; that the baser, or lower, part in us seeks to deny that fact about us, and the more indulgent we are with ourselves, the more difficult will it be for us to genuinely handle loss and grief of our own later, the more shall we seek comfort in the compassion of others, the less resilient

---

[33]"Kierkegaard, Wittgenstein, and a Method of 'Virtue Ethics,' " 164.
[34]"Kierkegaard, Wittgenstein, and a Method of 'Virtue Ethics,' " 164.

will the character of our moral fiber become to the exigencies of life. Adapting a remark of Kierkegaard, a Stoic might say to his disciple: the Stoic way of life, "and therefore the true are so foreign to a man by nature that it is with him as with the dog which can indeed learn to walk upright but still always prefers to walk on all fours."[35]

Third, and finally, suppose Christianity and, say, Hinduism both respond in nearly identical ways to another's grief; both responses are neighborly. Then, this area of our common humanity will not enable us to settle the question as to which of the two grammars of faith is correct; we shall have to turn our attention to more recondite areas and see how the grammars succeed, or fail, there. For instance, how would a Christian or a Hindu treat animals? How would each treat nature and the environment? What implications would such treatments have on their diets or the manners of their habitats? Here the incompatibility of the two grammars might become stark and it is not clear how *this* conflict is to be traced, if at all, to *our* common humanity. Thus, when Roberts says, "But Christianity might appeal to a non-Christian in ways that do not presuppose the full panoply of Christian beliefs, but only some more generically human activities,"[36] he may be right in other (simpler?) cases, but not in the one presently imagined. The Hindu might claim that animals have lives which are intrinsically valuable (which is why he is a vegetarian), he might not even eat certain plants (like carrots, beets, and potatoes), and these claims of his cannot be understood unless his lifeview is understood. A Hindu's lifeview is informed by distinct concepts like *karma* (fate), *ahimsa* (nonviolence), *dukha* (suffering), *atman* (soul), and *Brahman* (Absolute Reality).[37] In such cases, the arguments on both sides will, and must, be advanced in the full panoply of their respective beliefs, and in the absence of a proper understanding of these beliefs conversion might be deeply suspect.

Anthony Rudd asks, "[W]hy does Kierkegaard call the passionate commitment to an objective uncertainty 'truth'?" And declares:

I shall approach this question by distinguishing three successively stronger theses, each of which Kierkegaard holds. . . . The first thesis

---

[35]*Works of Love*, 229.
[36]"Kierkegaard, Wittgenstein, and a Method of 'Virtue Ethics,' " 161.
[37]Words in parentheses are fairly loose translations.

is that objective thought about ethics and religion is not enough—knowledge of 'existential' truths is worthless unless one allows them to change one's life. The second thesis is that there cannot be genuine objective knowledge about ethics and religion—someone who thinks that he has understood ethics and religion objectively has simply misunderstood them. The third thesis is that 'truth' can be attributed not only to ideas, but to attitudes; not only to beliefs but to the spirit in which they are held; not only to propositions, but to human lives.[38]

Would this save Kierkegaard from the charge of irrationalism? Consider any two religions, R (say, Christianity) and R* (say, Hinduism). Both religions maintain that merely knowing, or mouthing, the dogmas of their respective religions is not enough—the dogmas must transform one's life, they must permeate one's thought, speech, and deed. Second, the knowledge of these religions is not something objective; one learns through participation, enactment—studying the scripture and engaging in prayer and ritual. The attempt to understand the religion, while staying at a distance, will only result in an understanding that is a caricature of the real thing. Finally, "truth," both religions will maintain, can be attributed not only to the dogmas of their respective religions, to the fundamental ideas, but also to the attitudes of the believers: to the spirit in which they are held by them and to the lives that are guided by their dogmas. R might point to individuals who profess to be the followers of R, but are very poor examples of it; R might also point to individuals who profess not to follow it, but are indeed good practitioners of it; finally, R might point to individuals who are on the borderline between faith and apostasy. R* can easily be seen to make parallel claims.

An epistemologist might chalk up this argument.

> An objective uncertainty attends upon the basic propositions of both R and R*, their being passionately held by their believers notwithstanding. Either that objective uncertainty is equal in both religions or it is not. If the uncertainty in R is equal to the uncertainty in R*, then the choice between the religions is entirely arbitrary: one might as well be a Hindu polytheist as a Christian monotheist. On the other hand, if the uncertainty in R is unequal to the uncertainty in R* (say, it is greater), then the choice between the two religions is not only not arbitrary, but

---

[38]*Kierkegaard and the Limits of the Ethical*, 56.

it is a function of a criterion or criteria that displays the difference in their objective uncertainty.

Such an argument stands regardless of whether the assessment is made from within the respective systems or from outside them. If the uncertainty is indeed *objective*, then it is quite conceivable to make it from a neutral standpoint. But suppose not, for all that has been said. Then, the individual assessing the objective uncertainty has not only experienced R, but R* as well. If he has not experienced them, one can hardly speak of any arbitration at all, let alone a fair arbitration of their relative worth. Let us say he finds R* convincing: he assesses the relative worth of the two religions from *within* the fold of R*. This assessment is not that of a neutral observer, yet he now has *reasons* for why he chooses R* over R. It is no less a criterion of his choice, notwithstanding that it is not the criterion of a neutral observer.[39] However, please note: it must *also* be true of him that when he was practicing R he was not similarly persuaded of R being superior to R*. Otherwise, his assessment of which should be the favored religion would simply be a function of the religion he has espoused when he judges the issue.[40]

---

[39]Thus Judge Wilhelm:

There are situations in life to which it would be ridiculous, or a kind of insanity, to apply an either/or; but also, there are people whose souls are too disjointed to grasp what such a dilemma implies, whose personalities lack the energy to be able to say with feeling: either/or . . . I think of the moment when, later in life, I stood at the crossroads, when my soul was matured in the hour of decision. I think of the many less important, yet for me not indifferent, occasions in life where choice was what mattered. For although there is only one situation where this phrase has its absolute meaning, namely where it points on the one hand to truth, righteousness, and holiness, and on the other to desire and susceptibility, and to dim passions and perdition, it is important to choose rightly even when the choice in itself is harmless; to test oneself so as never to have to begin a retreat to the point one started out from, and thank God for having nothing worse to reproach oneself for than wasting time.

Kierkegaard, *Either/Or: A Fragment of Life*, 477.

[40]Taking a cue from the last footnote: it should not be the case that Judge Wilhelm would reverse himself were he to opt for an aesthetic view of life, and calling his earlier life dull, ensnaring, and deceptive.

Consequently, either there exists criterion or criteria which enable
us to decide which religion or ethical system to espouse; or, our choice
is arbitrary.

I do not know how to respond to the skeptic.

NEITHER/NOR

Perhaps someone else might respond thus. To the supposition "that someone confronts the choice between them [the ethical and the aesthetic
mode of living and regarding life], as yet having embraced neither,"[41] one
might counter,

---

[41]MacIntyre, *After Virtue: A Study in Moral Theory*, 40.

Alastair Hannay in the introduction to his translation of Kierkegaard's
Either/Or: A Fragment of Life, entertains that very possibility in its much
stronger form. Where MacIntyre considers an individual who is *about* to choose,
having chosen neither, nor knowing what principles of choice are around, Hannay
considers an individual who, *after* having deliberated on both choices, chooses
neither: "at least from the fictitious editor's [Victor Eremita's] point of view, the
proper conclusion to draw from reading *Either/Or* is 'neither/nor' " (7). This is
sitting on the fence, *par excellence*, between selves. Kierkegaard himself, thinks
Hannay, might have wanted us to assume that Victor Eremita did occupy "some
vantage point superior to the two he presents, . . . and that we should therefore
somehow seek in deficiencies of both views the basis of a third" (7). Consequently, it is puzzling when Hannay later says, "So 'either' there is a great deal
of indirect persuasion and subterfuge, hardly a good advertisement at least for a
supposedly *ethical* lifeview, 'or' the radical choice reading is mistaken" (13).

It is puzzling for two reasons. First, one might equally say for the "neither/
nor" option that there is too much indirect persuasion and subterfuge; that, if
Kierkegaard had wanted us to adopt neither of the two alternatives, he should
simply have come out—in the person of Victor Eremita, so to speak—and said
so. Thus, not running the risk that we might make the wrong choice and choose
the ethical; or, worse, choose the aesthetic lifeview. But, second, and significantly, the indirect persuasion need not be a subterfuge at all. Here, I borrow the
argument from Hannay himself. Hannay cites Kierkegaard on indirect communication: "It means that one doesn't begin *directly* with what one wants to com-
municate, but . . . going along with the other's delusion" (*Kierkegaard*, 56).
Then, Hannay himself: "Where false pictures paralyse a person's will and understanding, any form of direct communication is useless. One must first apply a
'corrosive'; but this corrosive is the negative, and in communication the negative
is to precisely to deceive" (*Kierkegaard*, 57).

Well then, that someone is a self-deluded aesthete. For Kierkegaard, there is no sitting on the fence between selves. If you have not chosen, you are an aesthete, but if you are really facing the choice, you have already chosen to choose. There simply is no earnestly facing the choice *qua* an individual who has yet to choose, for to acknowledge the choice is to affirm that you have a self, which marks the second, not the first, stage on life's way. And that, in one breath, is why Kierkegaard believed he only needed to "present the reader with an ultimate choice."[42]

Exegesis aside, this is a puzzling philosophical position. It almost seems as if the problem is defined away. Either you have a self or not. An aesthete has no self, if he thinks he has a choice as to which life to choose. For, by definition, a self is only a self when it has chosen or, at least, sees that there is a choice. The objector, Gordon D. Marino, is careful to say that a self is a self even when he has chosen to choose. Now, a self is an ethical self when, having chosen to choose, it chooses the ethical; a self is no less an ethical self when it has only chosen to choose. But, the latter is oddly described as a position in which a choice is to be made because that self, by definition, has no real choice: it cannot choose the nonethical option. If it could, and did, then it would not be a self. (It would be a self-deluded aesthete.) In any case, its choice would have to be governed by a criterion or criteria. This argument is designed to show that enough selfhood must be conferred on the aesthete for him to be in a position to make a choice between the two kinds of lives.

Kierkegaard:

He chooses himself, not in a finite sense, for then this 'self' would be something finite along with other finite things, but in an absolute sense. And still he chooses himself and not another. This self he thus chooses is infinitely concrete, for it is himself, and yet it is absolutely different from his former self, for he has chosen it absolutely. This self did not exist previously, for it came into existence through the choice, and yet it has been in existence, for it was indeed "he himself." The choice here makes the two dialectical movements at once: what is chosen does not exist and comes into existence through the choice, and what is chosen exists, otherwise it would not be a choice. For if the thing I chose did not exist but became absolute through the choice itself, I would not

---

[42]Gordon D. Marino, "The Place of Reason in Kierkegaard's Ethics," 52-53.

have chosen, I would have created. But I do not create myself, I choose myself. Therefore while nature has been created out of nothing, while I myself *qua* my immediate personal existence have been created out of nothing, as free spirit I am born of the principle of contradiction, or born by virtue of the fact that I chose myself.[43]

History of an Individual

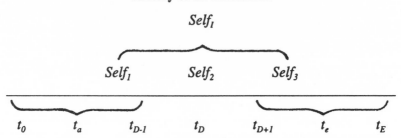

Self₁ ... *Self₁ Self₂ Self₃* ... t_0 t_a t_{D-1} t_D t_{D+1} t_e t_E

An individual is born at t_0 and lives the life of an aesthete until t_D; his life will end at t_E; between t_D and t_E he lives an ethical life. The big decision in his life, whether he is going to choose himself, comes at t_D.[44] Here, then, are some puzzles from which I cannot free myself. Before t_D, he is not an ethical self, he is an aesthete; and, therefore, by the aforesaid argument, cannot choose between the life of an aesthete and the ethical

---

[43]Kierkegaard, *Either/Or: A Fragment of Life*, 517-18.

[44]Does Kierkegaard even recognize the possibility of such a moment? Yes, he does: "What it amounts to is nothing less than that the real meaning of life, after all, is sorrow, and being the unhappiest is the happiest thing of all. At first glance this does not look like an aesthetic view of life, for its slogan can scarcely be pleasure. Neither, however, is it ethical, but it lies at the dangerous transition between the aesthetic and ethical, where the soul is so easily seduced by one or another version of the theory of predestination" (Kierkegaard, *Either/Or: A Fragment of Life*, 529-30).

There is this passage, too, in *Fear and Trembling*: "The category I shall consider in more detail is the *interesting*, a category that especially now—since the age lives in *discrimine rerum* [at a turning point in history]—has become very important, for it is actually the category of the turning point. . . . Furthermore, the interesting is the border category, a *confinium* [border territory] between aesthetics and ethics. Accordingly, this examination must constantly wander into the territory of ethics, while in order to be of consequence it must seize the problem with esthetic fervor and concupiscence" (82-83).

life. After t_D, *ex hypothesi*, the choice has already been made. What, then, at t_D? There are three alternatives as to where t_D might belong. Either (1) in the set to which t_a belongs; or (2) in the set to which t_e belongs; or (3) in neither of those sets, but a different set: it may or may not be the sole member of this third set. In the first alternative, there is no possibility of choice since he is still an aesthete; in the second alternative, the choice has already been made; and, finally, the third alternative is not a possibility. Why? To repeat: "For Kierkegaard, there is no sitting on the fence between selves. If you have not chosen, you are an aesthete, but if you are really facing the choice, you have already chosen to choose."[45]

Let us say t_D is the moment when the individual has "chosen to choose" and t_{D+1} the moment when he specifically chooses the ethical life. Then, three questions would arise. First, on what rational grounds, if any, was the individual moved from t_{D-1} (he has not chosen to choose) to t_D (he has chosen to choose)? Second, to what set does t_{D-1} belong: to the set to which t_a belongs or to the set to which t_D belongs? In either case, we clearly run into the same sequence of problems. Third, on what rational grounds, if any, was the individual moved from t_D (he has chosen to choose) to t_{D+1} (he has chosen the ethical life as the rational one)? Is there any difference between the rational grounds used in the two transitions from t_{D-1} to t_D and from t_D to t_{D+1}, respectively?

Kierkegaard is also saying, first, that $Self_3$ is "infinitely concrete," chosen "in an absolute sense," and is "absolutely different from his former self," namely, $Self_1$, which self he presumably chose in a finite sense, not absolutely. *Ergo*, $Self_1 \neq Self_3$. What, if any, is the relationship between $Self_1$ and $Self_3$? Second, both $Self_3$ did exist previously and $Self_3$ did not exist previously: it did exist previously because if it had not, then Kierkegaard would have created himself ab initio, and not chosen it; it did not exist previously because if it had, then (I am extrapolating now) what Kierkegaard should have chosen to become, he already was. How could this be explained away? Third, what is the relationship between $Self_2$ (assuming it to exist), on the one hand, and $Self_1$ and $Self_3$, on the other hand? Fourth, is there an overarching, or an underlying, $Self_1$, say,

---

[45]Marino, "The Place of Reason in Kierkegaard's Ethics," 53.

a pure ego?[46] Is this the self that ultimately unifies these various selves? Might it be that $Self_1 = Self_3$?[47]

Consider George B. Connell's rather pertinent question: "If in order to choose ethically in a given situation I must have chosen to make such choice my policy, why is it not necessary to choose to choose ethically?"[48] Connell offers the following by way of an answer:

> It is the very totality of this choice that nullifies the threat of infinite regression. The self, though free and responsible, is not at its own disposal in the simplistic sense that it can without difficulty convert the wish to be ethical into effective willing. It is not in a prior act of the self but rather in a spontaneous gathering together of all the aspects of the self in taking responsibility for itself that ethical selfhood originates. Thus while the self chooses to choose, it does not choose to do so.[49]

This is a rather difficult passage. First, there is no prior act and yet there is a choice—*how*? Second, does not a clear wish to be ethical (regardless of whether it is followed by an effective will) confer selfhood on an individual, thus making him ethical? Is not an aesthete distinguished just by the fact that he does not even have this wish? Third, what, and especially, *who*, converts wishing into willing, if the self is not at its own disposal? What factors block the conversion, and why? What overcomes the block? What reasons, if any, go into the conversion, especially if the conversion is spontaneous? Fourth, there is "a spontaneous gathering together of *all* the aspects of the self in taking responsibility for itself." But, there is no self unless there is an ethical self; that, at least, was Marino's point of insistence. Fifth, what self is it that does the gathering? Is it the gathering of all aspects of the self which makes into "the very totality of this choice"? Why is the gathering of all aspects required? Could a partial gathering not suffice, bringing other aspects

---

[46]"So there is something in him that is absolute in relation to everything else, something whereby he is the one he is, even if the change he obtains through his wish were the greatest possible" (Kierkegaard, *Either/Or: A Fragment of Life*, 517).

[47]I leave the task of finding a solution to these problems in far more capable hands than mine.

[48]"Judge William's Theonomous Ethics," 58.

[49]"Judge William's Theonomous Ethics," 68n.10.

(less central?) of the self gradually into the fold? Sixth, is "a spontaneous gathering together of all the aspects of the self in taking responsibility for itself" required before "a spontaneous gathering together of all the aspects of the self in taking responsibility for itself" can be made? If so, the infinite regression is easily established; if not, it is hard to see how this kind of spontaneity—serendipity—can be made to govern an individual's ethical being.

What ejects an individual out of the aesthete's life space? Passion? Not quite, the objector thinks. It is false to believe that "the infallibility of the first genuine choice follows from the passion with which it is made—and that is that. It isn't. Of course, once the inwardness, which earmarks the ethical is present, the choice is made."[50] But, that inwardness is not present unless it is attended by a proper passion; and, so, the issue revolves around the question, What brings that passion about which will eject the aesthete from his present mode of life?

"And what renders the choice of the ethical a criterionless choice? . . . And if the proof is in the act of the choice? It makes no difference. If a converted Don Juan cannot provide the next Don Juan with compelling reasons to follow his lead, his conversion is without a basis in reason."[51] And if a Don Juan were to convince *no one* to follow his lead, would the proof still lie in the act of the choice? Why, then, whatever your act of choice, happily, for you, your proof lies in your choice. Clearly, matters cannot rest at such an impasse, nor does Marino think they need to.

Here we come to an interesting exegetical fork. "[T]here is more continuity (equilibrium) between the ethical and the aesthetic," than one might allow; so much so that "True, every desire will appear differently according to the categories through which it is conceived, but both the Judge and Kierkegaard suppose that there is enough continuity to reason the aesthete out of one conception and toward another."[52] Such reasons

---

[50]Marino, "The Place of Reason in Kierkegaard's Ethics," 53.

[51]Marino, "The Place of Reason in Kierkegaard's Ethics," 54.

[52]Marino, "The Place of Reason in Kierkegaard's Ethics," 55. Kierkegaard himself does not make things easy: "[Y]our thought has taken everything from you but it has given you nothing in its stead. The next instant some little triviality captivates you. You look upon it, indeed, with all the superiority and pride your overbearing thought gives you. . . . In this way, once it is people you

are ultimately built on the goal of happiness—there is a *telos* after all. The reasons are tied to the *telos*; anyone who accepts the *telos*, therefore, will accept the Judge's arguments and pursue the ethical life. At least in part, his arguments will show that the life of the aesthete does not bring as much happiness as the life of the ethical; the balance sheet of reason— neither chance nor demonstration—will dictate that one must live the ethical life.

Given the earlier arguments of the objector, though, these reasons are useless, at best; perpetuating an epistemic illusion, at worst. Recall: There is no self poised between the self of the aesthete and the self of the ethical; consequently, there is no self eagerly debating which lifestyle will promote most happiness.[53] And, if reasons will instruct the individual as to which form of life he should adopt, what then is the role of passion? Is it, after all, second fiddle to reason?

THE PRINCIPLE OF CONTRADICTION[54]

Not having sought refuge in God, one needs to band together. Therefore, says Kierkegaard, people

> would have to agree on something in which it is a contradiction to be more than one. The idolized positive principle of sociality in our age is the consuming, demoralizing principle that in the thralldom of reflection transforms even virtues into *vitia splendida* [glittering vices]. And what is the basis of this other than a disregard for the separation of the religious individual before God in the responsibility of eternity. When dismay commences at this point, one seeks comfort in company, and thus reflection captures the individual for his whole life. (86, 53)

But, says Kierkegaard: "This is why eventually not even a very gifted person is able to liberate himself from reflection, for he soon realizes he

---

have to deal with, your nature exhibits a high degree of faithlessness, *for which one cannot blame you morally, however, since you are outside the category of the ethical*" (Kierkegaard, *Either/Or: A Fragment of Life*, 507; my emphasis).

[53]To which individual? After all, the aesthete has no self. Rudd clearly takes a similar view to Kierkegaard, as does Marino. Or, else, Rudd's seeking of support for his view through a unique reading of Wittgenstein would become incomprehensible. See Rudd, *Kierkegaard and the Limits of the Ethical*, 50-54.

[54]I now to return to the pages of *The Present Age*.

is merely a fraction in something utterly trivial and misses the infinite liberation of the religious life" (85, 53). So, the strong claim: "rescue comes only through the essentiality of religious in the particular individual" (88, 56). Assuming that Sarah Wylcott is a preeminently gifted woman, and that she does not merely seek consolation in company (nothing in her character or history would entice her to do that), she might very well become conscious of being content with herself, banding people together, being a fractional part of a venture she has launched—hardly a trivial enterprise—and, yet, not being enslaved to "the devouring and demoralizing" positive principle of association. Consequently, it is unclear why she should be regarded as having failed to achieve freedom, given what her life now exhibits. To say that it is not the infinite freedom of religion is straightforwardly a case of *petitio principii*.

Sarah Wylcott instantiates the *principle of contradiction*. What is this Kierkegaardian principle?

> The existential expression of nullifying the principle of contradiction [says Kierkegaard] is to be in contradiction to oneself. The creative omnipotence implicit in the passion of absolute disjunction that leads the individual resolutely to make up his mind is transformed into the extensity of prudence and reflection—that is, by knowing and being everything possible to be in contradiction to oneself, that is, to be nothing at all. The principle of contradiction strengthens the individual in faithfulness to himself, so that, just like that constant number three Socrates speaks of so beautifully,[55] which would rather suffer anything and everything than become a number four or even a very large round number, he would rather be something small, if still faithful to himself, than all sorts of things in contradiction to himself. (97, 68-69)

One must be true to oneself; and not know everything and be everything: in that way one loses faithfulness to oneself; one dampens the discerning and differentiating passion. Those who live the life of reflection, as do most who live in the present age, live in opposition to this principle. But not Sarah Wylcott.

---

[55]Plato: "Thus we shall say, shan't we, that three will sooner perish, will undergo anything else whatever, sooner than abide coming to be even, while remaining three?" (*Phaedo* 104c, p. 62; see esp. 61-63).

What, then, is it to be at one with oneself? *How* can one be one with oneself? Moreover, why should one be one with oneself? Listen to Socrates in *Lysis*:

> God himself makes them friends by bringing them to one another. I think the sort of thing they say is this: "God always brings like to like."
> . . .
> "Well," I said, "are they right?"
> "Possibly," he replied.
> "Possibly half-right," I said, "but possibly even wholly right, only we don't understand them properly. . . .
> "But I think what they mean is that good men are like one another and therefore friends, whereas bad men (as is in fact said of them) are never like even their own selves, but are capricious and unstable, and anything which is unlike and at variance with itself would hardly become like or friend to anything else."[56]

To stretch the Socratic metaphor no more than necessary: in order for the number three to be true to itself and not want to be any other number, no matter how large and round, it must *know* itself. Only the failure to know itself, its ignorance, will drive it to have fancy desires and ambitions, both unnatural and unbecoming; say, it dreams of becoming א. And when it knows itself, it shall then be faithful to itself in being the best number three it can be. I draw on an old distinction of Terence Parsons between what he calls *general* essences and *individual* essences. Parsons's characterization is too simple and precise to be improved upon: "let us

---

[56]Plato, *Early Socratic Dialogues*, 146-47. Nor is this in Plato an isolated instance of showing the consequence of a house divided against itself. *Republic* teaches very much the same lesson: see 350d-52d, esp. 352a.

Aristotle hums the same tune, but with an explanation. "But wicked men," says Aristotle, "have no steadfastness (for they do not remain even like to themselves). . . . And having nothing lovable in them they have no feeling of love to themselves. Therefore also such men do not rejoice or grieve with themselves; for their soul is rent by faction, and one element in it by reason of its wickedness grieves when it abstains from certain acts, while the other part is pleased, and one draws them this way and the other that, as if they were pulling them in pieces." This, Aristotle concludes, "is the height of wretchedness" (*Nicomachean Ethics*, 206 and 229). The entire chap. 4 of book IX is relevant, although I cite only a brief passage from it.

dichotomize essentialist doctrines into two kinds. One kind has to do with what I shall call *individual* essences and the other with what I shall call *general* essences. The former doctrine makes some claim to the effect that some or all objects have characteristics (or properties) which are so intimately associated with the object that nothing else *could* (with emphasis on the "could") have precisely those characteristics without being that object."[57]

Kierkegaard's point then seems to be this. An engineer must be an engineer; a skiff plower a plower of skiffs; a paleontologist, a paleontologist. Try and make a gifted viola player into any one of these things and, unsurprisingly, he does not fit in: neither his mind nor his environment will be at peace with one another. There is enormity and unnaturalness in asking Rembrandt to do the work of building a city's sewer system; or asking a sewer system builder to be a Rembrandt. Not even a da Vinci can know and do everything. But, then, the principle of contradiction has a profound and powerful implication. It is this: we need to try to know *who* we are for unless we know who we are, we might haplessly and ignorantly live against the principle of contradiction. Then, does passion have the differentiating power? Does understanding? Passion might unify, for Kierkegaard speaks of passion as the unifying principle; indeed, one might say it is a positive unifying principle, while envy is the negative unifying principle (81, 47). Passion might bind into a whole, what understanding might differentiate, disentangle, view, review, conjoin, collate, or provide an overview, without which, what passion binds, unifies, or provides the force to be faithful to, would not be worth much. Without understanding, what passion binds may fly in the face of the principle of contradiction.

Combining Parsons with Socrates might yield something interestingly Kierkegaardian. Kierkegaard is deeply concerned about individuals not being lost in the faceless, characterless crowd, for that would rob an

---

[57]Terence Parsons, "Essentialism and Quantified Modal Logic," 73. Parsons then goes on to state that this doctrine is stronger than the thesis of Identity of Indiscernibles in two ways. First, it forbids any two objects sharing the same individual essences; second, if the world had been different, then any object that had the same individual essences that object A possesses in the actual world would have been A. Parsons, alas, does not go on to specify the doctrine of individual essences in any greater detail than what he has already done.

individual of the very individuality which is his saving grace. Such an individual "would rather be something small, if still faithful to himself, than all sorts of things in contradiction to himself" (97, 68-69). In a genuine act, the individual responds, or should respond, with the full force of what is unique in him; this is one reason why he does not join a group. Such an individual, at ease with what is unique in him, will be at ease with himself—will be a friend, will be good, as Socrates says. But when an individual is at variance with what is unique in him, he is ill at ease with himself; and such an individual is a threat both to himself and to others.

So far, so good. But it conceals the important role of understanding. On this view it is crucial—if anything, more so—for the individual to come to an understanding of who he really is: what *this* individual essence of his is. For the harmony in his life is ultimately dependent on this knowledge, although no doubt the will is also required to live a life in accordance with that knowledge. Nor is this all the knowledge he is to possess. For he must have knowledge of his general essence, in virtue of which he is, shall we say, a member of the *homo sapiens* species. Yet more, of course, he must have knowledge of what it is to be moral. So Sarah Wylcott comes to an understanding of her unique self, her individual essence; she distinguishes herself from the others in her environment; she does not join the crowd. But not anything she chooses to do in the light of her knowledge is right, fair, or just. For her to be right, fair, or just, she would have to act in accordance with the knowledge of good and evil.

Assume, then, that being in tune with one's individual essence enables one to be content with oneself. Socrates, unhappy about talk of individual essences, might ask some such questions as these. What is it about one's unique self that one should be content with it? Why should we not transform at least some type of selves into other kinds and get them to be content with their new selves? To illustrate the point of the questions, consider the following. A hardened criminal, a drug addict, a habitual sex offender, or a frequent larcenist may each have their unique individual essences, such that, quoting Parsons, anyone who has those individual essences will *be* that person. Why, Socrates might ask, should such an individual be content with himself as *that* individual? Why ought he not to be asked to be content with himself as a duly transformed moral agent?

Kierkegaard—and I with him—might well argue in this context that moral principles while necessary may not be sufficient to inform a moral agent as to what he should do in a particular situation. To illustrate: a gifted doctor, who also happens to be a concert pianist, forsakes his established lifestyle and goes into the heart of Africa to heal the sick; a Sienese governor sits in a public square with a begging bowl in hand, seeking contributions from passerbys for a ransom for his imprisoned friend until he has collected enough. No moral theory can dictate that each ought to have done what each, in fact, did; neither can any moral theory decide that not doing any of it would have been immoral. So that, if Schweitzer had not gone into the heart of Africa, he would have been immoral as Provenzan Salvani would have been if he had not—in just the way he did—come to the aid of his friend rotting in King Charles's prison.[58]

A moral theory paints in broad strokes, and allows a variety of ways in which one can be moral: each way an individual picks to be moral is his declaration of his uniqueness, an exhibition of his individual essence(s). Thus, when Kierkegaard asks an individual not to join the crowd, he does not mean to say, "Do not ever do what the crowd does," so much as (a) consult the moral principles and (b) make sure that what you do is not only in conformity with the moral principles, but also with what is your individual genius. When both (a) and (b) are satisfied, then it matters not whether the individual does, or does not, do what the crowd does. *Ergo*, a mafia don who claims to act in conformity with his particular genius is not moral since he is in clear violation of (a); but also, had Schweitzer not gone to Africa, thus not heeding what his genius dictated to him, he would have been in violation of (b), and hence, perhaps, morally amiss. Had Schweitzer done merely what others in his community did, Kierkegaard might have ventured that Schweitzer was only mimicking the crowd or mob. If this is correct, it makes it patently obvious why knowledge of oneself is so utterly important. Might it be that when the true moral theory gets to be written, it will prescribe so accurately what each individual's duty is that it will circumvent the need for clause (b)? Or, will (b) never be replaced?

---

[58]Thomas Caldecot Chubb, *Dante and His World*, 115-16.

One of our general essences might be that we are all equal before God. My argument is that insofar as I choose to live, and perform deeds, I do so not solely on the basis of that general essence—which I grant, for the sake of argument, is a necessary condition—but also on the basis of my individual essences, or of my knowledge of my individual essences. (My actions, of course, may loudly declare that I am concealing that knowledge from myself.) This I claim is also a necessary condition. I may very well be what I am *par accident*, or as a gift from God. But I am only an agent of Good when I choose to act as *this* particular individual.

The circle of rightness, fairness, and justice is sufficiently wide to allow distinct approaches, designed by individuals in possession of unique individual essences, to rest squarely within it, but not so wide or accommodating as to allow everything in. But clearly, then, authenticity or uniqueness is not enough; we also need an understanding of what we morally ought to do. Kierkegaard might respond that he is asking the individual to respond in the fullness of that knowledge which he fails to do when he is led or forced into a decision by a crowd: the vital moral decision is not his; it is someone else's. That response does not undercut the indispensability of understanding; it only emphasizes that that understanding must be genuine, must be *his*, and must be the ultimate motivating factor.

Chapter 5

STAGES OF SELF-KNOWLEDGE

This chapter offers a theory of understanding, more precisely a theory of *self*-understanding. What significant elements or stages there are in this process of understanding are better served by two literary texts: Christopher Marlowe's *The Tragical History of the Life and Death of Doctor Faustus* and Isaac Bashevis Singer's *The Penitent*. Perhaps this theory of understanding may in turn cast some light on these texts, but that is not my primary aim.

I begin by briefly exploring the old Socratic maxim. Attempting to *know oneself* leads one to know one's physical and psychological characteristics; but one's self is not exhausted by those characteristics because a human being is essentially marked by moral characteristics as well. It follows that a moral theory is imperative in guiding one's knowledge about oneself. One's identity is relative to one's characteristics—physical, psychological, and moral; the worth of one's characteristics is relative to one's life plan; the worth of the latter is judged by a moral theory. Once again, one needs a moral theory not only to determine one's identity but also to measure the worth of one's life plan. As one journeys—Socrates's word—towards that self-knowledge, putting into practice the moral theory one has uncovered so far, one's experiences and dispositions are transformed and these then serve as indispensable epistemic guides in discovering, understanding, and justifying the next phase of the theory, and, so, the next aspect of oneself. There are, I argue, six essential stages of self-understanding, and I end by showing some of the interconnections between these stages.

THE SOCRATIC MAXIM

Know thyself. This maxim has always puzzled me. I could have understood, even been persuaded, if Socrates had said "Know great men" or "Know great books" or "Know great phenomena." And then I would have set out forthwith to do as he bid. But *Know myself*? Examine a life of routines of dishwashing, lecturing, putting out the garbage, attending committees, going to movies, walking, and drinking teas? I could see no rationale for that exercise, and, yet, Socrates would have enjoined us to make it our central, and endless occupation. However, understanding the rationale of that maxim is not my chief task in this part of the essay, although I do say something about it. It is rather to explore the Socratic adage in order to locate his differences with Kierkegaard. So I venture, through this exploration, to resolve some such questions as these: If Socrates epitomizes reason and Kierkegaard faith, how precisely should their differences be understood? What, if any, are their common grounds? What are the impasses? What, and how, can reconciliation be effected? And, who emerges less scathed?

Why, then, should I know myself? There are certain physical characteristics of me which I can easily identify, some not that easily; but most of these are not of any importance, or are not important to my self-knowledge.[1] What I cannot identify easily generally requires a deep and detailed scientific theory, such as the one about my genes, eyes, brain, or kidneys. I also have certain psychological characteristics, some of which are likewise easy to identify, some stubbornly difficult; and many of these are of considerable importance, or are important to my self-knowledge. Here, too, I might require a profound psychological theory to enable me to discover my psychological traits and qualities, such as anxiety, paraphrenia, agoraphobia, an inferiority complex, aggressiveness, masochism, and so on. As a rule, the physical and psychological theories overlap and interconnect.

---

[1]This is the traditional answer. Yet, I wonder. Surely, my DNA sequence is not that unimportant to me. It may determine the likelihood of a child of mine suffering from Down's syndrome, my suffering from Alzheimer's disease, or my being a victim of schizophrenia. Nor does this view take into account the brute contingencies of life. Let us suppose that the gene that makes possible brilliant mathematical work cannot be had without the gene for serious depression. Should I know this to be my makeup, and assuming that the gene for depression can be eliminated through genetic engineering, ought I to opt out of being a mathematician? But the brute contingencies of life, like a gunshot wound, may eliminate me before the dreaded disease takes its toll. Or, the cure for depression may be found in my lifetime. Presently, I have left untouched the question of which physical characteristics are constitutive, or necessary, for my identity or self-knowledge.

While the physical and psychological characteristics are significant characteristics of my identity, they are not all the characteristics I possess; I also possess moral characteristics. These characteristics I cannot identify—and, therefore, I cannot identify myself—unless I have an adequate moral theory. So, an initial inquiry about who I am has ineluctably led into an inquiry about a moral theory. At no point in my life, can I complete the task of fully discovering and understanding a moral theory; *ipso facto*, at no point in my life, can I complete the task of fully discovering and understanding myself, my identity. Correspondingly, the more I discover and understand a moral theory, the better I understand myself.

What is an important characteristic is relative to a life plan—a meaning of life—I should think. Socrates' characteristics of being short, stubby, snub-nosed, and having protruding eyes are of no importance to his life as a philosopher, soldier, and an occasional participant in his community's political affairs. But to an actress, her looks may be of vital importance to her life plan. If one's identity is closely linked to one's life plan, then the worth of one's life plan is one's crucial characteristic, and if the worth of one's life plan is decided by the moral theory, then a moral theory is imperative for determining one's identity, and for determining which of one's physical and psychological characteristics are important. There is this to consider, too: Is one's life plan a contingent aspect of oneself? Do we have two notions of identity, one primary and the other—the one under discussion—secondary, so that the latter is foisted on the former? For purposes of self-knowledge, which is supposed to have connection with wisdom, it is hard to see the present notion cast in a secondary role.

Such a process of self-examination makes an utterly important demand on the would-be self-inquirer: put to practice what you know if you wish to have more moral knowledge. What comes to the same thing: put to practice what you know if you wish to have more self-knowledge. It follows that failure to do so will perpetuate ignorance: willful neglect to do the moral thing will lead to self-deception. A moral theory offers a (*the?*) pathway towards the good. In the absence of such a theory, we cannot know the good, let alone the path to that good. In the absence of any theory, our actions or deeds will be random, unconnected. In the presence of a false moral theory, our deeds will be connected, but will be pushed away from the good. The correct moral theory offers a clear picture of what we should do in a moral situation; it acts as a guide.

Socrates' other view—one I find hard to share—is that moral knowledge alone will enable us to do the moral thing. But we can come in fair proximity of that view—moral knowledge cannot be had in the absence of moral practice—if we add this: the possibility of understanding and discovering the next phase of the moral theory, or the possibility of rejecting its mistaken parts, depends upon putting the dicta of the present phase of the theory into practice. The practice transforms one's experiences and dispositions which attune one's gaze in the right direction. These experiences and dispositions then serve as indispensable epistemic guides in understanding and discovering the next phase of the theory. The doing of moral deeds deepens our moral understanding in a way no amount of theoretical knowledge by itself would; the tutored understanding learns to cast off the errors in the theory, to remold the theory, and makes us act in accordance with its fresh insights and understanding. On this view, one's moral personality develops alongside the moral theory. The failure to put the theory into practice leads to corruption of one's experiences and dispositions, and these become defective moral compasses—they lead to further moral chaos.

Such a process of self-examination requires knowledge of full and adequate physical, psychological, and moral theory. The acquisition of such knowledge is an endless process; therefore, the task of knowing oneself is endless. This, in short, is the reason behind the Socratic maxim.

THE SIX STAGES

Say Nehemiah of Sodom becomes reflective, starts to examine himself, and is in the process of saving himself. There are six stages he might undergo.

Stage 1. The problem of who he, Nehemiah, is, and what his moral shortcomings are; how might he become ethical? This is the stage calling for the knowledge of particulars, especially about the particular, Nehemiah.

Stage 2. Nehemiah asks himself, What is this society of Sodom in which he lives, and to what extent is an individual the result of being a member of that society? This is the stage calling for the knowledge of universals.[2]

---

[2]This is not to advocate the false claim that the knowledge of particulars and

Stage 3. The first two stages have created enough doubt about his ethical stature in his own mind for Nehemiah to embark on an ethical investigation. He cannot tell, precisely, what his present life is worth, let alone be able to give a reason for an ethical assessment of his life as a whole, unless he knows what is good and just, what his rights and duties are, and what should be the nature of a society that would give him a better chance to realize those values and fulfill his obligations. This is the stage calling for the knowledge of moral principles.

Stage 4. In the light of his ethical knowledge, he slowly comes to the recognition of how evil his ways and deeds are. This is the stage of acknowledging low self-worth; or it is the step of error recognition. This stage is indispensable to the next stage.

Stage 5. The stage of faith. Here, he acknowledges, or avows, faith in God.

Stage 6. Once the leap of faith has been made, then comes the full task of rearranging one's life in accordance with one's faith and beliefs. Old ways must give way to new ones.

This is my contention: unless he genuinely arrives at self-knowledge, knowledge of the corruption of his ways, there cannot, *per impossible*, be a genuine leap of faith. If there is no error recognition, then, no amount of acknowledging God can save him. The transition to stage 5 must be mediated by self-knowledge or stage 4, or it is not worth much. Or, minimally this: he who arrives at stage 5, via stage 4, has more faith, is more redeemed, than he who knows not stage 4, but has managed to bungle through stage 5. Understanding is utterly indispensable.

What would such stages look like for a man going in the opposite direction, from faith to apostasy? Anthony Kenny describes such a journey in *A Path from Rome: An Autobiography* as does Edward O. Wilson in his scintillating autobiography, *Naturalist*. The first three stages would be quite similar, I imagine. The fourth stage would be filled with

---

the knowledge of universals are sharply separate, independent things, that one could have the one without the other. But it is true that in some of our knowledge-seeking activity one of them plays a far more dominant role than the other. When I examine myself, my knowledge of universals becomes a backdrop against which I carry out my self-examination. When I seek knowledge of universals, my knowledge of particulars, in its turn, provides me with the backdrop of my knowledge-seeking activity.

suggestions or conjectures about self-deception, pursuit of grandeur by a different route, lack of moral courage against overwhelming odds, fear of mortality, the desire to find a meaningful life running amuck, and so on. Will there, then, be something corresponding to the fifth stage, a leap to a humanist credo?

Schematically, then:

Stages of Self-Knowledge

Stage 1   *Knowledge of Particulars*
        (Knowledge of himself, his particular history, his particular surroundings, his particular station in life)
Stage 2   *Knowledge of Universals*
        (Knowledge of his society's economic, social, political, and cultural substance, structure, and history)
Stage 3   *Knowledge of Moral Principles*
        (Knowledge of right conduct, rights, and duties; knowledge of the principles of governing a just and good society)
Stage 4   *The Step of Error Recognition*
        (Knowledge of the error of his ways, the falseness of his life-form, the corruption of his society)
Stage 5   *The Leap of Faith*
        (The point of transition)
Stage 6   *The Task of Rebuilding One's Life*
        (The individual musters enough will to change his life-form, habits, designs, and hopes, in accordance with his new faith and beliefs)

Stage 1. Knowledge of Particulars. Whether one sees one's life as a single narrative, or a cluster of narratives, with or without a common direction, to keep focus on the particulars of one's life is not nearly as easy as it is imagined. This is due to the fact that already stages 2 and 3 are implicated, but not only for that reason. It may also have to do with poor memory, inability to focus, not knowing how to dwell on a particular.[3] If one were to slice a single life, thus far lived, into relatively short, arbitrary intervals, each interval would have a *node*, from each

---

[3]Hence, the strange-seeming advice from Zen Buddhism: When you see a tree, become that tree.

node would proceed several *lines*, and from each line would hang several *knots*, events, episodes, or things of lesser moment. A node occupies the center stage of our consciousness; it is impregnated with significance, not much of it do we normally even articulate. The several lines emerging from each node poach their own smaller significance from that node. Lines, in turn, support still less significant knots and things. And these knots will lead to the next node, if any. The *life net* is a congeries of nodes, lines, and knots. Most if not all of us remember only a few nodes, lines, and knots of our life net; a few, like Lady Macbeth, become fixated on a handful of these;[4] and those who search for a meaningful life[5] often look for a sheltering, or even a shattering, node or two.

Joseph Shapiro has turned to repentance. He has become a *baal tshuvah*.[6] He had kept a mistress who milked him for money; he had made good, through bribery and corruption, in the real estate business; and he was cheating on his wife. He did not like his lifestyle. One day, as he mulls over his ways, his mistress and her daughter have so violent a fight, in his presence, that he is afraid one of them will kill the other, and so violent has the situation become that he runs away from it, and thus essentially runs away from the man he has become. During this interval of time, this scene between the mother and her daughter serves him as a powerful node. The knots of the connecting line—two other lines starting from this node pertain to the parent-child antagonists—are his returning home to discover the infidelity of his wife, his abandoning his wife and going to live in a hotel, ordering his first vegetarian breakfast, withdrawing large amounts of cash from the bank, and going to a Hasidic house of prayer. These connect to the next node: his being in the presence of the desperately ailing rabbi, from Maidenek, an embodiment of the old and revered form of Jewishness, and this in turn

---

[4]It would be interesting to study, from the present perspective, certain psychological traits such as obsessiveness, compulsiveness, reckless envy, unrelenting hatred, and certain forms of neurosis and depression.

[5]The ancient skeptic's view provides a puzzle. He claims that every view is equally plausible (*isosthenia*), he has the capacity for suspending judgment (*epoche*), and such a form of life would lead to tranquility (*ataraxia*). Can the skeptic do without a life net? Can all his knots be nodes and his nodes knots? See Myles F. Burnyeat, "Can the Skeptic Live his Skepticism?" 117-48.

[6]Isaac Bashevis Singer, *The Penitent*, 5. Hereafter cited as *The Penitent*.

takes him to other knots: his offering money to the rabbi and the other nine members of the group with whom he performed the *minyan*, finding an apartment nearby, purchasing two holy books, leaving New York for Israel, and so on. Things are not always that perspicuous. For example, consider Shapiro's flirtation with the young woman on the plane to Rome: is it to be connected to the node about violence (saying, he hasn't changed a bit) or to the node concerning the rabbi (saying, he lives in utter shame)? Or to both?[7]

We ride roughshod over particulars as of no great importance. We think that if we have the right moral map and the knowledge of universals, the rest is mere application of these principles in getting to know oneself and the particulars that happen to oneself. But, I think, it is a largely untraversed philosophical territory to show the importance of particulars of the self: to show how the injunction, *know thyself*, is to be linked to the knowledge of the particulars about oneself, and vice versa; how such an injunction cannot be carried out in the absence of knowledge of such particulars; and, how, for all our knowledge about either the knowledge of universals (stage 2) or knowledge of moral principles (stage 3), it is from the knowledge of particulars, and from dwelling in them, that our firmness of conviction, the rightness of our cause, is planted and nurtured.

Stage 2. Knowledge of Universals. Joseph Shapiro constantly derides society as he has experienced it in New York, as well as in Tel Aviv, Jerusalem, or in the kibbutzim. Namely, that these are the societies in which might wins over right, politicians are utterly corrupt, lawyers are despicable, victims and witnesses are abused by an inapt legal system, leftists have their own idolatries, modern women are whores, the world at large sells itself to become like a pimp or prostitute of Hollywood, modern literature and drama glorify torture, adultery, and evil, modern culture generally is made of the self-same cloth, and Hebrew, the language of worship, is mangled to serve modern needs of commerce and

---

[7]Death is difficult to pin down in this scheme. This is assuredly something that is going to happen to every mortal, many are obsessed by their eventual demise, and for some this produces significant alterations in their lives. Is death, which still lies in one's future, then, a node? Or, perhaps—a severe heart patient tells me—the nodes are those moments when the expectation of one's own death becomes especially vivid.

business. Such is the culture and the substance and the structure of the society he despises.

This, against the background of general knowledge of other things. What real Jewishness is, what its women were like, what it suffered in history: the destruction of the Temple, the Wailing Wall, the commercialization of religion,[8] the ravages of Stalin and Lenin against the Jews in the Diaspora (indeed, that without the Diaspora, which some Jews were prone to condemn, the old Jewishness would not have survived), the unimaginable terror of the Holocaust.[9]

But so long as knowledge is as general as that, it is difficult to see what bearing it can have on a particular individual's ability to know himself. The individual must see himself wrapped up in the particularities of his life: his escaping from Lublinka, his serving as God's cossack in Russia. Unless such general knowledge has seeped into the skin of the individual, tangled inextricably with the particularities of his life, or permeated his circumstances, thought, and deed, it can have little or no impact on him, no real assist in his drive for self-knowledge. Many of us ordinary folk may bemoan the goings-on in Hollywood, the state of our prison systems, the inefficiency of our automobile industry, but they have no discernible tempo in our reflections about ourselves—unless one is a Hollywood account executive, a prison guard, or an auto mechanic. Several such sketches collectively provide a background against which we place ourselves in society, and their significance ends when they have provided us with such a picture. Such a general picture can never—

---

[8]This is a trite generalization, although Shapiro does make it (*The Penitent*, 56-57). But when an individual in his own concrete, distinctive way faces, or is a participant in, the commercialization of his religion, the color changes, and his awareness of his so observing or doing can prompt a significant deed.

[9]There is no doubt that under this rubric I should also mention scientific knowledge: of psychoanalysis, economics, political and sociological theory, and such (notwithstanding Shapiro's denouncing of them, *The Penitent*, 66), but the pattern, extent, and focus of what and how much of this kind of knowledge is necessary will vary from individual to individual. Here I continue to tilt in favor of particularities even when the order of discussion is general or universal knowledge. The Holocaust has an important lesson to teach, but what etches the lesson firmly in the mind, as nothing else does as effectively, is your being in Lublinka, Warsaw, or Maidenek.

never—make a man escape from an evil condition, or keep him clinging to something good, but the knowledge of some particular about him can.[10]

We have this uncanny ability to take a larger view of things, but in so doing we blur ourselves and our particulars; and then, with just as much ease, we can flip the focus to take a close-up view of ourselves, and in so doing blur the distant scenery. The larger picture provides the geography in which we are located; the particulars about ourselves provide the local coloring which prompts us to act. Both are important, and the proper *balance* between them is utterly crucial. To act by ignoring the particulars, or by focusing wholly on the larger picture, is often wrong. (Perhaps, a philosopher's feeling that his theory seems to have no connection with real issues and real people may stem from a recognition of just such a mistake?) On the other hand, to act by ignoring the larger picture, or by focusing wholly on the particulars, is often mistaken, too. (Perhaps this is the kind of mistake made by men given to no reflection or understanding at all.) What is a proper balance between these two things need not be the same for all or even the same for one individual in all circumstances. What is a proper balance for the father of a nation is not so for a hair stylist.

Stage 3. Knowledge of Moral Principles. This is what Socrates eagerly sought to discover. Spend your life each day, he said, in talk of virtue and courage and duty and justice so that you protect, preserve, and promote the best possible state of your soul (P 32-33). Without the knowledge of these moral notions and principles, it is impossible to examine one's life; self-knowledge is not possible without such knowledge. The moral principles provide a map wherein we are able to locate, if we know the particulars of the self, where, in its journey, a self or a soul resides. Now, if moral principles are prerequisites for self-knowledge and self-

---

[10]Says Joseph Shapiro: "I must confess that at the time that I made this resolve, my faith wasn't yet that strong. I was still completely riddled with doubt and with what I might even call heresy. I went away from evil, you might say, not so much out of love for Moredecai as out of hate for Haman. I was filled with a raging disgust against the world and against the civilization of which I was a part. I ran like a beast runs from a forest fire, like a man fleeing from a pursuing enemy" (*The Penitent*, 112).

Take away the nodes in his life, and his general knowledge would not have budged him an inch from New York.

knowledge necessary for the having of faith (and not a surrogate or a poor substitute for it), then knowledge of moral principles is necessary for proper faith. The role of understanding is assured in the life of faith.

Stage 4. The Step of Error Recognition. So deeply had he sinned that he cries:

the serpent that tempted Eve may be saved, but not Faustus.[11]

Earlier, Johannes Faustus had come to acknowledge the error of his ways and the need to repent, but he did not do so. Here is how that transpires:

Good Angel:	Faustus, repent; yet God will pity thee.
Bad Angel:	Thou art a spirit; God cannot pity thee.
Faustus:	Who buzzeth in my ears I am a spirit?
	Be I a devil, yet God may pity me;
	Yea, God will pity me if I repent.
Bad Angel:	Ay, but Faustus never shall repent. *Exeunt* Angels.
Faustus:	My heart is harden'd, I cannot repent.
	Scarce can I name salvation, faith, or heaven,
	But fearful echoes thunders in mine ears,
	"Faustus, thou art damn'd!"[12]

There are four alternatives. First, Faustus was able to repent, but unwilling to do so; second, he was able and willing; third, he was unable to repent and unwilling; and, lastly, he was unable, but willing. Which of these alternatives was true of Faustus? The second alternative is surely false of Faustus for he did not repent in the twenty-four-year lease he had with Lucifer. Likewise, the third and fourth alternatives pose no interesting problems: if Faustus was simply unable to repent—his will, say, being wholly in the hands of Mephistophiles—then his willingness or unwillingness to repent is, at best, piquant. Until virtually the very last, Faustus was able, I think, but unwilling to repent. What I wish in brief to examine here is to what extent his unwillingness was influenced by his lack of understanding. And, if he did become unable, to what extent was this a matter of a lack of understanding, too. For I wish to underscore the

---

[11]Christopher Marlowe, *The Tragical History of the Life and Death of Doctor Faustus*, 96. Hereafter, cited as *Doctor Faustus*.

[12]*Doctor Faustus*, 35.

thesis that understanding is indispensable: without it neither repenting, nor faith, is possible.

The foregoing passage poses an interesting query or two. For instance, after Faustus affirmed unhesitatingly

> Be I a devil, yet God may pity me;
> Yea, God will pity me if I repent

the Bad Angel plants a thought in his mind to the effect that "No, Faustus, you will do no such thing." And, suddenly, a solitary line later, Faustus just as strongly affirms that he will not repent. The rationale of the transition from one stage of thought to the next is difficult to follow. Is one's refusal—like one's affirmation—sudden, uncomprehending, instantaneous, solely a matter of passion? Or was Faustus's refusal to acknowledge the error of his ways the consequence of his ignorance, his lack of understanding? Was Faustus's refusal, ultimately, to be understood in terms of his false beliefs? For example, Faustus had declared:

> I think hell's a fable.[13]

Not an isolated thought, this.

By contrast, Joseph Shapiro recognized the error of his ways—"I myself was part of this system,"[14] a system that was corrupt to the core—and reshaped his faith and fate.

Stage 5. The Leap of Faith. When does the leap occur? Is it slow in its progress, like the recovery from a serious illness? Is there ever a time in one's life when the leap becomes impossible to take? How, if at all, is understanding interwoven with this step?

The first warning from the Good Angel comes early (scene 1):

> O Faustus, lay that damned book aside[15]

The book is a book of conjuring. Faustus brazenly ignores the warning. Even Mephistophiles warns him, but that also has little effect. A little later, the Good Angel admonishes thus:

---

[13]*Doctor Faustus*, 31.
[14]*The Penitent*, 31.
[15]*Doctor Faustus*, 10.

Faustus repent; yet God will pity thee.[16]

No change of heart, yet. After a short tête-à-tête with Mephistophiles, the Good Angel returns to say:

Never too late, if Faustus will repent.[17]

The Bad Angel tries to frighten Faustus, with threats of extreme physical violence, only to find the Good Angel inducing in him hope and courage:

Repent, and they shall never raze thy skin.[18]

Into scene 18 an old man enters, and repeatedly warns Faustus:

Yet, yet, thou hast an amiable soul,
If sin by custom grow not into nature:
Then, Faustus, will repentance come too late.[19]

He can still repent. But Faustus falters, contemplates suicide. He cowers under a threat from Mephistophiles, and repents now of having disobeyed Mephistophiles's "sovereign lord." In the next and penultimate scene, three scholars enter, and commiserate with a deeply distraught Faustus. One of them says, "Yet, Faustus call on God."[20] And, just before they leave, another one of them says, "Pray thou, and we will pray, that God may have mercy upon thee."[21] Apparently, he might have still repented, but he did not. And then the Good Angel appears for the last time, and says:

O Faustus, if thou hadst given ear to me,
Innumerable joys had follow'd thee;
But thou didst love the world.[22]

---

[16]*Doctor Faustus*, 35.
[17]*Doctor Faustus*, 39.
[18]*Doctor Faustus*, 39.
[19]*Doctor Faustus*, 90.
[20]*Doctor Faustus*, 96.
[21]*Doctor Faustus*, 97.
[22]*Doctor Faustus*, 98.

As it exits, with the Bad Angel, the clock strikes eleven. An hour of Faustus in utter terror follows. With nature at its most foreboding, he comes to his end at midnight.

When, in that one hour, or a little more, did Faustus lose the right, or even the capacity, to repent and be forgiven, and why? The aim is not to show that any argument that justifies that there was such a time has a slope that is slippery, but rather that Faustus's damnation may lie in his failure of understanding. Was it, perhaps, the case that he never did lose this right but was incorrigibly stubborn to the end? Was it simply the case of a corrupt will? Or, a case of ignorance? Faustus's refusal to repent rested on his lack of knowledge; or overestimating what he knew; or deprecating good advice; or the simple inability, for all his dialectical skills, to see his way through; or all of the above.

Some time later, Faustus did lose his capacity to repent. The old man was on the mark when he warned:

> If sin by custom grow not into nature:
> Then, Faustus, will repentance come too late.[23]

A will is usually in the firm grip of one's beliefs or understanding. A will that constantly executes deeds on the basis of a lack of understanding becomes powerless against true beliefs. The true beliefs need to make the will pause, then slowly make it see their side of the story, then win it over, and, finally, utterly conquer it. This takes time *and* patience *and* learning *and* doing things according to the wisdom of one's faith. Then real understanding will dawn and with it the full realization of the enormity of one's sins, certainly of Faustus's sins. Thus, unsurprisingly, Faustus cannot overcome himself, at the very end, and repent. There was

---

[23]*Doctor Faustus*, 90. And thus Plato in *Lysis*:

"So, what is neither bad nor good becomes the friend of the good because of the presence of bad—"

"I think so."

"—but obviously *before* it becomes bad itself through the bad it possesses. Once it had become bad it would certainly not desire the good or be its friend any longer, because we said it was impossible for bad to be friend to good."

"It is impossible" (*Early Socratic Dialogues*, 151).

no time left to know one's faults. Haunted by the demons, he could not say what the old man could in the fullness of his faith:

> Satan begins to sift me with his pride
> As in this furnace God shall try my faith,
> My faith, vile hell, shall triumph over thee.[24]

From Kierkegaard's perspective there was too much cleverness in Faustus; from the present point of view, not just a little ignorance either.

Consider this bit of the conversation between the Good Spirit and Joseph Shapiro. " 'What concrete steps can I take now?' I asked the voice, and it replied, 'Go to a house of prayer and pray.' 'Without faith?' I countered, and the voice said: 'You have more faith than you know.' "[25] Towards the end Shapiro says, "Faith is not an easy thing to acquire. Long after I had become a Jew with a beard and earlocks, I still lacked faith. But faith gradually grew within me."[26] It is also the last thing he says: "This faith keeps growing in me all the time."[27]

When had Shapiro leapt to faith? When he escaped from the house of his mistress? When he acknowledged that someone tapping on his shoulder asking him to serve as the tenth man for the *minyan* was no accident? When he told the cab driver to take him to Kennedy Airport? When he met Sarah? Or when, having met Sarah, he resolved to marry her and to have a family? What came to fruition *then* had been a long time in the making. If there was progress in the affirmation of the old Jewish faith, it was surely marked by incremental progress in self-knowledge in the life of the repentant.[28] It was no sudden thing.

---

[24]*Doctor Faustus*, 94. John D. Jump, the editor of *Doctor Faustus*, urges a comparison between Marlowe's use of "sift," and Luke 22:31 (KJV): "Satan hath desired to have you, that he may sift you as wheat."

[25]*The Penitent*, 46.

[26]*The Penitent*, 161.

[27]*The Penitent*, 164.

[28]Shapiro's life amply illustrates that understanding, without the attendant deed, would not be sufficient for self-knowledge. Both are required: "And as a general rule, there is no other way in which the human spirit can acquire self-knowledge except by trying its own strength in answering, not in word but in deed, what may be called the interrogation of temptation. And then, if God acknowledges the task performed, there is an example of a spirit truly devoted

I should say a word or two—at Louis H. Mackey's urging—about what I mean by "saved" or "salvation." First, I am proposing a theory of understanding, but I am not assuming any particular definition of salvation; it is the last stage one arrives at having gone through the first four stages I have delineated. Thus, one might be an Aristotelian and think of salvation as a life of contemplation (no leap of faith there); or one might be a Jew and think of oneself as saved only if one's life embodied the principles of Torah (what Shapiro essentially tried to do); or one might be a Christian and think of being saved only as one who believes in Jesus as one's savior. The theory should exhibit considerable power if it can be successfully applied in such a variety of cases. I leave it to my critic to show that my theory of understanding is actually quite religion-specific and fails in a particular case.

Second, one might argue that to be a Christian, at least in the Kierkegaardian sense, is to make the leap of faith, and that leap is to the absurd. Or so Saint Paul admonishes. A. S. Byatt diagnoses our failure thus:

> No mere human can stand in the fire and not be consumed. Not that I have not dreamed of working in the furnace—as Shadrach, Meshach and Abednego—But we latter-day Reasonable Beings have not the miracle-working Passion of the old believers.[29]

Consequently, one believes *against* understanding, not in it or in harmony with it. Faith, so understood, has nothing to do with understanding; it is, perhaps, even a hindrance. "A man who still preserves his understanding must come to the verdict that only a god bereft of understanding could concoct such a teaching [as Christianity]."[30] Let us accept this. Even so, we need to distinguish two cases: (a) an individual, A, who has full knowledge of the things referred to in the earlier stages—knowledge of particulars, universals, moral principles, and recognition of error—makes the leap to the absurd; (b) an individual, B, who has virtually no knowledge of the things referred to in the earlier stages, makes the leap to the absurd, too. *Ex hypothesi*, both A and B have faith, but does it follow that they have equal faith? Does not A have to struggle far greater against

---

to God, with the solidity given by the strength of grace, instead of the inflation of the empty boast" (Augustine, *The City of God*, 693-94).

[29]*Possession: A Romance*, 195.

[30]Kierkegaard, *The Sickness unto Death*, 126.

his understanding than B? Should we not speak of a *scale of faith*? Should both individuals, A and B, be put at the same point on the scale? Or, as I think, should not A be placed much higher on the scale than B?

Kierkegaard's most vehement objection would have been reserved for stages 4 and 5, respectively, and for the transition between them. I deem stage 4 to be central and quite essential to the moving to stage 5. Kierkegaard would undoubtedly argue that not only is it not essential, the step completely miscasts faith and religion. It miscasts them because it avers that religious claims must eventually be understood intellectually.

In response to the foregoing argument, Mackey wrote:

> In the *Concluding Unscientific Postscript* especially, Johannes Climacus argues that reflection cannot lead to understanding. The process of thought—the dialectic—is not constructive but purely negative. It multiplies possibilities but cannot ground a choice among them. (Paul Weiss once said that God can do nothing because he knows everything.) Right or wrong, this argument is part of Kierkegaard's anti-Hegelian polemic and has to be dealt with by anyone who would chide him with neglecting understanding.[31]

As an entry, let me begin with Weiss's statement. God *did* do something: he created the world. Let us ignore that, and provide a Leibnizian answer. God knew everything, and every possibility. But not all the possibilities did he bring to fruition. How was God able to eliminate all possibilities but one, or even several? I argue that God's choice was grounded in his understanding: because He understood that some possibilities were evil, and others which He brought to fruition were not. Perhaps, then, what Weiss meant was just this: God is so utterly clear about the possibilities, so utterly clear about the criterion to be used for judging these possibilities, that His choice lacks the dialectic movement and is instantaneous. Just as an individual Cartesian reasoner perceives in an instant the truth of the *cogito*, so does God perceive in the twinkling of an eye the truth of all there is, and of the right choice to be made.

But we humans are different. It is true that the process of thought multiplies possibilities—something Kierkegaard insisted on in *Sickness unto Death*—but *before* the choice is made one has to perceive the correctness of that choice and the correctness of the choice cannot be

---

[31]Personal communication, 6 August 1997.

grounded in the will, only a decision to live in accordance with the possibility, acknowledged to be the right one, can be so grounded.

Kierkegaard avers that religious claims are beyond thought and reason; they simply have to be accepted on *authority*. Here is what Kierkegaard says:

> What, exactly, have the errors of exegesis and philosophy done in order to confuse Christianity, and how have they confused Christianity? Quite briefly and categorically, they have simply forced back the sphere of paradox-religion into the sphere of aesthetics. . . . If the sphere of paradox religion is abolished, or explained away in aesthetics, an Apostle becomes neither more nor less than a genius, and then—good night, Christianity! *Esprit* and the Spirit, revelation and originality, a call from God and genius, all end by meaning more or less the same.[32]

Kierkegaard's argument would be that there is nothing endless about an affirmation of faith; once you have declared and professed it, you do not deepen it by contemplating, reasoning and reflecting about it. You accept it on authority, and that is it. To try to find a deep, or deeper, reason for the affirmation of faith is to do a disservice to the paradox-religion.[33] It does not need intellectual support; indeed, it cannot have it. It

---

[32]*The Present Age, and Of the Difference between a Genius and an Apostle*, 89.

[33]*The Inquisitor*: The blessed St. Athanasius has laid it down in his creed that those who cannot understand are damned. It is not enough to be simple. It is not enough even to be what simple people call good. The simplicity of a darkened mind is no better than the simplicity of a beast.

Joan: There is great wisdom in the simplicity of a beast, let me tell you; and sometimes great foolishness in the wisdom of scholars.   (Bernard Shaw, *Saint Joan*, 132-33.)

Was Shaw echoing Kierkegaard? "The more the wise person thinks about the simple (that there can be any question of a longer preoccupation with it already shows that it is not so easy after all), the more difficult it becomes for him. Yet he feels gripped by a deep humanness that reconciles him with all of life: that the difference between the wise person and the simplest person is this little evanescent difference *that the simple person knows the essential* and the wise person little by little *comes to know* that he knows it or *comes to know* that he does not know it, but what they know is the same" (Kierkegaard, *Concluding Unscientific Postscript to Philosophical Fragments* 1:160).

must needs stand on its own legs. St. Paul does neither himself nor the paradox-religion any service by proclaiming it to be profound, deep, or elegant.[34]

Stage 6. The Task of Rebuilding One's Life. Shapiro has returned to his old faith. He has married Sarah, who presumably bears the yoke of the Torah as did the women of yesteryears, has had children, and has thus commenced the rebuilding of his life that was shattered when he once lived in New York.[35]

THE INTERCONNECTION OF THE STAGES

To fill in some of the larger, essential details. The simplest postulate is to assume that there will be a cyclical occurrence of these stages; one does not arrive at full knowledge of oneself in one fell swoop, nor can it end arbitrarily in an earlier stage (unless one stops being an inquirer, of course). The primary reason why this process will continue in an endless cycle is simple: there is no end in sight about what one can know about morals or ethics, and the other sciences, and these are prerequisites for knowing oneself. A self might be a pile or a cluster of layers,[36] or that which is hidden behind a cluster of layers.[37] On the first view, the individual who is trying to understand himself is one who, with each complete cycle, has covered the distance marked by a single layer, and who, with the next cycle, proceeds to the next layer lying below it, and so on downward and deeper. If, as on the second view, the self is the reality beneath the layers, then the completion of each cycle will show why it was an *illusion* to identify one's self with the layer just traversed. One arrives at the knowledge of one's self only *after* one has traversed

---

[34]*The Present Age, and Of the Difference between a Genius and an Apostle*, 89-90.

[35]The stages here are, undoubtedly, not independent of the five stages in chap. 1 nor of the stages in chap. 4. Their exact relationships are worth exploring, but I am not going to pursue that inquiry here.

[36]Not quite the Humean doctrine which identifies the self as a bundle of impressions and ideas. By contrast, a pile is a more complex notion than a bundle, and nothing yet is said about what it is a pile *of*. Nor is there a notion of depth attached to the Humean notion of self which is strongly implied in the notion of a pile of layers.

[37]This is essentially an Eastern doctrine.

all the layers. It is not necessary to assume an infinite number of layers in order to conclude that one cannot know oneself; it is sufficient to postulate enough layers that cannot be traversed in a single lifetime.

The Eastern doctrine, at this point, gets ecstatic: in *Svetasvatara Upanishad*, for example, the self (*atman*) is identified with the total, ultimate reality, God (*Brahman*). There is also the Buddhist doctrine of no-self theory of self. This doctrine says that the self is, like all other things, emptiness (*sunyata*), in other words, absence of own-being (*svabhav*). It would be fascinating to work out the consequences for the Socratic maxim if any of these metaphysical views of self were correct. What notion of self did Socrates or his arguments presuppose? Buddha had argued that it was the wrong conception of one's self which was the ultimate cause of so much of one's suffering. If the Socratic view is different from the Buddhist view, and if suffering is caused also in the Socratic view by having a wrong conception of one's self, what is the nature of *that* suffering? How does the nature of salvation in the Socratic view differ from the Buddhist view, and to what extent is it the result of having a different view of the self?

The stages are scarcely self-contained units succeeding each other in a nice one-way procession. Interconnections abound. For example, the knowledge of particulars at stage 1 will become more focused and enriched as one has more knowledge of moral principles at stage 3. As that happens, error recognition will occur also, stage 4, and that can scarcely happen without it leading, in turn, to more knowledge of particulars, stage 1. Stage 5 will inform stage 1, and stage 1, in conjunction with stages 2 and 3, will lead to stage 6. This in turn will lead back to stage 1. One thing is perspicuous: stage 1 lies at the center of things.

The interconnections may be depicted thus:

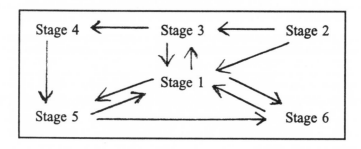

The present view of self-knowledge offers an account of *humility*. It can distinguish between humility and modesty; it can also distinguish between humility and being merely humble—docile, servile. It does so in terms of understanding.

By now, it is a truism that one cannot have even provisional self-knowledge unless it is based on a good bit of understanding. A cardinal feature of the stages of self-examination is the step of error recognition, stage 4. Here a man comes to terms with the failure of his attempts to know himself for he is bound to encounter, repeatedly, such failures in his Socratic journey towards self-knowledge;[38] and these failures induce in him the requisite humility: "I know that I do not even know the subject closest at hand: myself. How dare I believe I know anything else that is worth knowing?" Was Socrates' confession of being a know-nothing to be understood in this way? By contrast, a man who is modest is essentially one who has thrown his hands up at an earlier cycle, and said, "I'll never be able to know myself; I'll do something more manageable. But I'll learn not to boast." On the other hand, he who is merely humble, or docile (Socrates *docile*?), is perhaps so by nature, but he has not much inclination to learning or understanding. He is a cultivator of social graces: a man far removed from humility.[39] This picture offers a view of why humility is such a hard thing to achieve; so much so that one is always tempted to be satisfied with something less (in the hopes that it will pass off as something more?).

Might one become arrogant in knowing that while one knows that one does not know oneself, others falsely claim to know what in fact they do not know, not having traversed enough cycles, and failing? Their lack of humility serves witness to that. Or, might one become boastful in knowing that these others no longer pursue self-knowledge, and hence are less worthy than oneself who is engaged in such a pursuit? Of such an outstanding individual, what might Kierkegaard have said? Of two men

---

[38]"I must give you an account of my journeyings as if they were labors I had undertaken to prove the oracle irrefutable" (P 26).

[39]Plato put it precisely: "It follows, then, that good use of language, harmony, grace, and rhythm all depend on goodness of character. I'm not talking about the state which is actually stupidity, but which we gloss as goodness of character; I'm talking about when the mind really has equipped the character with moral goodness and excellence" (*Republic*, 99).

equally entitled to the claim that they know they do not know themselves, why is he who is humble better than he who is not? The answer, I think, lies in this: one might "pride and preen" (P 24), or be boastful of whatever one *has*, or what one possesses intrinsically, nonrelationally. And it must be something substantive. What one is boastful about here, on the other hand, is something relational. When I am just as destitute as my neighbor, my destitution is not offset by a whit by my knowing that I am destitute when my neighbor does not know that he is, too. Nor would his coming to know his true condition diminish my state.

We can view self-knowledge as being cumulative; or, we can think of it as having, at least once, a rupture-like effect in its growth. Let me explain. The crucial stage in this case is stage 5, the leap of faith. For Socrates, there is no such stage. Each successive cycle, assuming it to be properly carried out, would bring an individual closer and closer to knowledge of oneself. Perhaps, no human would ever have full knowledge of oneself; only God could. But it would, at least, be assured that we would have verisimilar knowledge about ourselves.

By contrast, on a view in which faith plays the central role, the function of stage 4 is, at least once, to rupture the life-form of an individual. To induce in the individual a state of despair, anguish, or suffering that will lead to faith, stage 5—Saul on the road to Damascus or Saint Augustine hearing *tolle lege, tolle lege.* Kierkegaard would argue that such a transition, the transition between stage 4 and stage 5, cannot occur on the basis of understanding, but on passion.[40] Indeed, that passion can bring us to stage 5, *whichever* cycle we are on, and once it occurs, it will permanently alter the direction of our life. My argument has been that a leap of faith based on ignorance is not worth much; thus, even when there is a leap, there should be understanding of oneself. The greater the understanding, the more powerful the leap. Both in the Socratic view, in which faith plays no role, and in the Kierkegaardian view, in which faith plays the dominant role, self-knowledge is essential. That task of seeking self-knowledge is best described by the schema I have offered.

[40]See chap. 7, n. 5.

Chapter 6

A PARADOX FOR FAUSTUS

Faustus:	Am I damned, Mephistopheles?
Mephistopheles:	You are.[1]
Faustus:	I know not why I did what I did.
Mephistopheles:	You do.
Faustus:	Gently, sweet Mephistopheles.
Mephistopheles:	You wished power and honor
	And fame and knowledge; to travel
	And spend time a-whoring; to make fun of
	Popes and cardinals and priests.
	Our appetites quench not easily:
	not for these things nor for wealth.
Faustus:	The truth you speak offends.
Mephistopheles:	I offend of necessity. I am commanded to speak
	The truth unless a sweet lie will win a soul
	For Lucifer.
Faustus:	How then will I know when you lie,
	That I might save my soul?
Mephistopheles:	That task is hopeless now.
	To the highest bidder in Hell
	Faustus already has auctioned away his soul.
	In any case, you cannot tell.

---

[1]"If someone were to ask me," writes Kierkegaard, "who is the more dangerous seducer, a Don Juan or a Faust, I would answer Faust. In Faust, a world has been destroyed, but for this reason he has at his disposal the most seductive tones, the double tones that quiver in two worlds at once, compared with which Don Juan's most baneful tenderness and sweetness are childish babbling. If someone were to ask me which victim is more to be lamented, a girl who is seduced by a Don Juan or by a Faust [I would answer that] there is no comparison—the one who is seduced by a Faust is utterly lost. Thus it is very profound that the legend puts 1,003 on Don Juan's list; Faust has only one, but she is also crushed on an entirely different scale. A girl who is seduced by a Don Juan has the world of spirit before her; a girl who is seduced by a Faust, for her even that is poisoned" (*Either/Or*, pt. 1 [1987], supplement, 377).

	For if you could discern it, lying would
	Lose its point, and I my hard-won soul.
Faustus:	Where were we? Ah, yes, greed is wrong.
	Not so all greed, surely.
Mephistopheles:	All forms of greed corrupt
	A man; mistresses of his sins, they rein not
	His spirit for rest and worship. They
	Harness the spirit to one thing—wealth, fame,
	Power, glory, hunting, food. In days of yore,
	They called it idolatry.
Faustus:	But is there such an evil
	As greed for knowledge?
Mephistopheles:	Aye; provides the deepest coloring
	For the darkening of the soul.
Faustus:	Why so? I thought man was created
	To hunt and hound knowledge,
	To disseminate and rejoice in it.
	Would the sun be sun if it cast not light
	And make spots of darkness sing?
	What is this you say: gather not knowledge?
Mephistopheles:	Yes, gather not knowledge;
	Faith requires it not:
	Faith is the only and ultimate thing.
	A simple affirmation will do.
	The rest is idle curiosity
	Up to no good.
	The kind that kills, maims, contorts the heart
	Of man. Then, it singeth not.
Faustus:	But mine sings when I know things.
	Come, recount the structure of the heavens:
	Of the sun and the moon, the wandering stars,
	Of Jupiter, Mars, Venus, and Mercury,
	Of the crystalline spheres, and of
	Conjunctions, oppositions, aspects, and eclipses.
Mephistopheles:	Mephistopheles is too tired to do this again.
	Though observe this coincidence:
	The whole heavens revolve in
	Twenty-four hours, and Faustus has asked
	For a lease on life for as many years.
Faustus:	In hopes that my life might have the harmony
	I note in the celestial order.
	This is the old idea of the cosmos
	Stamping its fundamental diagram

In the design of even the smallest things.
The macrocosm-microcosm thing.

Mephistopheles: So be it, if you believe in it.
I don't.

Faustus: Instruct me anew, then, about plants and herbs
And healing stones and fabulous minerals.
And, about seas and rains and thunderstorms,
And such sublunar phenomena:
As nature from its stock daily parcels out to man.

Mephistopheles: This, too, we have done;
Faustus knows it all.

Faustus: What, then, should Faustus do?
I have had you conjure up blind Homer,
And Homer did sing to me the parts
Of *The Iliad* I love the most;
And heard the ghostly voice of Amphion
That once rebuilt the walls of Thebes;
And saw great Alexander, and
The face that launched a thousand ships
(And as many tales).

Mephistopheles: Yes, so have you done.

Faustus: Who else shall I have you recall?

Mephistopheles: Whatever you command
I am, by contract, bound to perform.

Faustus: Abraham!

Mephistopheles: Who? Some friend of yours
Long since departed? A man of substance?
An unknown poet?

Faustus: Abraham, Mephistopheles! Prophet Abraham!

Mephistopheles: No, no, no, no, no!

Faustus: Why not? I thought I heard you say:
"Whatever you command
I am, by contract, bound to perform."

Mephistopheles: Yes, but not *that*.

Faustus: Why not?

Mephistopheles: I am unable for two reasons.

Faustus: Yes?

Mephistopheles: First, our contract cannot override
My prime allegiance: in all
Matters, my first and last obedience
Is to my lord Lucifer. That in no wise
Am I to do what endangers his enterprise,
To do a deed that forfeits a hard won soul

	Doomed to his dominion.
Faustus:	And the other reason?
Mephistopheles:	Stronger than the first. I simply, physically,
	Mentally, spiritually, or any other way, cannot.
Faustus:	Why so?
Mephistopheles:	You knoweth not the man Abraham.
Faustus:	I know him, too. He went to a Mount in Moriah:
	For God had bid him go there
	And sacrifice his only son.
Mephistopheles:	Easily said.
Faustus:	He rose early (did he sleep that night?),
	Saddled his donkey, loaded
	Split firewood, his retinue:
	All of two servants.
	Through Beersheba-desert the journey must have seemed long:
	For each step Abraham took forward
	Half a step the father in him must have
	Dragged him back. And this lasted three days
	Before he saw the fated mountain
	Where, he said to his men, he was to worship.
	Each day a witness to the conflict,
	Centered in a single man, of how
	The most powerful love of the father
	Gradually lost, yet resented not,
	To the most unswerving will of the prophet
	In his obedience to God.
Mephistopheles:	Easily said; easily said.
Faustus:	And how was it with the son?
Mephistopheles:	He, also, was firm.
	When Abraham called him, he too said:
	"Here I am." No questions asked:
	No wherefore, why, or for what guilt this?
Faustus:	What then cannot you tell me about them?
	Conjure them up for me.
Mephistopheles:	Ask me something else:
	Let me bring forth the spirit of Herod
	(Or Herod's whore),
	Nero, Nimrod, or Nebuchadnezzar,
	God-forsaken, God-despised, God-accursed men,
	Then go figure on your own
	What, by deepest contrast, Abraham might have been.
Faustus:	Nothingness is all you offer
	And expect I deduce from it what life is?

Mephistopheles:	You are on your own.
Faustus:	Why cannot you conjure them up for me
	That I might witness, silently,
	On my knees, if I have to,
	What happened in those blessed days?
Mephistopheles:	When Abraham went up
	The mountain, he left the donkey and
	His servants behind. For
	The servants could not have witnessed the deed.
Faustus:	Why not?
Mephistopheles:	I have this on unsubstantiated rumor:
	When the mountain learnt of God's command
	To Abraham, it said to the Almighty:
	"Let me not bear witness to what Abraham will do,
	Nor feel the son's innocent blood
	Drip into my soil;
	Let it dry itself on the firewood: for
	Not even I, O God, have the heart for this!"
	For like reason I am unable to conjure up
	The team of God-driven two: one very young, one very old.
Faustus:	Even so, try, Mephistopheles.
Mephistopheles:	You want each happening in the universe
	To be neatly packaged in a sentence or two,
	As if the happening, thing, or deed
	Were a bird one could cage
	And make it sing when one wants to.
Faustus:	But I want to witness the event, Mephistopheles,
	That I can convince myself of. . . .
Mephistopheles:	Convince yourself of what?
Faustus:	. . . Of what faith can do.
Mephistopheles:	Ask not for it. The deed is gone forever.
	Had I the strength to bring it back,
	And you the strength to witness it,
	I should lose you, and incur the wrath
	Of Lucifer.
Faustus:	Fear not, I shall honor my word.
Mephistopheles:	Meaningless words!
	Do you think this deed is like
	A fabulous monster out of Pliny's
	Natural History or the sweet
	Evening smell in the Rhine valley
	Or a cultivated chrysanthemum in the East,
	That you can observe, watch, or smell,

	Applaud and then go your way?
Faustus:	What is it that Mephistopheles fears?
Mephistopheles:	I fear not for myself, but for you.
	You will so calculate your loss,
	Should you witness Abraham's deed,
	That your cry and howl, and beating of breasts,
	Will make the neighbors run to you in fear
	That someone young, someone much loved,
	Had died: they not knowing
	That you, at last, have justly reckoned,
	The worth of what you have sold to us.
Faustus:	To take this risk or not:
	Let me be the judge of that.
Mephistopheles:	I cannot conjure him.
Faustus:	Why? Does that have anything to do
	With your second reason?
Mephistopheles:	Yes, Doctor Faustus.
Faustus:	What is it, Mephistopheles?
Mephistopheles:	I am a minister of Hell,
	Powerful, obedient to my lord Lucifer,
	And second only to him.
	But then, too, I am only an angel,
	If an accursed angel:
	While Abraham is Abraham.
Faustus:	I do not understand.
Mephistopheles:	Abraham is the friend of God.[2]
Faustus:	I still do not understand.
Mephistopheles:	You once told me: Had I as many souls

---

[2] In *The Nicomachean Ethics*, Aristotle says: "In such cases it is not possible to define exactly up to what point friends can remain friends; for much can be taken away and friendship remain, but when one party is removed to a great distance, as God is, the possibility of friendship ceases" (204).

However, here is what the Koran says in chap. 4, "Women," verse 124:

And who is there that has a fairer religion
than he who submits his will to God
being a good-doer, and who follows
the creed of Abraham, a man of pure faith?
And God took Abraham for a friend.

From *The Koran Interpreted*, trans. Arthur John Arberry, 119.

As there are stars in heaven, I should
Give 'em all to Mephistopheles.

Faustus: I did say that and I would.

Mephistopheles: Had you as many souls, my Faustus,
And witnessed Abraham's deed,
Each soul would curse thee
As many times as there are stars
To learn the havoc you have plagued them with
In the contract you have signed
With your blood.

Faustus: Is not my soul mine to give
To whomsoever it pleases me?
Hell hath no pains enough to tilt
The balance in its favor
For Faustus to sacrifice the joys you supply.

Mephistopheles: So be it; it is beyond argument.

Faustus: One more joy, then.

Mephistopheles: Yours is the command.

Faustus: Something fresh, something bold, something new.
The motion of the sun, moon, and stars I know;
Of inauspicious comets' trajectory, too;
I know the medicinal plants, and holy places,
I know the valleys and the mountains and the lakes
This mortal earth abounds in
And also those in the underworld;
I am tired of reviewing the past,
Reenacting History: it repeats itself
Often enough, I find, and the instruction is always the same:
The stupidity of men recoils on them
And such recoiling instructs them not.
Enough, enough!
Something different for Faustus's soul.

Mephistopheles: Yes?

Faustus: Indeed, I have it. Faustus's soul!

Mephistopheles: I understand it not, Doctor Faustus.

Faustus: Oh, Mephistopheles, it is a clever idea.

Mephistopheles: What is?

Faustus: I possess it; I own it; I am its master.
I cannot transact it for someone else's:
There cannot be bartering in souls.
You can have my boots, my astrolabe,
My collection of fossils and rare manuscripts,
In return for something you own,

	And these become yours as if I never possessed them
	And you always did.
	And, yet, Mephistopheles, I know it not.
Mephistopheles:	Know not what?
Faustus:	Know not my soul: Faustus's quiddity.
	Teach me about Faustus's soul.
Mephistopheles:	But you have bartered it away:
	A fair bargain, freely entered into,
	Designed to fulfill your dreams and wishes
	In exchange for which Lucifer will possess your soul
	On that Ultimate Day.
Faustus:	But the soul is *mine* as Lucifer
	Has his own; I have only joined his legion.
	In no wise can he be me.
	He may command Faustus, order, dispatch,
	Lead Faustus about: but not even in the lapse
	Of eternity of orders fulfilled will Lucifer *be* Faustus.
Mephistopheles:	What should I teach Faustus about Faustus?
Faustus:	Who *is* he, Mephistopheles?
Mephistopheles:	He is short, on this side of heavy,
	Has a sly smile, a slight squint in the left eye,
	Fan-like ears, a rich flowing beard,
	Fluent speech, upright gait,
	Not unpleasing to the eye on the whole.
Faustus:	Why thank you, Mephistopheles.
Mephistopheles:	I speak the truth.
Faustus:	Alas. But tell me about the man,
	Not about his physical self.
Mephistopheles:	Well versed in the arts and magic,
	Thrice-learned, much respected and vaunted
	For his rhetorical skill;
	Often magnanimous, heroic, but obdurate.
Faustus:	Anyone with a half-trained eye
	To peer through the looking glass of ordinary
	Sense could piece these things
	Together into a portrait.
	I ask you about the magic in the seed
	And you describe to me what all can see:
	The firm stalk, the expansive, ardent leaves,
	The colors that grace the temporary flowers,
	The soil the downward-invading roots clench.
Mephistopheles:	Ah, *that* magic!
Faustus:	Yes, Faustus's soul.

Mephistopheles: Why should you want to know that?
                    Is not Faustus happy with what Lucifer
                    Has conferred on him: new joys,
                    Fresh loves, and wild experiences?
                    What is to be had in Faustus's knowing himself?
Faustus: Take the whole of the Creation, Mephistopheles,
                    And divide it into two bits:
                    One that is within me and the other
                    The Creation minus it.
                    What is within is no match for what is
                    Without: the latter, in space and time enormous,
                    In history incomparable, in depth unfathomable.
                    And, yet, I can compass vast tracts
                    Of the external world: what the eyes, ears,
                    Nose, tongue, and touch can sketch,
                    And not know a solitary road, a lane, a by-lane even,
                    That leads to that thing internal,
                    The thing that is the Faustus seed.
Mephistopheles: But measure the enterprise, first.
                    Not each thing not known is worth knowing.
Faustus: This is so: I know not what festers in a cesspool.
                    I know it not, nor care I know it not.
Mephistopheles: Why then does Faustus want to know who he is?
Faustus: I am wholly concealed to myself.
                    My desires and ambitions are often as plain
                    To see as is my envy, or my hate, or my wrath.
                    But were I to know what propels my deed
                    And speech, I would know how to judge Faustus better,
                    What he should do, avoid, insist,
                    When gather courage, take a firm stand,
                    When desist, concede, retract, withdraw.
                    So Faustus can deepen himself.
                    A ripened Faustus is worth more than a raw one.
                    That is why Faustus would know who Faustus is.
Mephistopheles: I see.
Faustus: I know not always the source of my desires.
                    Take this, for example.
                    Why am I so addicted to learning,
                    To this damned necromancing art,
                    When other men can live out their
                    Lives well without it?
                    This I know not: why did I
                    Sell my soul to satisfy a desire I

	Do not wholly understand?
Mephistopheles:	Do you now regret your choice?
Faustus:	Should I? I know not the ultimate cause of my desire.
	This I did say;
	But not that that desire was wrong.
Mephistopheles:	Tell me clearly what you want.
Faustus:	Tell me this: what is the ultimate cause of my desires?
Mephistopheles:	I cannot do so.
Faustus:	The system of the stars and planets you can unveil,
	Why not things that move within me?
	One is lawlike; is the other lawless?
Mephistopheles:	No, although it is oftener true
	To suppose so.
Faustus:	One can be described; the other defies description?
Mephistopheles:	Both can be described.
Faustus:	One is complex; the other infinitely so?
Mephistopheles:	No, both are complex enough.
Faustus:	What then?
Mephistopheles:	Undertake this task yourself.
	I cannot aid in it for fear
	Of undermining our devils' joint enterprise.
Faustus:	How is that so?
Mephistopheles:	To teach you who you really are
	I need to unveil God's Plan and
	Ordinance.
Faustus:	How could a devil possibly know the
	Grand Design of the Architect?
Mephistopheles:	Only enough to know himself damned:
	No more.
Faustus:	Two questions, then, Mephistopheles.
	First, why do you need to know bits of
	The Plan to say merely who Faustus is;
	Second, should you tell me who I am,
	How then shall I your combined plans fizzle?
Mephistopheles:	Fair questions, these.
Faustus:	Well: then who is Faustus?
Mephistopheles:	Faustus knows his physical attributes:
	His height, weight, gait,
	Whether muscular or fat. . . .
Faustus:	Yes, yes, yes. . . .
Mephistopheles:	. . . Hair luster, eye and skin color,
	His shoe size, hat size, shirt size. . . .
Faustus:	Please, Mephistopheles.

Mephistopheles:	Well, then, to move on:
	Faustus knows several of his mental attributes:
	His character, desires, demeanor,
	Aims, hopes, lusts and loves. . . .
Faustus:	But where do they spring from?
Mephistopheles:	You hurry me, my friend.
Faustus:	Sorry, I shall be the essence of patience now.
Mephistopheles:	Your character and desires and loves
	Themselves have certain traits—
	Call them moral traits—
	These traits indict some desires and some loves,
	They commend others.
	For instance: Faustus's desire to mock
	And harry the Pope it condemns;
	To provide for Wagner it applauds.
Faustus:	But how do traits manage to divide
	My characteristics and dispositions thus
	Into vice and virtue?
Mephistopheles:	*That*, indeed, is the question.
Faustus:	I cannot see my way through.
Mephistopheles:	Part of God's Plan is the moral plan:
	What thou shouldst and what thou shouldst not.
	Beneath it I cannot see,
	Perhaps, only those can see
	Who have authority,
	And bring this Plan to mankind
	(Parenthetically, a mountain seems to be
	The favored place to unveil the Plan's parts).
Faustus:	And the Plan is what I need to know
	If I would know the traits
	That taint or honor me?
Mephistopheles:	Yes.
Faustus:	I see it now:
	Your collective plan is to defeat God's,
	And therefore you will not tell me
	God's Plan:
	In the event, I lose in knowing who I really am.
Mephistopheles:	Precisely.
Faustus:	Clever, clever, Mephistopheles.
Mephistopheles:	We think so.
Faustus:	And, yet, I think you err.
Mephistopheles:	Oh?
Faustus:	What is Faustus's deed worth

	Without the signature of Faustus's will?
Mephistopheles:	But you forget: you signed a contract
	And signed it in blood.
Faustus:	The deed is poor when the will
	Assents in curable ignorance.
Mephistopheles:	To increase our dominion
	I need consent; happily, not informed consent.
Faustus:	But is it then consent?
Mephistopheles:	Now speaks the syllogizer,
	Lull's disciple.
Faustus:	Think with me for a moment, Mephistopheles.
	Reconsider Abraham:
	Between the commandment of God
	To sacrifice his son,
	And the temptation of the father
	To keep him, Abraham is poised.
	Either he affirms his faith, or falls away.
	Take away the temptation, and
	The greatness of the deed sinks low;
	Take away the commandment,
	And it is only murder.
	Each half by itself diminishes Abraham;
	Together they make him the father of faith.
Mephistopheles:	What is your point?
Faustus:	Easy to see, now:
	Lucifer should demand of me, in like manner,
	What God did demand of Abraham.
Mephistopheles:	Go on.
Faustus:	Grant me knowledge of myself
	And an unhampered will.
	Then, if I freely choose
	Your master, knowing fully who I am,
	I shall be unto his legions
	What Abraham is unto nations.
	My soul will be to me
	What Abraham's son was to him;
	My will will be like Abraham's will
	At least in this: free and informed;
	And Lucifer's ordinance will be to me
	What God's commandment was to him
	Who made a pilgrimage to the Moriahean Mount.
Mephistopheles:	Do continue.
Faustus:	Then if, under those circumstances,

	With or without ceremony, I accept Lucifer's offer,
	You could flout the agreement in my face
	And hold me to the contract,
	If I try to violate or rescind it.
Mephistopheles:	If not?
Faustus:	If not I shall plead before God,
	Supreme Justice of the Universe,
	That my will was through ignorance won
	And that ignorance may be a just cause for pity,
	But hardly a cause for censure or blame.
	And that is how I shall wrest
	God's mercy on my soul and
	The membership in your dominion will be lessened by one.
Mephistopheles:	Self-induced, culpable ignorance is not
	A whit less offensive
	In God's measure
	Than a crime knowingly discharged.
	There is no room for pity for such a life,
	A life such as yours—
Faustus:	May God let me bury my past—
Mephistopheles:	A ploy God sees through.
Faustus:	But will He not acknowledge
	My efforts now,
	Efforts to gather knowledge
	And confront myself, and my past, with it?[3]
Mephistopheles:	And so we have come full circle:
	Knowledge is what saves.
Faustus:	Not only knowledge, Mephistopheles.
	There is also the question of the will.
Mephistopheles:	Reconsider your argument.
Faustus:	If there is reason to.
Mephistopheles:	The venture is self-defeating.
Faustus:	I sense a paradox.
Mephistopheles:	Self-knowledge, Faustus claims, is cardinal
	To the proper affirmation of faith.
	In its absence, faith is a poor, second-best thing,
	If faith at all.[4]

---

[3]The last twelve lines resulted from a query of Robert Edgeworth.

[4]The next fifty-nine lines were added in response to comments of Alastair Hannay and Anthony Rudd. Astonishingly, each made virtually the same point,

Faustus: Then, give it me.
Mephistopheles: Know you the Book of Life?[5]
Faustus: The Scriptures speak of it.
Mephistopheles: And the Book of Death?
Faustus: What of it?
Mephistopheles: It is with my lord, Lucifer.
Faustus: One book tells all, Mephistopheles,
                         For what is on one is not on the other,
                         And nothing escapes being on one of the two Books:
                         I need not know both. I want to know
                         Not merely who is on the Book of Life,
                         —Or on its hellish twin—
                         But for what reasons each lists a name.
Mephistopheles: One reason only.
Faustus: What might that reason be?
Mephistopheles: The reason lies in self-knowledge,
                         A reason a chimney sweeper might as easily know
                         As Faustus, a seasoned knowledge-gatherer.
Faustus: Self-knowledge, I thought, was hard to win,
                         Not even Socrates won it with a life enslaved
                         To the search for truth about justice, piety,
                         Courage: a retinue of virtues, and
                         Battles with orators, poets, and fools,
                         Craftsmen and friends, priests and politicians.
Mephistopheles: Poor Socrates! He never cast an inward look
                         But looked without.
Faustus: I've turned inward and wandered in the dark woods
                         Of my soul,—where a hooting owl of lust, hate, or envy
                         Scares even the habitual solitaire—
                         The better to know who I am.
                         Nothing you speak of have I stumbled
                         Upon in my journeys there.
Mephistopheles: But your inward gaze is always turned
                         Along a path ill-trod. For a thousand truths
                         That crown your labor, one truth escapes:
                         The truth that settles in what Book
                         The eternal Scribe shall write your name.

---

in almost the same language, and cited the same Kierkegaardian text, namely, *Sickness unto Death*.

[5]Saint Thomas Aquinas, *Truth*, vol. 1, question 7.

Faustus:	What truth is that?
Mephistopheles:	The truth, the truth, Faustus, which
	Too many arts and too many skills,
	By which you are possessed, deceive you
	By too many tricks to think it exists not.
Faustus:	What ill in turning inward as I do?
Mephistopheles:	The object of turning is ill.
Faustus:	I seek self-knowledge, toward self
	I turn. What sin in that?
Mephistopheles:	Turning toward oneself, longingly,
	Regretfully (as Lot's wife did
	Toward what she was forbidden),
	One stands impaled upon a spot, deluded
	One is making progress.
Faustus:	Tell me this: am in I the Book of Life?
Mephistopheles:	No one's privy to that book.
Faustus:	In the Book of Death?
Mephistopheles:	I know not all its contents.
	What I know of it, you are not there.
Faustus:	Name the price, and give me the knowledge
	Of my soul, knowledge so easy of access, you say,
	Yet lies hidden from me.
Mephistopheles:	If no knowledge of Faustus's soul,
	Then no saving of Faustus's soul.
	But if I give you that knowledge you crave,
	And extract from you a price,
	The price being your soul,
	Then this is what the Master of Wittenberg must weigh:
	If he wants to save his soul,
	He must have knowledge of his soul,
	If he must have knowledge of his soul,
	He must first lose his soul to my lord Lucifer.
	Ineluctably, if he wants to save his soul,
	He must first lose his soul.
Faustus:	Therefore: he must lose his soul.
Mephistopheles:	Yes, according to Aristotle: the Master of them that know.[6]
Faustus:	But only if I transact with you.
Mephistopheles:	This is so.
Faustus:	It would not affect the argument
	For someone venturing on his own

---

[6]So Aristotle is described by Dante.

	Towards knowledge of himself.
Mephistopheles:	This is true.
Faustus:	More: without that venture. . . .
Mephistopheles:	. . . His faith would be "a poor, second-best thing, If faith at all." I know.
Faustus:	*Sic probo*. But where does Faustus go from here?
Mephistopheles:	To us.
Faustus:	If I have already sold myself For a pittance, as if I were unto my soul What Joseph's brothers were to him, Then why should you not tell Me about myself? Ignorant about myself I am yours, No less yours for knowing myself.
Mephistopheles:	This is so, Faustus; this is so. But spare yourself the pain. The horror of your loss You cannot imagine. When the final version Of this tale about you, That you compel me to recount, ends, The terror that will seize you, The grief that will swell your mind and heart, Will seem to possess you longer than the time It takes to run through all the natural numbers.
Faustus:	I think you mean this well. This is the form of hell I have heard described. But better in my hand the description Of who this man is who suffers so Than that I should be damned Knowing not who I am.

Chapter 7

THE ROLE OF THE MESSENGER

The story of the forces that destroy a man—ambiguity, reflection, sapped springs of life, envy, *ressentiment*, leveling—by implication is also another story of how he is saved. He must become a man of passion that will restore the springs, flush away envy, and forestall the process of leveling. Yet, it is only a part, albeit a significant one, of that second story. He must also, first and last, become a man; that is, he must have faith, acknowledge God. The forces of the second story—equality of men, the greatest, the highest, finding oneself, authority, God—need their own telling. Thus far that story has also been silent about a messenger of God or an Apostle, the outstanding individual, and the proper relation between them and wherein lie their differences and similarities. Nor does it recount how an ordinary individual in virtue of his relation either to the Apostle or to an outstanding individual is saved. What, then, is that second story? That is the subject of my inquiry in this concluding part of the essay. While my arguments will question his other claims, my primary aim is to show that Kierkegaard's view leads to a paradox.[1]

ANTIQUITY AND THE PRESENT

Kierkegaard declares that

> the person who learns the most from the education and reaches the top does not become the man of distinction, the outstanding hero—this is forestalled by leveling, which is a utterly consistent, and he prevents it himself because he has grasped the meaning of leveling—no, he only becomes an essentially human being in the full sense of equality. This is the idea of religiousness. (88, 57)

Such an individual will learn, before God, to be content with himself, to learn to dominate himself, to learn as priest to be his own audience and

---

[1]This has, of course, nothing to do with the *kind of* paradoxes for which Kierkegaard has penchant.

as author to be his own reader—"for if the individual is unwilling to learn to be satisfied with himself in the essentiality of the religious life before God, to be satisfied with ruling over himself instead of over the world, . . . then he will not escape from reflection" (88-89, 57). This is attaining the highest.

This is also exhibiting understanding. He is a man who learns most from the process of leveling, such as the meaning of leveling, and having so learned he has become the greatest, not otherwise. He is a man who has gone through, at least, stages 1 through 4. But what he learns, one might object, are merely self-contentment, self-domination, and such, but no deep moral theory as is envisaged in stage 3. And it is this kind of learning, and nothing else, that teaches him to become a man, and nothing more. This objection confines the Kierkegaardian greatest man, inordinately. Such a man must, as would be demanded at stage 3, inquire why he must become his own audience or his own master, what the essential likeness he shares with others is, why all men are equal in the eyes of God,[2] and why he must accept it as the highest. To seek such answers is to seek escape from cleverness, not from reflection or under-standing. Nor having found the answers will he circulate them, and make them common currency, for that would impede others from achieving what he has achieved, solitarily. If neither satisfactory answers are provided either by himself or by the leveling process that now serves as his teacher and his guide nor does he even actively seek the answers, this greatest man is not as great as Kierkegaard portrays him to be; or his leap of faith was but an accidental, if lucky jump.

What one age applauds as the highest, another age may shrug away, and vice versa.

> The bleakness of antiquity was that the man of distinction was what *others could not be*; the inspiring aspect [of the modern era] will be that the person who has gained himself religiously is only what *all can be*. (92, 62)

Consider the Greeks. No run-of-the-mill Greek could aspire to be a Demosthenes or a Pericles, an Odysseus or Musaeus, an Ajax or an Achilles. For an ordinary Greek neither possessed the physical nor mental

---

[2]A. N. Wilson, *Jesus: A Life.*

prowess of these men, nor yet be destined to play great roles in Fate's affairs.[3] In modern times, the highest is something different. The highest is to find oneself. This is a paradigmatic expression of the importance of self-knowledge, one which we increasingly capture as we go through the six stages. Kierkegaard may mean a lot more, but, I assert, he must mean at least that. But when one has found oneself, one has achieved only what anyone could have achieved, had he chosen that path. Just how true is this claim?[4] In the present age, who corresponds to Achilles or Musaeus? Say, for the sake of argument, Eugene O'Neill, Mohandas Gandhi, Akiro Kurosawa, or Mother Teresa, to say nothing of Kierkegaard's examples: Holger Danske or Martin Luther (89, 58). I find it immensely implausible that a run-of-the-mill modern could aspire to write a *Long Day's Journey into Night*, be a father of a nation, make *The Seven Samurai*, or run the poorhouses in Calcutta.

Kierkegaard invites the reading that becoming religious, or finding oneself, is a one-step transition. Now you aren't, now you are, religious. To make such a transition is nothing less than to take the momentous step of affirmation of faith. Essentially, *any*one, *any*time, from *any* other stage can make a transition to stage 5. And such a transition would be equally good. What follows (stage 6) is merely working out the consequences of having taken that step just as what preceded it was merely a preliminary for it (stages 1-4). This is why, I suspect, he has a scale of energy and a scale of cleverness, but not a scale of understanding.[5] The view offered

---

[3]Recall Kierkegaard's enigmatic remark, "In modern times leveling is reflection's correlative to fate in antiquity" (84, 52).

[4]There is also this query: Why should the discovery of oneself be deemed something that anyone else could have done, had he tried? Some natures are wild, extremely rich, with labyrinthine personalities; some are rather simple. Contrast an Ezra Pound or a Yo Yo Ma with a happy Rick Mason with a car wash company in Simona, Nebraska. Why is the task of the discovery of oneself in each of these cases a task equal to any other? Or, is it that underlying each one of us is a common nature, not easily retrieved through self-examination, which makes it our common difficult task to discover?

[5]Consider the story of Theophilus. During the purge of Dicloteian, Theophilus was present at the torture and the decapitation of Saint Dorothea, and he mockingly asked her to send him apples and roses. She is said to have sent them to him. Seeing this miracle, he was converted, and in turn tortured, and decapitated. See, Gerard Manley Hopkins, *God's Grandeur and Other Poems*,

in chapter 1, on the other hand, suggests that the self-inquirer is one who
is rising through the cycle of five stages, in which both passion *and*
reflection are required. The self-inquirer is also one who rises through the
cycle of six stages of self-knowledge in which understanding plays a
cardinal role (subservient only to the leap of faith).[6] On this view, two
self-inquirers, say, a Socrates and a John Doe, may be on vastly different
points on the scale of understanding as they traverse these two cycles of
five and six stages, respectively. What they will have achieved by way
of self-discovery will be vastly unequal. Should they leap to faith (stage
5), their respective leap would be of immensely different orders. Thus,
not everyone can scale the true religious heights, or the heights of self-
knowledge. Perhaps, most of us will stop after a few rounds, lacking
Socrates' tenacity, intellect, desire for self-knowledge, or sheer heart.

I conclude that we are, surely, not so different from those in antiquity. That "the bleakness of antiquity was that the man of distinction was
what *others could not be*" is no less true of us, notwithstanding that what
we uphold as the ideal was not what was upheld in antiquity. If I am the
admirer, and a Gustav Mahler, Naguib Mahfouz, or Ramanujan, the object of my admiration, my sentiments are accurately portrayed thus:

> [T]he admirer is inspired by the thought of being a man just like the
> distinguished person, is humbled by the awareness of not having been
> able to accomplish this great thing himself, is ethically encouraged by
> the prototype to follow this exceptional man's example to the best of his
> ability. . . . (72, 38)

There is also this related puzzle. The process of leveling destroys distinction; it is a great equalizer of men. One would think that any process
producing or demonstrating equality will stand condemned in Kierkegaard
eyes for doing that. Not so. Not the religious process that leads one to
make the leap, even though when one has attained the highest, when one
has found oneself, and learnt most from the leveling, one "does not

---

51. Where, Kierkegaard might ask of us, was there room or role for understanding to occur in the conversion of Theophilus? One might counter: Is faith always
a one-step thing? If one step, is it always of the same order of intensity? If one
step, can it be anchored more deeply through understanding? In short, might
there be a *scale of faith*? See chap. 1, n. 7 and the attending text.

[6]When are these cycles in harmony, when out of sync?

become the man of distinction, the outstanding hero . . . "; rather, one has "only become an essentially human being in the full sense of equality. This is the idea of religiousness" (88, 57). The equality produced by the process of leveling is condemned; that produced by religion is exalted. But Kierkegaard never delineates what differentiates the two senses of equality. Albert Schweitzer, playing his broken-down piano, in the heart of Africa, may regard *himself* as being merely an ordinary man; I would dare hear a modern man say that of Schweitzer, let alone that he and Schweitzer were equals. To take it a step further: not only would this be *hubris*, but, also, to recognize the difference between him and us is what saves us—that we are rootless, superficial, sensate, and that he is not; that our lives are wasted, and his is not (96, 67)—from descending further into the morass of ordinariness. This is the essential recognition gained at stage 4.

He who has attained the highest has also achieved certainty. But no one can help another to attain either the highest or the certainty. If the unrecognizable

> provides one single man with that [certainty] directly, it means he is dismissed, for he would be unfaithful to God and would be assuming authority, because he would not in obeying God learn to love men infinitely by constraining himself rather than faithlessly constraining them by dominating them, even if they asked for it. (109, 83)

No, he will be "unwilling to deceive others by helping them" (90, 59). No, he cannot help another, who has to rise by his own bootstrings, for if he did, "it would be instantly obvious to a third party that the un-recognizable one was an authority, and then the third party would be prevented from attaining the highest" (109, 83). Therefore, exerting authority is taboo.

THE APOSTLE AND THE GENIUS: THE DIFFERENCES

This leads to an intractable paradox in Kierkegaard's *The Present Age*. To develop the paradox, let us delineate two differences and three similarities between an Apostle and an outstanding individual, say, a genius. The differences: First, an outstanding individual is born, not so an Apostle. Second, an Apostle has authority, not so an outstanding individual. The similarities: First, both the Apostle and the outstanding individual work for others, suffer for them. Second, neither of them can use authority or power to enforce faith. One's faith must be had freely, or not at all. Third, faith must come antecedently to accepting an Apostle or an outstanding individual. I begin with the details of the differences.

First, *sub specie aeternitatis*, in their essential or universal form or nature, an Apostle and an outstanding individual are different. An ordinary man is different from an outstanding individual, but he could conceivably have become what the other is. Mozart is a musical genius *par accident*, not essentially, so that an ordinary individual could have been that genius also. But a gift of Apostlehood makes a man essentially different from others. "A *genius* and an *apostle* are qualitatively distinct"[7] (L 105, 90).

> [The] genius is *born*. Already long before there can be any question to what extent the genius will devote his unusual gifts to God, or will not do it, he is a genius, he is a genius even though he doesn't do it. (L 106, 91)

Nikolai Vasilevich Gogol, author of *Dead Souls*, need not have used his literary gifts even to please men, let alone to relate them to God. He could have written all his novels for his own pleasure and benefit, kept them well hidden from the world, and when he was about to die, burnt everything he had written. But he would not have been any less a genius—perhaps an unrecognized genius, but a genius nevertheless.[8]

---

[7] I shall follow a referencing pattern similar to the one I adopted earlier in the book. The translation used here is by Walter Lowrie. For ease of reference, I note that the Dru translation, *Of the Difference between a Genius and an Apostle*, covers pp. 102-20 of the Lowrie translation entitled *On Authority and Revelation: The Book on Adler, or a Cycle of Ethicoreligious Essays*. Once again, there are two numbers in parentheses, this time with a prefix L: the first number refers to the pages of the Lowrie translation; the second refers to the pages of the Dru translation.

[8] After he had written the first volume of his greatest masterpiece that centered upon a rather unsavory character, Chichikov, Gogol toiled excruciatingly for almost seven years over the second volume of *Dead Souls*. In the second volume, he wanted to show how Chichikov would have been redeemed. A priest, Father Matthew Konstantinovsky, under whose spell Gogol fell, demanded that Gogol burn the second volume and, to atone for his sins for writing the first volume, enter a monastery. Gogol did as he was told on the night of February 24, 1852. He then confined himself to bed, refused food, and in intense agony died nine days later. See Nikolai Gogol, *Dead Souls*, 12.

Not so an Apostle: "For previously to becoming an apostle he possessed no potential possibility. Every man is equally near to being an apostle" (L 106, 92). The last claim is troubling: if essentially every man is equally near to becoming a musical genius as essentially every man is equally near to becoming an Apostle, what distinguishes a genius from an Apostle?

Kierkegaard might have countered with this: "A genius may perhaps be a century ahead of his age and hence stands there as a paradox, but in the end the race will assimilate what was once a paradox, so that it is no longer paradoxical" (L 106, 92). When Einstein first discovered the theory of relativity, Sir Arthur Eddington, the distinguished British physicist, was told that only three people in the world understood the theory. Sir Arthur is said to have asked: "Oh, who is the third?" Today, any senior physics major has a fair idea of what the theory is about. What was once thought to be paradoxical has now been assimilated by the *Homo sapiens*.

But becoming an Apostle is not like learning physics; that is, anyone who knows enough (of *moral* theory?) can become an Apostle. It is rather being singled out for a mission by God. This answer is inadequate. The issue raised by the objection is not whether one could know enough to be singled out by God for the task; the issue rather is whether God could have selected *anyone* to do His task. Thus, just as Mozart had the gift of music from God but an ordinary individual did not, so Mozart and that

---

Had Gogol did with all of his works what he did with the second part of his novel, which no one had laid eyes on, the world would have been bereft by that much, but Gogol would have been no less a genius.

There is a bizarre, but rough, parallel in the story of Adolph Peter Adler. Adler was born during the year before Kierkegaard was born. He was an arch-Hegelian, had earned the coveted degree of Magister Artium, and published four learned tracts. Kierkegaard had wanted to become a pastor, but had not become one. Adler, on the other hand, despite his learning, had become a pastor and cared for his parishioners. Then, writes Walter Lowrie, in "1842, he had a 'vision of light' which turned him against Hegel. Jesus Christ bade him burn his earlier books and manuscripts and dictated to him the greater part of a big book which he entitled *Several Sermons* and published at his own expense in 1843." In 1844, he was suspended by Bishop Minster on the "ground that his mind was deranged." Unlike Gogol, he did not die shortly thereafter, or of grief. Instead, said Kierkegaard, he used the small pension the Church allowed him, in leisure, to write against the Church. See, Lowrie's introduction to Kierkegaard's *On Authority and Revelation: The Book on Adler, or a Cycle of Ethicoreligious Essays*, ix.

individual could have had their roles reversed; likewise, just as Moses had the gift of prophecy from God but an ordinary individual travelling with him in the Sinai desert did not, so, too, Moses and that individual could have had their roles reversed.

Kierkegaard's view on prophecy or Apostlehood raises questions. For instance, could God have made an utterly impious man, who undergoes no transformation of life or character, a prophet? Perhaps, had God done so, that might have been the ultimate test of one's faith. For, I would be asked to have faith and believe in this man contrary to everything I know about him, and in defiance of what I know other prophets to have been. How can I, with any degree of rationality, believe that the man who is before me—a veritable rake, gambler, drunkard, and seeped in pomp and circumstance, in the past, present, and promising to be so in the future— can be a prophet of God, indeed, can have any connection with God? Such a man would destroy the last vestige of distinction between a prophet and a false prophet. Was there ever, in the history of any religion, such a man and acknowledged by his community, even if grudgingly, to be a prophet or an Apostle?

Learning, knowledge, and wisdom, then, seem prerequisites. But it by no means follows, of course, that if a man should have these he shall be a prophet or an Apostle. (And, yet, why not? Might it not be part of God's grand design that He obliges Himself, as ultimate evidence of His justice, to confer prophecy on anyone who has risen that high? Thus Moses was selected to come near the Lord, but neither Aaron, Nadab, Abihu, nor seventy of the elders of Israel, because only Moses had reached the plane where prophecy must be conferred: "Moses alone shall come near to the LORD; but the others shall not come near" [Exodus 24:2 RSV].)

Ultimately, even for such a man prophecy must be a gift from God. Consider Baruch, son of Neriah. Jeremiah taught and trained him, and Baruch set himself the task of becoming a prophet; yet he was prevented from becoming one. The son of Neriah cried: "Woe is me! for the Lord has added sorrow to my pain; I am weary with my groaning, and I find no rest" (Jeremiah 45:3 RSV). And so he was told through his teacher and prophet, Jeremiah: "Thus says the LORD: Behold, what I have built I am breaking down, and what I have planted I am plucking up—that is, the whole land. And do you seek great things for yourself? Seek them not" (Jeremiah 45:4-5a RSV). Moses Maimonides concludes, "It is possible to say that this is a clear statement that prophecy is too *great a thing for Baruch.*"[9]

So, the movement from being an ordinary man to a prophet involves knowledge, understanding, and wisdom. The prophet, then, has his own transition to make from stage 3 (stage 4, too?) to stage 5. In his stage 3, the prophet has arrived at enormous knowledge and wisdom which takes him—and I do not know if that is a leap of faith or what—to stage 5, which for the prophet is a stage not only of faith, but a stage of being conferred with prophethood. The corollary to ordinary men is then evident. An ordinary man arrives at some knowledge, far, far below that of the prophet. He then goes to stage 4 where he recognizes the error of his ways. But if he is now to make the leap of faith and, say, acknowledge the prophet in his community, then the ordinary man must, minimally, have self-knowledge too, and whatever else that entails. Nothing, I surmise, could have pleased Kierkegaard less.

Second difference: an Apostle has authority, an outstanding individual does not. *"In the sphere of immanence authority,"* says Kierkegaard, *"cannot be thought, or it can be thought only as vanishing"* (L 111, 97). It follows that the Apostle can rightfully exert his authority.

> The elect man should according to God's ordinance assert his divine authority to chase away all impertinent people who will not obey him but argue. And instead of obeying, men transform an apostle into an examinee who comes as it were to the market place with a new doctrine. (L 110, 96)

Not so the outstanding individual: If he tried to exert his authority, "he would be unfaithful to God and would be assuming authority, because he would not in obeying God learn to love men infinitely by constraining himself rather than faithlessly constraining them by dominating them" (109, 83). The Apostle has authority directly from God, he is in the

---

[9]I had thought the thoughts behind this and the last paragraph clearly and independently only to learn, alas, that they had been said incomparably well more than 800 years ago by Moses Maimonides (1135–1204). See *The Guide of the Perplexed*, vol. 2, chap. 32. There are some small differences, though. Maimonides is interested in theology (I took the example of Baruch and Moses from him); I am accenting the philosophical in showing the importance of the role of understanding and wisdom. Also, I take Maimonides to deny the speculation in parentheses in the paragraph above.

sphere of transcendence. By contrast, a genius is in the sphere of immanence and has no authority (L 105, 90-91). Therefore, the outstanding
individual must not exercise his authority.[10] Authority in the field of
immanence was clearly transitory. This is enigmatic in two ways. First,
if the outstanding individual *has* no authority, Kierkegaard cannot enjoin
him not to exercise what he does not have. Such an individual can only
play at having authority; he cannot act wrongly by acting authoritatively
when he ought not have done so. Second, nothing prevents the outstanding individual from declaring: "The only rightful authority one can have
is from God; I have no such authority. But I adjure you, by what my
genius dictates, to follow the path of God as I understand it (or what the
Apostle has told me; or, . . .)."

Divine authority is a different matter. It is not transitory; it cannot
become common currency; it is had directly from God. Kierkegaard says:

> If such an elect man has a doctrine to communicate according to a
> divine order, and another man (let us imagine it) has found out for
> himself the same doctrine, then are these two nevertheless not equal; for
> the first is by reason of his paradoxical specific quality (the divine
> authority) different from every other man and from the qualification of
> essential likeness and equality which immanently lies at the basis of all
> other human differences. (L 112, 99)

Consider Saint Paul and Socrates. Suppose Saint Paul is the man who
brings forth a doctrine by divine command, and suppose that Socrates
after years of reflection brings forth the same doctrine.[11] The two men,
Kierkegaard would aver, are different, and not all of eternity could
obliterate that difference. But here is a puzzle. Suppose we do not argue
that the two men are equal in *that* respect: we concede that the one had
a direct command from God, the other had to work things out for

---

[10]Jesus did not always reveal his authority: see Mark 8:27-30; 11:27-33.
Also, even in messengers, or apostles, authority and power are often intermixed:
see Mark 6:7-13.

[11]I understand Cardinal John Newman to deny just this possibility: "In all
cases there is a margin left for faith in the word of the Church. He who believes
the dogmas of the Church only because he has reasoned them out of History, is
scarcely a Catholic." Quoted in Avery Dulles, "Historians and the Reality of
Christ," 25.

himself. Both Saint Paul and Socrates live their lives in full accordance with identical principles; *both* relate themselves to God. Should we regard, nevertheless, the life of one differently from the life of the other? Wherein lies that difference?[12]

THE APOSTLE AND THE GENIUS: THE SIMILARITIES

Now for the details of the similarities. First, an Apostle works for others, and if need be, he suffers for them. "An Apostle has no other proof but his own assertion, and at the most by his willingness to suffer everything for the sake of the doctrine" (L 117-18, 105). But so too must an outstanding, or the unrecognizable, individual suffer for the sake of others:

> He does not dare to defeat leveling outright—he would be dismissed for that, since it would be acting with authority—but in suffering he will defeat it and thereby experience in turn the law of his existence, which is not to rule, to guide, to lead, but in suffering to serve, to help indirectly. (109, 83)

There is evidently a problem here. In *Of the Difference between a Genius and an Apostle*, Kierkegaard maintained that a genius exists for himself, whilst an Apostle exists for others. The latter exists *in order that* (L 120, 108); not so the former. The text of *The Present Age* has a different view. I reconcile the conflict in this way: a genius may be self-sufficient, and may not exert himself for others, but he may do so, if he chooses (109, 83). It is not difficult to imagine an artist, a poet, a musician, a novelist, and so on, to engage in his task, or trade, without any external purpose, without any *in order that*. But it is difficult to imagine a man who embarks upon an ethical inquiry to be indifferent about what he knows and let his knowledge die with him. He may not teach or instruct for a variety of reasons—reasons that conspicuously would not move an Apostle—such as fear of reprisals, ridicule, or even physical harm.[13] But that in the absence of such reasons he should make

---

[12]How is *this* for a metaphysical conjecture? God has so designed the universe that he who has faith is on the straight path. But he who relies on reason will, in time, after trial and error, guesswork, and weeding out of guesses, eventually arrive at the same path.

[13]Baruch Spinoza hid his *magnum opus*, *Ethics*, fearing it would be misunderstood, destroyed, mangled. Better, he thought, that it be stored away and

serious efforts to conceal his work is incomprehensible. If his moral
views lead to salvation, happiness, or to a good life, then concealing
those views from others borders on gross selfishness, and it would be
hard to justify that deed on his own moral grounds.

Second, neither the Apostle nor the outstanding individual can use
power to coerce an individual to accept faith.

> In case it were true in real life (let us imagine it) that an apostle had
> power in a worldly sense, had great influence and powerful connections
> by the force of which he is victorious over the opinions and judgments
> of men—in case he employed this power he would *eo ipso* have lost his
> cause. (L 118, 105)

The third similarity will be touched upon later.

These differences and similarities are stated in bold and brief, but
they constitute the essence of the Kierkegaardian view.

A TALE FOR TWO MODELS

Let me weave a tale. In the second century, Marcus Aurelius Antoninus,[14]
wandering in the forests by the Danube, during his last campaign, en-
counters a hunting party. One of them, Polybius, is more alert and sensi-
tive than the others and attracts Marcus's attention. They sit by a stream,
Marcus reciting to Polybius parts of his recent compositions, *To Himself*

---

its fortunes decided by time than by men not ready for it. This from a man who
was not easily scared: he calmly faced the mob, who wanted to tear him apart
thinking him to be a spy, than to have them burn down his old landlady's house.

[14]The origin of this tale probably has its roots in what I long ago read in
John Stuart Mill:

> Let us add one more example, the most striking of all, if the impressiveness
> of error is measured by the wisdom and virtue of him who falls into it. If
> ever anyone, possessed of power, had grounds for thinking himself the best
> and most enlightened among his contemporaries, it was the Emperor Marcus
> Aurelius. . . . This man, a better Christian in all but the dogmatic sense of
> the word, than almost any of the ostensibly Christian sovereigns who have
> since reigned, persecuted Christianity. . . . To my mind this is one of the
> most tragical facts of history. It is a bitter thought, how different a thing the
> Christianity of the world might have been, if the Christian faith had been
> adopted as the religion of the empire under the auspices of Marcus Aurelius
> instead of those of Constantine. (*On Liberty and Other Writings*, 28-29)

(now called *Meditations*). Polybius, at an impressionable age, marvels at Marcus's cleverness and remembers snippets from that talk.

> All of us are creatures of a day; the rememberer and the remembered alike.
>
> In all you do or say or think, recollect that at any time the power of withdrawal from life is in your own hands.
>
> Though men may hinder you from following the paths of reason, they can never succeed in deflecting you from sound action.
>
> For a human soul, the greatest of self-afflicted wrongs is to make itself (so far as it is able to do so) a kind of tumour or abscess on the universe.
>
> When beset from without by circumstance, be unperturbed; when prompted from within to action, be just and fair: in fine, let both will and deed issue in behavior that is social and fulfills the law of your being.
>
> All the cycles of creation since the beginning of time exhibit the same recurring pattern, so that it can make no difference whether you watch the identical spectacle for a hundred years, or for two hundred, or for ever.
>
> Happiness . . . means "a good god within"; that is, a good master-reason.
>
> Love nothing but that which comes to you woven in the pattern of your destiny.[15]

Polybius parts from Marcus, exhilarated. The vicissitudes of life have not wrecked him, yet. Polybius is naturally happy, contented; he loves wine, women, and hunting. Later in life, his prattling is filled with "Marcus said this," and "Marcus said that." But there is no evident change in his form of life; he is no Stoic. Kierkegaard would undoubtedly have said that whether Marcus had authority or not (and, of course, he did not), Polybius is not saved. Polybius might have the exact content of the *Meditations* memorized and even understood aright, but that has only increased his capacity for right action, if even that. Unless his inwardness has changed, transformed—unless Polybius himself makes the leap, thus bringing the intensity in line with the scope—Polybius is not, and cannot, be saved.

---

[15]Marcus Aurelius, *Meditations*, 72, 48, 169, 50, 145, 50, 108, and 115, respectively.

There is, yet, this cardinal question. Can Polybius be saved by Marcus Aurelius, even if Polybius's inwardness has changed, and Polybius has not merely turned into a clever talker after his encounter with the author of *Meditations*? This question naturally arises because Marcus Aurelius had no authority, none from God. (His views are merely cleverness?) Consequently, unless what transforms Polybius, his inwardness, is the message an Apostle brings, or unless he is transformed by the messenger whose injunctions are in accord with those of the Apostle, Polybius ought not to be regarded as saved. If an outstanding individual is to play any significant role in the life of an ordinary individual, his own must be linked to that of the Apostle—or he will not save anyone, himself included, whether he talks, remains silent, or properly balances talk and silence.

The second tale is nearly identical to the first. It occurs in the century before. In place of Marcus substitute an Apostle, in place of Polybius substitute Isaac, a wandering mendicant, now in Patara. They sit under an oak, and the Apostle declares his message to Isaac, and exercises his rightful authority. Isaac, too, is enamored with what the Apostle tells him.

> For the Spirit searches everything, even the depths of God. For what person knows a man's thoughts except the spirit of the man which is in him? So also no one comprehends the thoughts of God except the Spirit of God. (1 Corinthians 2:10b-11 RSV)

> He who plants and he who waters are equal, and each shall receive his wages according to his labor. For we are God's fellow workers; you are God's field, God's building. (1 Corinthians 3:8-9 RSV)

> Let no one deceive himself. If anyone among you who thinks that he is wise in this age, let him become a fool that he may become wise. (1 Corinthians 3:18 RSV)

> Though our outer nature is wasting away, our inner nature is being renewed every day. (2 Corinthians 4:16b RSV)

> But let each one test his own work, and then his reason to boast will be in himself alone and not in his neighbor. For each man will have to bear his own load. (Galatians 6:4-5 RSV)

> Let no one deceive you with empty words, for it is because of these things that the wrath of God comes upon the sons of disobedience. (Ephesians 5:6 RSV)

> Stand therefore, having girded your loins with truth, and having put on the breastplate of righteousness, and having shod your feet with the equipment of the gospel of peace. . . . (Ephesians 6:14-15 RSV)

> [A]mong men who are depraved in mind and bereft of the truth,
> [imagine] that godliness is a means of gain. There is great gain in
> godliness with contentment. . . . (1 Timothy 6:5-6 RSV)

Isaac too, like Polybius, is young, innocent, untouched by concerns
that are not ephemeral. He, too, remembers the Apostle as a clever talker.
Later, Isaac's talk is often peppered with recollections from what the
Apostle had said to him under the shade of that large oak tree. The
company would laugh a laugh of honest approval, Isaac would attend to
the food and drink, and then call it a day. The gaiety would be over, the
company would disperse, and Isaac would go home. This is how Isaac
would spend the rest of his days. Isaac is just as surely not saved—unless
he transforms his inwardness. *That* even the Apostle cannot help him do.

The affirmation of faith (stage 5) is paramount. I suggest that Kierkegaard is offering two models for understanding how that affirmation
comes about, and that, I shall argue, these models are at variance with
each other. Here, then, is a reconstruction. The first model of affirmation
is *under the tutelage of an outstanding individual.* The second model of
affirmation is *under the tutelage of an Apostle.* Let us begin with the first
model of affirmation.

The outstanding individual, a Marcus Aurelius, is enjoined to perform
a dual task: not to exert his authority and to work for others. This outstanding individual knows who the servants of the leveling process are,
and that they are evil. But he dare not directly oppose them, lest he give
himself away.

> The unrecognizables recognize the servants of leveling but dare not use
> power or authority against them, for then there would be a regression,
> because it would be instantly obvious to a third party that the unrecog-
> nizable one was an authority, and then the third party would be
> prevented from attaining the highest. (109, 83)

Polybius must not know that Marcus Aurelius, the unrecognizable, is an
authority, or he would be prevented from attaining to the highest.

Against the tide of leveling, Marcus Aurelius can only help by
suffering. But how exactly does the silence of the outstanding individual
procure for the third person the attainment of the highest? Or, for that
matter, how exactly, by the breaking of his silence, does the outstanding
individual *prevent* the third person from attaining the highest? Kierkegaard does not offer even a provisional, hesitant answer; yet the answer

is so crucial. This much we know: he who has *not* made the leap of faith, will regard the suffering of the outstanding individual as a failure (109, 83). "The fool should have known what was coming to him. What a pompous speech! No wonder he ended up drinking the hemlock," he will say. But he who has made the leap of faith "will have a vague idea that it was his victory" (109, 83), but then he can have no certainty. Only the outstanding individual can allay what remaining iota of doubt he has. But the outstanding individual will not allay it for he has been enjoined to remain silent. If he does not remain silent, he ruins it for the other who would be prevented from attaining the highest.

Recall what Kierkegaard said about reasoning:

> What does it mean *to be loquacious*? It is annulled passionate disjunction between subjectivity and objectivity. As abstract thought, loquacity is not sufficiently profound dialectically; as conception and conviction, it lacks full-blooded individuality. (103, 76)

Someone, say, Polybius, has firsthand knowledge of the outstanding individual as the latter attends to things in his daily life. Polybius sees him as maintaining the delicate balance between silence and chatter; subjectivity and objectivity; having real love; and keeping a sharp distinction between form and content.[16] Conversations with the outstanding individual yield only reasoning which yet does not translate into full-blooded individuality, conviction, or faith. Both experiences and conversations provide Polybius the platform from which to make the leap. That leap is subjectivity. Once he makes the leap, although he is not certain of it, and acts in accordance with that leap of faith, Polybius is saved. The outstanding individual has provoked Polybius's faith, but has not teased it out of him solely through objectivity or reasoning. He has offered Polybius no epistemic certainty. Had he done so, Polybius would not have attained the highest. Presumably, had Polybius been offered epistemic certainty, he would have mimicked the behavior of the outstanding individual, relied on mere objective reasoning, become prey to reflection,

---

[16]You undoubtedly recognize that I have bestowed on the outstanding individual just those qualities Kierkegaard himself discusses in the section where he delineates the "concrete attributes of the reflexion of the present age in domestic and social life" (97-105, 69-78). See chap. 3, 46.

and not have arrived at the full-blooded individuality of his subjective opinion or conviction. Therein would have lain his failure.

Now, the second model of affirmation, *under the tutelage of an Apostle*. With an Apostle, the story is so different; or, so it is made to seem. An Apostle has his authority from God. He declares himself as the carrier of God's messages, and enjoins his listeners to live and act in obedience to that message. He, too, must suffer in his task. But how can an ordinary individual be saved by an Apostle, saved, that is, in the strict Kierkegaardian sense? Consider Isaac again. He looks up to the activity of the Apostle, converses with him, and so on—just as he did before. Except this time, the Apostle is not reticent, but declares his authority and conveys his message to Isaac. This is only objectivity thus far. In fact, if Isaac sought certainty, the Apostle could grant him certainty, something an outstanding individual was enjoined *not* to do. But how, in this case, is Isaac saved by the Apostle's declaration of authority, or by his attempting to provide Isaac with certainty when, in the other case, had the outstanding individual provided Polybius with certainty, he would have ruined Polybius? Harshly, either the Apostle should make himself manifest or not. If he does, then those who follow him will not be saved, although he will have obeyed divine command. If he does not, then he will have transgressed the divine command, but he may succeed in saving individuals.

Kierkegaard himself thinks likewise. God having conferred authority on someone,

> they say to him, "From whom art thou?" He answers, "From God." But, lo, God cannot help his ambassador as a king can who gives him an accompaniment of soldiers or policemen, or his ring, or a letter in his handwriting which everybody recognizes—in short, God cannot be at men's service by providing them with a sensible certitude of the fact that an apostle is an apostle—this, too, would be nonsense. Even the miracle, if the apostle has his gift, gives no sensible certitude, for the miracle is the object of faith. (L 109, 95)

But then the two models of affirmation are remarkably similar, not to say identical. In both instances—the third similarity—an act of faith must *precede* an acceptance of what either the outstanding individual or the Apostle says or does. No amount of openness and talk by the outstanding individual will help the ordinary individual, if he has no faith; no amount of silence by the Apostle will convince him either.

This, then, is the paradox. *Either,* if the outstanding individual is wrong to exert his authority, then neither should the Apostle declare his authority from God. *Or,* if the Apostle should declare his authority from God, then the outstanding individual should exert his authority also. In short, either both should speak up or both should remain silent.

No Apostle can save an individual even when he exerts his rightful authority; *that,* first and last, the individual must do for himself. *He* must make that leap, no one else can do it for him. The Apostle, as well as the outstanding individual, can bring a horse water, but he cannot make him drink. Why, then, must an Apostle exert, announce, or proclaim his authority, but an outstanding individual must not? Kierkegaard's answer is that the Apostle has authority from God while the outstanding individual by exerting his authority fails to perform his God-appointed task and prevents another from attaining the highest. What is so confusing is *how,* exactly, does the Apostle, by exerting, announcing, or proclaiming his authority, save an individual while the outstanding individual prevents, say, the same individual, from being saved, especially since it is agreed that neither the Apostle nor the outstanding individual can do anything directly to save the individual? Indeed, if keeping silent is an essential way for a third party to come to the realization of the highest, why should the Apostle not keep silent also?

What is so difficult to understand is how could the saving of an individual depend upon the nature of the age, Apostle, or aid? And yet it does. "It will no longer be as it once was, that individuals could look to the nearest eminence for orientation when things got somewhat hazy before their eyes" (108, 81). If, on the one hand, he lives in a passionate age, he saves himself in one way: he seeks help from the great. In that age, there are heroes, Apostles, prophets, judges, company commanders, officers, or generals, who reveal their identity, are recognized, and the public accepts their authority (107, 80). The individual follows them with passion, and he is saved. If, on the other hand, he lives in the present reflective age, the individual saves himself in a different way: he can only seek help from himself. In that age there might be an outstanding individual or two. However, the outstanding individuals will conceal their identity, will be unrecognized, will not exert their respective authorities, although they will work for others. Not to conceal their identity is to prevent the highest possible achievements for individuals of that age. The ordinary individual will receive a glimmer about the worth of an outstanding individual, but no certainty, will follow him on his own steam, and be saved.

The only way out of the paradox is that individuals are saved in exactly one way. No man can truly be saved in the present or any passionate age, not even the outstanding individual, except through an Apostle. The Apostle has authority and must speak up; the outstanding individual has no authority, can offer no certainty if he tried, and may speak up, too, but only in the name of the Apostle. Without being linked to the Apostle, neither the ordinary individual nor, for that matter, the outstanding individual, can be saved. But, then, Kierkegaard should have said that.

PROPHECY?

"But I must cut this short," says Kierkegaard finally.

> Of course this can be of interest only as banter, for if it is true that every person has to work out his own salvation, then forecasting the future is at best tolerable only as a means of recreation, as an interesting game such as bowling or tilting the barrel. (109-10, 84)

> And since there is such an extraordinary quantity of prophecies, apocalypses, signs and insights in our age when so little is being done, there is probably nothing else to do but go along with it. . . . (105, 85)

Yes, he is ironical: if he is right, he says, no one will pay attention to him, an insignificant person; if he is wrong, then he will only have been "a prophet in the modern sense, for a modern prophet prophecies something, nothing more"[17] (105, 85). Speaking of the modern prophet, Kierkegaard might just as well have written the lines Euripides did:

---

[17]"For the literary review," wrote Kierkegaard in his *Journal* "of the novel *Two Ages* followed *Concluding Postscript* so closely that it is almost concurrent and is, after all, something written by me *qua* critic and not *qua* author; but it does contain in the last section a sketch of the future from the point of view of 'the single individual,' a sketch of the future that the year 1848 did not falsify." The Hongs comment: "In 1848 there was a culmination of political turmoil in Denmark and in most of Europe. On June 5, 1848, Denmark changed from an absolute monarchy to a constitutional monarchy" (*Eighteen Upbuilding Discourses*, xviii and n. 24).

What sort of man is a soothsayer or prophet?
I will tell you. If he is lucky
In his guessing even then he'll speak
A flock of lies and little truth, but
When his guess is wrong and unlucky,
Poof! like smoke he is nothing.[18]

These passages are difficult to fathom.[19] What, exactly, was Kierkegaard prophesying? Has he prophesied anything at all? Was he not only
admonishing? I find a passage from Plato's *Laches* helpful to understand
Kierkegaard:

> A prophet's only duty is to understand the signs of future events—to
> know whether someone is going to die, fall ill, go bankrupt, or be on
> the winning or losing side in a war or some other contest. But deciding
> which of these it's better for someone to suffer or not is surely no more
> the business of a prophet than it is of anyone else![20]

Kierkegaard is gently polemical. It is his parting shot at the present
age given to much information, and predicting the states of the world on
the basis of that information, thus yielding even more information. Even
if all this prophesying or predicting is true, it will not help. The modern
prophet will not have come an iota closer—and this was what Plato was
saying also—to getting anything right that really matters. For what
matters is neither the accuracy nor the correctness of one's prediction, but
whether a man has worked his way to salvation. Could a soothsayer
truthfully predict that future generations will live in a society in which no
one will labor to save himself or, to the contrary, nearly all will labor so,
to the *individual* the soothsayer will have failed to assist, and necessarily
so. The prophets of old were merely predictors, says Kierkegaard. They

---

[18]"Iphigenia in Aulis," 164.
[19]The reader of the Alexander Dru translation needs a warning. The section
of *The Present Age*, as of the book, does not end where the Dru translation ends;
toward the end there is some text missing which reverts the discussion back to
the novel, *Two Ages*; and, finally, the paragraph with which it ends actually
occurs few pages earlier in the text.
[20]Plato, *Early Socratic Dialogues*, 107.

did not bring anything about; it was God who did so. So he mockingly palms himself off as a modern prophet, as a predictor of things:

> we modern prophets, lacking the endorsement of Governance, perhaps could add a postscript as Thales did: What we prophesy will either happen or it will not happen, for the gods have bestowed the gift of prophecy also upon us. (106, 86)[21]

Kierkegaard thus slyly suggests that, by that token, anyone can claim to be a prophet.

Kierkegaard had no divine sanction, yet he was a seer of our dark and murderous modern age. He prophesied what it will be and diagnosed its ills—an age of hypertrophic collectors and gatherers, users and decoders, storers and retrievers, packagers and dismantlers, creators and disseminators, purchasers and sellers of information. Let the final words Kierkegaard the seer might have spoken come from him who knew the human heart at its bleakest; I mean Aeschylus:

> Believe me if you will. What will it matter
> If you won't? It comes when it comes,
> And soon you'll see it face to face
> And say the seer was all too true.[22]

---

[21]What Thales is supposed to have said is mere fabrication, or else I am unable to find it in the doxographic tradition. Though, as we know, through Aristotle's testimony, Thales cornered the market of olive presses in Meletus and Chios, having predicted a heavy crop in the coming season, based on his knowledge of meteorology, and was able to make himself rich by subsequently leasing the presses at outrageous prices. Thus, Thales demonstrated that he was indifferent to his poverty, and that had he wished he could just as well have shown that philosophy was useful by using it for purposes for which it was not primarily designed. See Aristotle, *Politics*, 32.

[22]"Agamemnon," *The Orestia*, 153.

Bibliography

Aeschylus. "Agamemnon." In *The Orestia*, 99-172. Translated by Robert Fagles. New York: Penguin Books, 1979.

Alighieri, Dante. *The Divine Comedy: Purgatorio*. Translated, with a commentary, by Charles S. Singleton. Princeton NJ: Princeton University Press, 1977.

Arberry, Arthur John, translator. *The Koran Interpreted*. New York: Macmillan Publishing Company, 1955.

Aristotle. *Politics*. Translated by Sir Ernest Barker. New York: Oxford University Press, 1995.

_____. *The Nicomachean Ethics*. Translated by William David Ross. Revised by J. O. Urmson and J. L. Ackrill. New York: Oxford University Press, 1980.

Augustine, Saint. *Concerning the City of God against the Pagans*. A new translation by Henry Bettenson with an introduction by John O'Meara. New York: Penguin Books, 1984.

Aurelius, Marcus. *Meditations*. Translated by Maxwell Staniforth. New York: Penguin Books, 1964.

Bayley, John. "Elegy for Iris." *The New Yorker* (27 July 1998): 45-61.

Burnyeat, Myles F. "Can the Skeptic Live His Skepticism?" In *The Skeptical Tradition*, 117-48. Edited by Myles Burnyeat. Berkeley: University of California Press, 1983.

Byatt, A. S. *Possession: A Romance*. London: Vintage Books, 1991.

Chubb, Thomas C. *Dante and His World*. Boston: Little, Brown, and Company, 1966.

Connell, George B. "Judge William's Theonomous Ethics." In *Foundations of Kierkegaard's Vision of Community: Religion, Ethics, and Politics in Kierkegaard*, 56-70. Edited by George B. Connell and C. Stephen Evans. Atlantic Highlands NJ: Humanities Press International, 1992.

Dulles, Avery. "Historians and The Reality of Christ." *First Things: A Monthly Journal of Religion and Public Life* 28 (December 1992): 20-25.

Dummett, Michael. "Wittgenstein's Philosophy of Mathematics." In *Wittgenstein: The Philosophical Investigations*, 420-27. Edited by George Pitcher. London: Macmillan, 1968.

Emerson, Ralph Waldo. *The Heart of Emerson's Journals*. Edited by Bliss Perry. New York: Houghton Mifflin Company, 1926.

Euripides. "Iphigenia in Aulis." In *Euripides III: The Complete Greek Tragedies*, 7:107-201. Edited by David Greene and Richmond Lattimore. New York: The Modern Library, 1959.

Evans, C. Stephen. *Passionate Reason: Making Sense of Kierkegaard's Philosophical Fragments*. Bloomington: Indiana University Press, 1992.

Gogol, Nikolai. *Dead Souls*. Translated with an introduction by David Magarshack. New York: Penguin Books, 1961.

Hannay, Alastair. *Kierkegaard*. New York: Routledge, 1993.

Hardin, Garett. "The Tragedy of the Commons." *Science* 162 (December 1968): 1243-48.

Hare, R. M. *The Language of Morals*. Oxford: Clarendon Press, 1952.

Harvey, Peter. *An Introduction to Buddhism: Teachings, History, and Practices*. New York: Cambridge University Press, 1990.

Hendrickson, Robert, editor. *American Literary Anecdotes*. New York: Penguin Books, 1992.

Herodotus. *The Histories*. New edition. New York: Penguin Books, 1996.

Hopkins, Gerard Manley. *God's Grandeur and Other Poems*. New York: Dover Publications, 1995.

Hume, David. "Idea of a Perfect Commonwealth." In *Essays: Moral, Political, and Literary*, 512-29. Edited by Eugene F. Miller. Indianapolis: Liberty Fund, Inc., 1987.

Kenny, Anthony. *A Path from Rome: An Autobiography*. London: Sidgwick & Jackson, 1985.

Kierkegaard, Søren. *Either/Or: A Fragment of Life*. Translated by Alastair Hannay. New York: Penguin Books, 1992.

————. *Concluding Unscientific Postscript to Philosophical Fragments*. Volume 1. Edited and translated by Howard V. Hong and Edna H. Hong. Princeton: Princeton University Press, 1992.

————. *Eighteen Upbuilding Discourses*. Edited and translated by Howard H. Hong and Edna H. Hong. Princeton: Princeton University Press, 1988.

————. *Stages on Life's Way*. Edited and translated by Howard H. Hong and Edna H. Hong. Princeton: Princeton University Press, 1988.

————. *Either/Or*. Part 1 and 2. Edited and translated by Howard V. Hong and Edna H. Hong. Princeton: Princeton University Press, 1987.

————. *Fear and Trembling*. Edited and translated by Howard V. Hong and Edna H. Hong. Princeton: Princeton University Press, 1983.

————. *The Sickness Unto Death: A Christian Psychological Exposition for Upbuilding and Awakening*. Edited and translated by Howard V. Hong and Edna H. Hong. Princeton: Princeton University Press, 1980.

_____. *Two Ages: The Age of Revolution and the Present Age, A Literary Review*. Edited and translated by Howard V. Hong and Edna H. Hong. Princeton: Princeton University Press, 1978.

_____. *The Present Age, and Of the Difference between a Genius and an Apostle*. Translated by Alexander Dru. Introduction by Walter Kaufmann. New York: Harper Torchbooks, 1962. Originally published (with "Has a Man the Right to Let Himself Be Put to Death for the Truth?") under the title *The Present Age and Two Minor Ethicoreligious Treatises* (1940).

_____. *On Authority and Revelation: The Book on Adler, or a Cycle of Ethicoreligious Essays*. Translated by Walter Lowrie. Princeton: Princeton University Press, 1955.

_____. *Training in Christianity*. Edited and translated by Walter Lowrie. Princeton: Princeton University Press, 1944.

_____. *The Point of View for My Work as an Author*. Translated by Walter Lowrie. New York: Oxford University Press, 1939.

Kirmmse, Bruce H. "Call Me Ishmael—Call Everyone Ishmael." In *Foundations of Kierkegaard's Vision of Community: Religion, Ethics, and Politics in Kierkegaard*, 161-82. Edited by George B. Connell and C. Stephen Evans. Atlantic Highlands NJ: Humanities Press International, 1992.

_____. *Kierkegaard: In Golden Age Denmark*. Bloomington: Indiana University Press, 1990.

Kitcher, Philip. *The Advancement of Science. Science without Legend, Objectivity without Illusions*. New York/Oxford: Oxford University Press, 1993.

_____. "The Cognitive Division of Labor," *The Journal of Philosophy* (January 1990): 1-22.

Locke, John. *A Letter concerning Toleration*. Works, volume 2. London: 1727.

MacIntyre, Alasdair. *After Virtue: A Study in Moral Theory*. Notre Dame IN: University of Notre Dame Press, 1984.

Maimonides, Moses. *The Guide of the Perplexed*. Translated and with an introduction and notes by Shlomo Pines. Chicago: University of Chicago Press, 1963.

Marino, Gordon D. "The Place of Reason in Kierkegaard's Ethics," *Kierkegaardiana* 18 (1996): 49-64.

Marlowe, Christopher. *The Tragical History of the Life and Death of Doctor Faustus*. Edited by John D. Jump. London: Methuen, 1965.

May, Herbert G., and Bruce M. Metzger, editors. *The New Oxford Annotated Bible with the Apocrypha. Revised Standard Version*. Expanded edition. New York: Oxford University Press, 1977.

Meier, John P. *A Marginal Jew: Rethinking the Historical Jesus*. Volume 2. *Mentor, Message, and Miracles*. New York: Doubleday, 1994.

Mill, John Stuart. *On Liberty and Other Writings*. Cambridge: Cambridge University Press, 1991.

Milton, John. *The Poetical Works of John Milton*. Revised Edition. Edited by Helen Darbishire. New York: Oxford University Press, 1958.

Morrison, Toni. *The Bluest Eye*. New York: Holt, Rinehart, and Winston, 1970.

Murdoch, Iris. *Metaphysics as a Guide to Morals*. New York: Penguin Books, 1992.

_____. *The Message to the Planet*. New York: Penguin Books, 1989.

Niebuhr, H. Richard. *The Responsible Self: An Essay in Christian Moral Philosophy*. New York: Harper & Row, 1963.

Nozick, Robert. *The Examined Life: Philosophical Meditations*. New York: Simon and Schuster, 1989.

_____. *Anarchy, State, and Utopia*. New York: Basic Books, Inc., 1975.

Parsons, Terence. "Essentialism and Quantified Modal Logic." In *Reference and Modality*, 73-87. Edited by Leonard Linsky. New York: Oxford University Press, 1971.

Perkins, Robert L. "Envy as Personal Phenomenon and as Politics." In *International Kierkegaard Commentary: Two Ages*, 107-32. Edited by Robert L. Perkins. Macon GA: Mercer University Press, 1984.

Plantinga, Alvin. "Justification and Theism," *Faith and Philosophy* 4/4 (1987): 403-26.

Plato. *Phaedo*. Translated by David Gallop. New York: Penguin Books, 1993.

_____. *Republic*. Translated by Robin Waterfield. New York: Oxford University Press, 1993.

_____. *The Trial and Death of Socrates*. Translated by G. M. A. Grube. Indianapplis IN: Hackett Publishing Company, 1988.

_____. *Early Socratic Dialogues*. Edited by Trevor J. Saunders. New York: Penguin Books, 1987.

_____. *Phaedrus and Letters VII and VIII*. New York: Penguin Books, 1973.

_____. *The Symposium*. Translated by Walter Hamilton. New York: Penguin Books, 1951.

Popper, Karl. *Objective Knowledge: An Evolutionary Approach*. Revised edition. Oxford: Clarendon Press, 1979.

Rawls, John. *A Theory of Justice*. Cambridge: Harvard University Press, 1971.

Rilke, Rainer Maria. *The Notebooks of Malte Laurids Brigge*. Translated by Stephen Mitchell. New York: Random House, 1983.

Roberts, Robert C. "Kierkegaard, Wittgenstein, and a Method of 'Virtue Ethics.' " In *Kierkegaard in Post/Modernity*, 142-66. Edited by Martin J. Matustick and Merold Westphal. Bloomington: Indiana University Press, 1995.

Ross, Sir David. *Aristotle*. London: Methuen, 1964.

Rousseau, Jean-Jacques. *On the Social Contract*. Translated and edited by Donald A. Cress. Introduced by Peter Gay. Indianpolis: Hackett Publishing Company, 1987.

Rudd, Anthony. *Kierkegaard and the Limits of the Ethical*. New York: Oxford University Press, 1993.

Russell, Bertrand. "A Free Man's Worship." In *The Basic Writings of Bertrand Russell, 1903–1959*, 66-72. Edited by Robert E. Egner and Lester E. Dennon. London: George Allen & Unwin, 1961.

Sanders, E. P. *The Historical Figure of Jesus*. New York: Penguin Books, 1993.

Sarkar, Husain. "The Task of Group Rationality: The Subjectivist's View. Part 1." *Studies in History and Philosophy of Science* 28/2 (June 1997): 267-88.

————. *A Theory of Method*. Berkeley: University of California Press, 1983.

Shaw, Bernard. *Saint Joan*. New York: Penguin Books, 1946.

Singer, Issac B. *The Penitent*. New York: Farrar, Straus, Giroux, 1983.

Spinoza, Benedict de. *The Ethics*. Translated by R. H. M. Elwes. New York: Dover Publications, 1951.

Taylor, Charles. *Sources of the Self: The Making of the Modern Identity*. Cambridge MA: Harvard University Press, 1989.

Toynbee, Paget. *Dante Dictionary*. Oxford: Clarendon Press, 1898.

Westphal, Merold. *Kierkegaard's Critique of Reason and Society*. Macon GA: Mercer University Press, 1987.

————. "Kierkegaard's Sociology." In *International Kierkegaard Commentary: Two Ages*, 133-54. Edited by Robert L. Perkins. Macon GA: Mercer University Press, 1984.

Williams, Bernard. *Morality: An Introduction to Ethics*. New York: Cambridge University Press, 1976.

Wilson, A. N. *Jesus: A Life*. New York: W. W. Norton, 1992.

Wilson, E. O. *Naturalist*. Washington DC: Island Press, 1994.

Wittgenstein, Ludwig. *Philosophical Investigations*. Translated by G. E. M. Anscombe. Oxford: Basil Blackwell, 1967.

————. *Remarks on the Foundations of Mathematics*. Edited by G. H. von Wright, R. Rhees, and G. E. M. Anscombe. Cambridge MA: MIT Press, 1967.

Zola, Emile. *The Masterpiece*. New York: Oxford University Press, 1993.

INDEXES

NAME INDEX